Skipper from Leith

The History of Robert Barton
of Over Barnton

By

W. Stanford Reid

McGill University
Montreal

a . *University of Pennsylvania Press*

Library of Congress Catalog Card Number: 61-6623

Printed in Great Britain by
Spottiswoode, Ballantyne and Co. Ltd.
London and Colchester

To

Mrs. Fraser and
the late Mr. Llewellyn Fraser

Uncle Lal and Aunt Lil

Contents

Ever since the publication of the works of Max Weber, Ernst Troeltsch, and R. H. Tawney on the relationship of the Reformation to the rising sixteenth century bourgeoisie, there has been a tendency in some quarters, although by no means universally, to regard the Protestant ethic as one of the major sources of the rise of modern industrial capitalism. This thesis has been based upon broad generalizations which have in turn looked for their support to rather dubious historical evidence. For instance, there has been a tendency to look to seventeenth century Puritans as trustworthy exponents of Calvin's economic views. One test of this interpretation lies in the study of the pre-Reformation capitalist. By such an investigation one should be able to ascertain—at least to some degree—whether his motivations and actions were of the typical post-Reformation pattern. It is partly for this purpose that the present work has been written.

The study of an individual bourgeois in Scotland, an area in which the development of the middle class has usually been ignored, is also important for wider understanding both of the middle class's sixteenth-century development and of the history of the country itself. It is hoped that the career of Robert Barton of Leith here described may throw some light upon the sixteenth-century middle class and upon pre-Reformation history in Scotland.

Robert Barton, in his economic, social, and political activities, can almost be said to epitomize Scotland in the first four decades of the sixteenth century. As one of the leading Scottish traders and financiers he was caught up in practically all the contemporary currents. He seems to have been a shrewd bargainer, a skilful business man, and at the same time a nationalistic supporter of any government which could unite Scotland and bring peace to the frequently faction-torn country. Thus, although he does not always appear in the forefront of the historical scene, he was of no little importance as one of the chief financial powers behind the government, particularly during the period following the disaster of Flodden Field.

His activities and interests were not, however, limited to his own country. He was heavily involved in the domestic policies of Denmark, had an important influence in establishing a Scottish staple in Holland, and was continually traveling to France on business for the government. As a consequence he became well known, either favourably or unfavourably, in most of the trading centers along the European Atlantic seaboard. He was one of that driving class of men who influenced so strongly the history of northwestern Europe at the beginning of the modern period.

He is, of course, by no means entirely unknown; he is referred to in standard histories, in introductions to collections of historical documents, and even in a few specialized studies. Nevertheless, there has grown up so much erroneous tradition concerning Robert Barton that the facts have practically disappeared from sight. The present writer has attempted to dissolve the unhistorical elements in the popular accounts and build on a firm foundation of fact. This has involved research extending from Copenhagen in the north, to Madrid and Lisbon in the south, to say nothing of considerable time spent in Scottish and English archives, libraries, and muniment rooms.

As far as possible he has dealt with all the relevant manuscript as well as all the printed sources available.

In his travels on the trail of Robert Barton, the author has always received the greatest kindness and courtesy from those in charge of the various repositories of documents. Especially he would single out the help given by Dr. A. T. McInnis and Miss Marion Miller of Her Majesty's General Register House, Edinburgh. To all the keepers of the records which he has examined he would express his gratitude for their patience and willingness to give him aid.

The author is also deeply appreciative of the interest, encouragement, and advice which he has received from Dr. F. Cyril James, Principal and Vice-Chancellor of McGill University, while wrestling with the problems involved in this work.

None of his research in Europe would have been possible, however, had it not been for the generosity of the American Philosophical Society, Philadelphia, who helped to finance two expeditions abroad, and of McGill University, Montreal, who made a grant for the third. To both these organizations the author is very grateful.

To Mrs. L. VerHagen, Mrs. P. Russel, and Mrs. P. Silvester who have typed and retyped pages, he would also extend his very hearty thanks.

Finally, like most authors, the present writer would acknowledge his indebtedness to his research assistant, his reviser, his proofreader and his house critic: his wife who has worked unfailingly with him both in his research and in his writing.

W. STANFORD REID

Montreal, Canada

Skipper from Leith

I

Scotland at the End of the Fifteenth Century

Scotland in the last decade of the fifteenth century, when Robert Barton was beginning his career, was a very different country from what it is today. The Middle Ages were just beginning to ebb, America was unknown, and the Industrial Revolution with its factories, its shipyards, and its slums was far in the future. Consequently it would seem wise, before plunging into the story of Robert's career, to take a quick glance at the character of the country in which he was to wield no small influence for the next forty to fifty years.

To begin with, the physical aspect of the land was very different. It was much more heavily wooded, than it is today, particularly in the Lowlands and the far north, and there were numerous large areas of bog. For example, the now famous Princes Street Gardens was at that time merely a shallow marshy lake. Even the cultivated land was not at all what a farmer of the twentieth century would expect, for methods of agriculture were extremely primitive. Physically Scotland was rough, difficult, and inhospitable.

Settlements were few and far between. The usual unit of

country society was not the "nucleated" village as in England, but rather the Celtic hamlet straggling alongside the meandering tracks which were at best mere excuses for roads. Dominating the hamlets, and the landscape generally, countless feudal towers rose gaunt and bleak from hilltops or from islands situated either on the broad expanse of a loch or off the coast surrounded by the sea. Some were well-built and extensive fortifications, deserving the term castle, such as those at Stirling, Linlithgow, Edinburgh, or Dunvegan. Most, however, like Castle Stewart in Nairnshire or Castle Borthwick near Edinburgh, were simple towers made to withstand the attacks of raiders but incapable of defending themselves against an army equipped with artillery. In these hamlets and towers lived the larger part of Scotland's population. Yet one would also find small towns or burghs located at rivers' mouths, fords or bridges, and crossroads, behind whose walls was gradually developing an urban culture. Such was the outward aspect of Scotland around 1500.

It would be a mistake, however, to think of Scotland simply as a rude country dominated by poverty. To understand it one must see the pattern and dynamics of its way of life.

At the apex of both government and society stood the king. In 1488 James III had been murdered by his rebellious nobles, while fleeing from the Battle of Sauchieburn, and his son, James IV, who had been on the rebels' side, now professing deep remorse occupied the throne.[1] He was an able albeit romantic person who had the ambition to make Scotland an important factor in European politics. Yet he apparently realized that this would be impossible unless he had adequate force at his command— force attained by the creation of a navy, for his country was not wealthy and his army was but an uncertain feudal levy. James I and James III had both taken some initial steps in this direction, the latter going as far as to obtain two ships, the *Flower* and the *Yellow Caravel*, which he placed under the command of the former Leith merchant-sailor, Sir Andrew Wood of Largo.[2]

Thus when James IV ascended the throne he needed only expand the program already commenced by his unpopular father. He had, however, the great advantage of the support of most of the people coupled with almost dictatorial political power. Consequently everything seemed to favor his plans.

That his authority was very great, at least in theory, is indicated by the constitution of the Scottish government of the time. There was a parliament or Estates which supposedly ruled the country through commissions, but was largely under the control of the feudal faction in power.[3] Of much greater importance was the Secret Council of the king made up of the ecclesiastical and lay magnates to whom at the beginning of James IV's reign were added the parliamentary law officers, the auditors "of causes." This body, sometimes referred to as the Privy Council, was in truth the instrument of the king, and by it James IV succeeded in controlling the government absolutely.[4] Moreover, since the whole financial system of the government, centered around the royal feudal revenues and customs duties, was regarded as the king's own personal possession, he could direct the country's economic life to whatever ends he desired.

If James was to maintain his absolute power, however, he would have to control the major noble families. Scotland during the Middle Ages had developed a system of feudal immunities known as "regalities", which gave the holders of such rights virtual royal authority within their own lands. In these areas the king's writ did not run except in cases of murder, rape, arson, and treason. The result was that the nobility could, as they had done in preceding reigns, form alliances between themselves almost like independent monarchs, mass their forces, and defy the king. From this James IV was saved to a considerable extent by his own personal influence and popularity. Moreover, he did not commit his father's fatal mistake of ignoring the nobility. Instead, by including them in his council and household, and by allowing them to participate in the direction of the country's affairs, he satisfied their pride.[5]

This body of magnates formed the wealthiest lay group in the realm. With wide powers over their vassals and extensive lands, if they had any business sense at all they were able to count on large and stable incomes so that many seem to have found it comparatively easy both to pay for the upkeep of castles and private armies and to live as petty kings. Consequently they do not seem to have been greatly affected by the economic changes of the day.[6]

Subordinate to the great magnates was the large class of lesser nobility and lairds. These individuals might be the vassals of some great earl or lord, or they might hold their land directly from the crown. Their positions both politically and economically were not entirely secure. They possessed few economic resources and—partially as a result—they had little say in parliament. Since serfdom had long since disappeared from Scotland and rents were relatively low, those gentry who aspired to a standard of living beyond that of their forefathers often found it difficult to make ends meet. Since most of the profitable ecclesiastical positions were monopolized by the king or the great nobles, the lairds' chief hope seemed to rest in some form of alliance with the middle class.

The second important element in Scottish society was the church. Although threatened in earlier days by the soaring ambition of English prelates, particularly the Archbishop of York, the Scottish clergy had succeeded in maintaining their independence, the Archbishopric of St. Andrews being created in the reign of James III (1466) followed by a further archbishopric, Glasgow, in 1492.[7] Successful in preventing control by foreigners, the church was nonetheless in very much the same state as its sister institutions in other countries. The only difference was that the Renaissance does not appear to have had any great influence. The three universities founded during the fifteenth century, St. Andrews, Glasgow, and Aberdeen, continued to be largely medieval in their outlook until the Reformation. A number of individuals, of course, felt the impact of the revival of letters, but the clergy as a whole had little interest in what was going on beyond the bounds of their own parishes, or at best beyond those of their own country.[8]

Yet relative isolation from the major intellectual movements on the Continent had not kept the church pure. Indeed, one might even say its isolation helped to cause even greater deterioration in many spheres of its life. Some have estimated that it owned two-thirds of the land in the country, which of itself was a great danger, for since land was wealth, men were often attracted to holy orders by a desire to control part of these material possessions. Ignorance and extreme youthfulness were no bar to preferment if one had the proper patrons, the result being a generally low level of learning and morality throughout the ranks of the clergy.[9]

Usually the higher offices in the church were held by scions (frequently illegitimate) of the great families, who received their benefices by virtue of political influence. The nobility naturally favoured this because it provided both political and economic power for their children, and the king agreed, for it kept his nobles in a good mood and gave him an excuse to follow their practice.[10] Because of this state of affairs, the church, to a considerable extent ignoring her spiritual functions, was becoming more and more involved in politics and in the exploitation of her economic possessions. One can see, therefore, that she would have relatively little religious impact upon the people as a whole.

One religious group, frequently ignored, no doubt did have some influence: it was the Scottish Lollards. Its members seem to have had their spiritual origins in the teachings both of refugee English Lollards who had fled across the border early in the fifteenth century, and of wandering Bohemians who had brought to the east coast some of the doctrines of Jan Hus. Although relatively little is heard of them during the century, one gathers that by 1450 they were of some importance in the southwest of Scotland among the lower ranks of the gentry. It is also possible that their new ideas, and in particular their rejection of much of the church's authority, would appeal to the middle class traders in the towns. The rise of this dissentient religious element undoubtedly reflected the current dissatisfaction with the church's spiritual condition.[11]

Lower in the social hierarchy than the nobility and the clergy were the members of the mercantile class who dwelt within the burghs. Of an inferior order and relatively few in number, the Scottish merchants were beginning to assume more importance. As Froissart pointed out in the fourteenth century, Scotland in his day found it necessary to import all of its iron, most of its textiles, and much of its food,[12] and this situation had not changed materially by 1500. Consequently Scotland was still very dependent upon the activity and enterprise of her trading class.

But what had the Scots to offer in exchange for the needed goods? The answer is to be found primarily in the large flocks of sheep owned by the monasteries situated on the southern uplands and along the shores of Moray Firth, and by great land-owners such as the Earl of Huntly. Wool, wool-fells (fleeces with the skin still attached), and hides formed the staple Scottish exports. Other raw materials—cured fish such as salmon, herring, and cod; skins of the martin and the rabbit; beeswax and tallow; and some pearls from the oyster beds of the east coast—helped to provide the wherewithal for Scots to make their purchases. The only manufactured goods the merchants sent to the foreign markets were a little rough cloth and plaiding.

None of these commodities was exported in large quantities,

for the average consignment of wool per merchant seems to have been no more than a single sack weighing between 24 and 40 stone, along with a few lasts of hides and a few barrels of salmon.[13] Merchants dealing in large quantities of export goods must have been few.[14] But if Scotland were to continue to exist as a nation, let alone exercise any influence in Continental affairs, it was obvious that the merchants whether great or small held positions of strategic importance.[15]

One might naturally expect Scotland's best cutomer to be her nearest neighbour, England, but this was not the case. Almost continuous warfare, whether officially recognized or not, had been the dominant feature of the two countries' relations since the beginning of the fourteenth century, a state of affairs that had not promoted exchange of goods. Moreover, English trade restrictions and controls, coupled with the fact that London, the chief English port, could be reached only after a long and often dangerous voyage down the east coast, discouraged commercial intercourse at least by sea. That the English were interested, however, in fostering overland trade is indicated by their establishing Berwick and Carlisle in 1482 as legal ports of entry for Scottish goods. Apparently this action was taken in the hope that Scottish wools from the southern uplands might be sent to England for re-export, the merchants of Berwick being permitted to ship them directly to the Netherlands without taking them to the English wool staple at Calais. Yet despite this, little was accomplished; even by 1600 England was of no great economic significance in the Scottish commercial pattern.[16]

Of much greater importance was France. Since the latter part of the thirteenth century she had been Scotland's "auld ally", which fact made trade relations between the two countries quite natural. Rouen and Dieppe were the two principal ports to which, and from which, the Scots brought goods. Wool, fish, leather, and skins went to these markets, while from them came cloth, silk, sugar, and spices.[17] Indeed the trade became so important during the fifteenth century that settlements of Scottish merchants were established in both of these towns.[18] From two other French ports, La Rochelle and Bordeaux, the Scots brought home their wine, which coming by way of the west coat would seem to have been the basis of prosperity of Ayr and Dumbarton.[19] Yet trade with France suffered numerous hindrances both natural and human, not the least of these being English privateers during peace and warships during open hostilities. There was always considerable risk in sailing to a French port, a hard fact which clearly did not aid in promoting trade between the two countries.

Equal to, and in some respects more important than the trade with France was Scotland's commerce with what might be called the "northern triplice," the Hanseatic League, Denmark, and Holland. As there was a continual struggle going on among these three for control of the trade of the Baltic and the North Sea coast, Scotland was bound to become involved. In some respects this never-ending conflict aided, and in others hindered Scottish commerce so that it is a little hard to evaluate its total effect. Nevertheless it is quite clear that the constant struggle did influence Scotland's economic position.

The story of the Hanseatic League is largely that of the rise of Lübeck, which by 1490 had gained complete control of the organization. Made up of a group of north German cities, the League had been formed for the purpose of trading Baltic wares with the outside world both east and west. By 1350 it had become the principal trading organization of northern Europe with the objective of bringing all countries within the region under its economic sway. In this rise to power and influence, Lübeck gained the predominance because it controlled the shortest land route from the Baltic to the North Sea and the Rhineland. By dint of persuasion backed by strongarm methods, the Lübeckers succeeded in gaining a monopoly of both the dried fish trade between Bergen in Norway and the cities east of the Elbe, and the Baltic grain and salt exports to the west. As long as the Øresund was kept closed to non-Hanseatic vessels, Lübeck could control the commerce of the Baltic as well as much of that with the countries lying beyond. It was this position of power that the Hansa had secured by the middle of the fifteenth century.[20]

Up to this time, by virtue of its control of Scandinavian trade, the League had succeeded in preventing the Danes from admitting outsiders freely to the Baltic. By 1470, however, the situation was changing, for foreign vessels were carrying goods as far east as Danzig and Königsberg. The only answer to this threat to their monopoly was to force the King of Denmark to block the Øresund more effectively. But at this point the rising nationalism of the time played its part. The Danes who dominated the whole of Scandinavia, supported by the foreign traders, refused to close the entrance to the Baltic.[21] The result was continuous warfare, the Lübeckers doing everything they could to stir up trouble for the rulers of Denmark in order to regain control of what they regarded as their God-given monopoly.

Danish opposition to the Hansa, however, had not only an economic but also a political origin which had become apparent on the accession to the throne of Christian I, Duke of Oldenburg. In order to gain recognition as king, Christian had been obliged to acknowledge the monarchy to be elective, but he had hoped that once in power, he would become a ruler in deed as well as in theory. One of his first moves in attempting to achieve this end was to curtail the Hanseatic economic control of his kingdom. This was a difficult task since he possessed no great naval or military forces, and had little money. He therefore reinforced his rather feeble feudal Danish army with contingents from his ducal territories, and at the same time took steps to make alliances with various other European crowned heads. The culmination of his efforts was the marriage of his daughter to James III of Scotland. Thus, the Scots became involved in Danish problems for more than purely economic reasons.[22]

Although Christian I never succeeded entirely in shaking off the tentacles of the Hansa, his son Hans I, who ascended the throne in 1481, determined to attain that objective as well as to establish complete Danish control over Sweden and Norway. Unfortunately, however, an alliance between his brother Frederick, Duke of Oldenburg, the Hansa, and the Swedes meant that only by continuous warfare could he achieve his ends.

In this struggle the Scots played a considerable part. Early in the fifteenth century by attempting to circumvent Hanseatic restrictions they had come into serious conflict with the German authorities. However, so successful were they that by the end of the century Aberdeen and Dundee were carrying on a lucrative trade in Baltic goods.[23] When the Lubeckers in the latter part of the fifteenth century attempted to close the Øresund by force, the Scots gave their support to the Danes, with the result that thereafter, owing to Danish friendship, they were able to trade freely throughout the area. In this way both international politics and economic opportunity encouraged the Scots to expand their trading activities towards the north.

Scotland's expansion was nothing, however, compared to that of Holland's growing interest in the Baltic area. As far as the Danes were concerned this Dutch development was all to the good, for through it they hoped to gain the support of the nation which was becoming the middleman of northern Europe. During the fifteenth century, Antwerp had been slowly forging ahead of Bruges. She had adopted liberal policies to attract foreigners away from the older centers of trade, and had taken the practical step of deepening and widening the channel of the River Scheldt, so that by 1490 most oceangoing vessels from the south and west could sail safely into her spacious harbor.[24] From the north there were two routes to Antwerp, one inside the islands, the other by way of the open sea, entering Dutch territory through the Veergat, just east of the Island of Walcheren. The former was undoubtedly more important for local and western Danish trade, but the Hansa ships coming from the Baltic seem to have preferred the western route, for they found Veere and Middelburg on Walcheren to be good markets in which to buy imports from the south. It was to these cities that the Scots also came, since their traditional enemies the English monopolized Antwerp.[25] Veere, Middelburg, and Antwerp thus became rivals striving to attract foreign trade to their own particular markets by every possible means.[26]

It is at this point that one sees the importance of blood relationships. All the Island of Walcheren, except Middelburg, Arnemuiden, and Rammeken, was controlled by the Van Borselen family which was doubly related to the Scottish ruling house. James II's sister Mary had married Wolphaerts, son of Henry, Lord of Campveere, while James II himself had married Mary of Guelderland.[27] This connection exercised no little influence on Scottish trade policy, for the Scots had a tendency to carry their goods to the Van Borselen possessions, where the latter because of their Scottish connections were always prepared to give them every possible advantage.

Thus at the beginning of the sixteenth century Scotland found itself in a somewhat favoured position. On the outer rim of the North Sea, Edinburgh, Dundee, Aberdeen, and the other east coast ports had direct access across the North Sea to Norway, Denmark, the Baltic, and the Netherlands. Moreover, the merchants who plied these routes found that there was a constant demand for their goods. Consequently the Scots were well on the way to achieving a greater economic prosperity than they had ever known before.

The towns or burghs from which the Scottish traders set out on their ventures to foreign parts were usually "royal burghs," that is they had been founded by royal charter. Among their special privileges, the most important was a virtual monopoly of trade in the area surrounding them, extending sometimes to the whole of the shire.[28] By this right they controlled all business transactions, determined that certain types of industrial activity be kept within the town walls, and ensured that all trading of goods was carried on within the burgh limits. Nonburgesses were forbidden to buy from foreign merchants until the burgesses had first made their purchases, and very frequently the town authorities would make a "common bargain" (i.e. purchase goods in bulk) in which the burgesses alone had a right to participate.[29] Naturally the many nonburgess town dwellers objected, while at the same time the citizens of burghs founded by nobles or ecclesiastics insisted that they should have equal rights with the royal burghs. The latter, however, fought hard against any infringement of their monopolistic claims, insisting that they should be left in their exalted position because they helped pay part of the government's expenses. But with expanding trade making its influence felt, it was difficult to maintain such outmoded fashions. By 1500 the royal burghs' restrictive monopolies were beginning to show signs of wear.[30]

As the internal government of the royal burghs had developed slowly during the Middle Ages and without very much planning, it is not easily described. By 1490 the town administration was controlled by representatives of the wealthy commercial class organized as a Merchant Guild. Indeed, at times it is even difficult to distinguish clearly between the guild and the local civil authorities. Thus urban life was controlled by the "middle class," which, on the one hand strove to keep the artisans and unskilled laborers subservient, and on the other fought hard to prevent the feudal aristocracy from interfering with its rights and freedoms. The burgesses jealously maintained their monopoly of the burgh courts and their right to dominate the local market, endeavouring to exclude any who were not members of the guild.[31]

The royal government's oversight of the burgh administrations at the end of the fifteenth century was inclined to be rather vague and uncertain. Its principal interest seems to have been the collection of taxes, a duty performed by the Comptroller of the Royal Household.[32] Beyond this, however, little attempt was made by royal officials to interfere with the activities of the burgesses. The only real effort to control was in parliament's legislation concerning trade, by which it was hoped commerce would be directed into the channels most profitable for the country. Not infrequently, of course, these statutes were the outcome of recommendations by the burghs themselves.[33] It was probably because of this regulation by parliament that there is no sign of the rise, as in England, of the chartered company; the merchants, particularly of the east coast ports, acting under the government's supervision had no need of a special body to direct their activities. As commerce was a national affair of great importance, they were supposed to act in the national interest.[34]

Since the trade of the fifteenth century unlike that of today was directed towards Europe, it fell largely under the domination of the east coast towns. Of these Edinburgh ranked first, for it was not only the country's political, but also its commercial capital. Dundee and Aberdeen were in competition for second place, and after them came Perth, Haddington, and St. Andrews.[35] Edinburgh, however, situated on the Firth of Forth, one of the best roadsteads in Scotland, and the closest to the Continental trade centers, was in a position to advance its economic fortunes beyond those of any other Scottish burgh.

At this point it might be well to stop for a moment to take a closer look at Edinburgh. Although the largest and most important of the Scottish urban centers, it was still very small when compared with its present physical extent. Lying to the east of the Castle, it had really but one thoroughfare, the High Street, the whole town being little more than a concentrated hamlet sitting on the ridge bounded to the north by a sharp declivity falling away to the North Loch, now Princes Street Gardens, and to the south by the hollow in which runs the Cowgate. During the middle of the fifteenth century a wall was built from the base of the Castle Rock eastward along the brow of the slope overlooking the Cowgate, as far as Leith Wynd at which point it turned northward to the east end of the North Loch which was regarded as the town's northern defense. East of the wall, and continuing the High Street, was the Canongate belonging to the monks of Holyrood Abbey. Here and on the Cowgate to the south, during the latter part of the fifteenth century, nobles and wealthy citizens were building fashionable residences. On the other hand, it was within the walls that most of the burgh's inhabitants carried on their activities, cramped and confined through lack of space, in narrow closes and wynds. Such was the country's capital city.[36]

Not only was it the capital, but as a royal burgh Edinburgh possessed many privileges. A very important one was the right of anyone who owned a "borrowage" within the town, who had lived there for a year and a day, and who had taken the necessary oaths of fealty, to be a burgess. This regulation opened the door for rising men to achieve the desired position more easily than in many other towns. While some of the burgesses might not favour such a rule, it did increase the number of those paying taxes and liable for military service on the burgh walls, thus relieving the strain on the individuals already enjoying burgess-right.[37] Much more important was the right of the "town" to hold two fairs, one for eight days after Trinity Day in June and the other for eight days at the feast of All Saints. Likewise the city authorities had the privilege of establishing weekly markets. Furthermore, the Edinburgh merchants were free of the payment, throughout the country, of all customs duties on salt and skins. Parallel to its economic privileges was political power, for the burgh possessed extensive rights of self-government, the baillies and provost having the privilege of calling a peremptory court on three weeks' notice to deal with all types of suits and of decreeing new statutes and regulations for the city and its inhabitants.[38] To be a burgess of Edinburgh was a privilege and an honor of a very high order.

One further right was Edinburgh's control of Leith. A number of inland towns were overlords of seacoast ports through which they carried on their seaward trade. Linlithgow held Blackness, Elgin had Lossie and Spey, and most important of all, Edinburgh was lord of Leith, a relationship which gave rise to much conflict and controversy.[39]

Leith's subservience to Edinburgh seems to have commenced on May 31, 1398, when the former's feudal superior, Sir Robert Logan of Restalrig, granted to the city of Edinburgh the privilege of extending the port at Leith, and promised that he would renounce for himself, his heirs and the indwellers of Leith, the keeping of taverns for wine, mills for grinding flour, and all shops for retailing goods. To this grant the inhabitants of Leith do not seem to have taken too kindly, for in January, 1454, the Laird of Restalrig signed another agreement with Edinburgh, stating that he would see that the Leith men maintained its terms and would protect citizens of Edinburgh from attack.[40] By this time, however, royal authority had added to the privileges of the Edinburgh burgesses. James I had granted them the right to collect taxes on every ship entering the port, charging strangers and even the men of Leith a higher rate of duty than citizens of Edinburgh. In 1436 it was ordered that all victuals coming into Leith be taken immediately to the Edinburgh Tolbooth, where they were to be priced and sold, the burgesses having first choice. From this time on, greater and greater powers were given to the Edinburgh town council, James III going beyond anything which had been known before. By 1485 no Edinburgh merchant was permitted to take a Leith man into partnership, neither could he allow him to act as his factor, nor could he participate with Leith inhabitants in the freighting of ships.[41] As far as possible the people of Leith were to be kept permanently in the position of stevedores and fishermen, totally dependent upon the merchants living around the Castle Rock. Here was a cause for grievance which, because of the development of trade, was bound to lead to increasing conflict.

Thus the expansion and growth of trade had its repercussions on the life of the country. Although the Western Highlands and Islands were little affected, on the east coast and particularly in the towns, changes were beginning to take place such as might presage almost a social revolution.

One such development was that the increased demand for goods brought the trader to the fore. Although the merchant and urban trading center had long been recognized as necessities, they had also been regarded almost as parasites living off the work of others. If a man risked his life in going abroad for business, he might be given the benefit of the doubt since he was maintaining the nation's balance of trade, but if he stayed at home he was likely to be considered a monopolist preying upon society's need for goods.[42] The truth is, however, that the merchant did not make a very great profit on any article. Power and Postan point out that the average English wool merchant probably made no more than £2 on a sack of wool, although this might be increased by playing with exchange rates.[43] It was constant saving, working to the utmost of one's ability, taking risks in lending money, and occasionally indulging in some piracy on the high seas that combined to bring the merchant large gains and eventual wealth.[44] As the burgesses accumulated liquid wealth either individually or corporately they in turn became suppliers of funds to the impoverished gentry. It is not surprising, therefore, that during the latter part of the fifteenth century a growing number of lairds seem to have been borrowing money from the townsmen. Moreover, often in connection with such transactions intermarriage between the two groups seems to have taken place. At the same time the merchant frequently purchased properties which had escheated to the crown. The middle class was in this way rising to a higher status in society, making its position more secure and at the same time increasing its influence in the life of the country.

As a group these men were—perhaps by nature and training, but most certainly by necessity—the most enterprising element in the country. Before them lay continually the possibilities of large fortunes and honor, objectives which could be attained, however, only by taking great risks. As they grew in wealth and power they usually became more self-sufficient and individualistic, refusing to allow others to encroach upon what they considered to be their rights. They were inclined to believe in freedom—for themselves. This attitude in turn obliged them to examine everything carefully and critically, a tendency which they further developed when on their constant travels they were forced to deal with new ideas, new concepts, and new practices. Intellectually they were the most advanced element in the population simply because they had to be if they were to survive in the competition of business.[45]

This alertness of the middle class showed itself in many different ways, the most obvious, of course, being in the methods of trade. Not only were they prepared to venture to almost unknown lands with their goods in hope of winning a profit, but what is more, they were also quite willing to break any and all trade regulations if they felt that such action would bring them more money. Ecclesiastical censures and time-honored custom meant little in the search for wealth. This point of view in turn, had its repercussions upon the government. For one thing, the men of the middle class began to take an increasing part in what might be called the civil service, filling posts which had formerly been held by clerics; or they made names for themselves as naval commanders. At the same time they were of the opinion that they should have a greater voice in the government of the country itself. Another side of the middle class's intellectual iconoclasm was its attitude toward the church. In many cases the burgesses were quite prepared to turn away from the old medieval ecclesiastical organization with its "idle" clergy, its ownership of more than half of Scotland's lands, its insufficient doctrines, and its anachronistic economic regulations. The middle class which was coming to the top around 1500 in Scotland was an explosive force which might well bring about a radical revolution. Out of this background came Robert Barton.

Letters of Marque

One English writer, J. Stedman, has claimed that the Bartons of Leith were originally of Yorkshire stock and that their name was really Bertram, Bertrahame, or something similar; but without proof his assertion is scarcely worthy of serious consideration, especially as there is no indication that the name Barton or Bertoun was ever interchangeable with Bertram.[1] The name Barton signifies Briton, which may indicate that the family originally came from the old western British kingdom of Strathclyde whose capital was Dumbarton. But whatever its origin, Robert's family does not seem to appear on the pages of history until some of its members met with disaster.

The earliest information available on the family is, most appropriately, connected with piracy, although in this case the Bartons were the victims. Some time during the latter half of the fifteenth century Juan Vasquez and Juan Pret, captains of two vessels forming part of a Portuguese fleet, off the port of Sluis attacked and captured a Scottish merchantman, identified by Stedman as the *Juliana*, owned and commanded by Robert's father, John Barton of Leith. The crew of the ship they either killed or set adrift in a boat, and the captured vessel they

carried off to Portugal.[2] In this apparent disaster lay the beginning of the Bartons' rise to fortune and fame, for as will be seen
in the succeeding pages, this event brought forth results which
were, for the Bartons, both unexpected and profitable.

Although Stedman states that this misadventure happened in
1476,[3] there are good reasons for placing it somewhat earlier.
For one thing John Barton appears to have been the captain of
the *Yellow Caravel* when she was almost wrecked at Berwick, in
1473. This vessel belonged to the king who, in peacetime,
rented it out to his captains for trading ventures. In November,
1474, she carried a Scottish ambassador to France ; in the
following April she was captured by the Duke of Gloucester but
was later returned.[4] It is obvious, even if Stedman should be
wrong about the name of the ship which was stolen by the
Portuguese, that it was not the *Yellow Caravel*, as there would
certainly have been mention made of her "royal" character in
later Scottish complaints. It may have been that by 1473 John
Barton had taken over the *Yellow Caravel* as a substitute for the
ship lost at Sluis. Moreover, the *Yellow Caravel* appears, as we
shall see, a number of times in the later history of the Bartons.
Thus the probable date for the seizure of John Barton's ship
would seem to be prior to 1473.

Perhaps a more accurate determination of the date can be
obtained by other means. Around 1470 Bruges had been designated the staple for Scottish exports, and to this city all
Scottish merchants were supposed to resort. Within three
years, however, the staple was removed owing to the treatment
meted out to the Scots by the local authorities. Rooseboom
believes that the seizure of the sails of Scots' ships lying at
anchor in the river Zwin was the reason for the change. It is
quite possible, too, that the failure of the local authorities to
protect such people as Barton may have been a contributing
cause. But whether this specific case of Portuguese piracy was
involved or not, since the Scots seem to have largely disappeared

from Bruges for some time after 1473, it is probable that the attack on Barton took place in the first three years of the 1470's.[5]

In the various extant accounts of the Portuguese misdemeanor many conflicting statements appear concerning the fate of John Barton. George Buchanan states flatly that he was killed in the fight. Stedman, however, with his usual omission of proof, claims that he, along with some of his crewmen, was put adrift-in a boat. Then, having returned home, he went to Lisbon to sue the pirates for recovery, but was murdered. It is a quaint story, but in the light of the evidence it seems to be somewhat fanciful.[6] In all the complaints made later concerning the Portuguese action, no mention is ever made of the death of John Barton either in the original attack or at Lisbon. What is more, there are references to a John Barton, senior, a sea captain and a resident of Leith, down to 1510, and it seems highly probable from various pieces of evidence that this was Robert's father.[7]

Apparently he brought the matter before James III, who endeavoured to settle it in his usual manner, by issuing him letters of marque against the Portuguese, which he then refused to put into commission. The date on which the King granted the letters we do not know, although J. C. Irons claims that it was in 1476.[8] The difficulty is that not having any copies of the original letters patent, one must be content to guess. More important is the fact that by this grant, the Bartons obtained recognition of their right to sail the seas despoiling the Portuguese until they had recouped themselves for John's losses. This was a privilege of which they were to avail themselves on numerous occasions.[9]

Before they could do anything with their letters of marque, however, a political revolution shook Scotland. In 1488 a group of disgruntled nobles who gained possession of young Prince James, the heir-apparent, rose in revolt against James III.

On June 11, 1488, the conflict came to an issue at Sauchieburn
where the rebels were victorious, the king being murdered
as he fled from the field. In this struggle it would seem that
the mercantile and seafaring element generally favored the
king, for before the victorious nobles knew of James' fate
they suspected that he had escaped to Sir Andrew Wood's
squadron, which had been sailing in the Forth near the site
of the battle. Although Wood swore that this was not so, the
nobles did not believe him and demanded that the skippers of
Leith capture his ships. To this, according to Lindsay of
Pitscottie, "On Captaine Bartone answeired and said thair was
not ten schipes in Scotland that would give Captane Woodes
twa schipes combatt ; for he was weill practised in warre, and
had such artilyrie and men that it was hard dealing with him
aither be sea or land."[10] This statement before the council of the
rebel lords by one who was apparently a recognized leader
seems to have clinched the matter, for no further action was
taken. The respect manifested by the skippers of Leith for the
opinion of this Captain Barton would indicate that he was not
only a man of experience and judgement, but was also intimately
acquainted with Wood's capacity as a naval commander. No
young man without a reputation could have carried the day
against the lords. Consequently the evidence seems to point to
John Barton, senior, as the man in question, the probable explanation of his presence at the council being that by now he had
given up the royal service to sail once more in a ship of his own.[11]

The loyalty of the seamen to James III experienced a quick
change once it was known that he was dead. The true king was
now James IV, to whom Wood, along with Leith captains such
as William Brounhill, David Falconer, and John Barton gave
their allegiance.[12] For the remainder of his reign James IV was
to enjoy the loyal support and wholehearted co-operation of
these men who were to aid him in fashioning Scotland into a
maritime power.

That Scotland needed a strong fleet became only too clear within a year of James' accession. Early in 1489 one of " the king's ships " was chased into Dumbarton by the English.[13] Why they made this attack is difficult to say, but the episode caused the Scots no little concern. Their worry at this time was nothing, however, to that aroused a little later in the year by the appearance in the Firth of Forth of five English vessels that attacked both ships and ports.[14] Lindsay of Pitscottie, who is not always trustworthy, says that nobody was willing to resist the searobbers until finally Sir Andrew Wood, perhaps in desperation, sailed out with the *Flower* and the *Yellow Caravel*, making contact with the marauders off the coast just opposite Dunbar. In the ensuing battle he captured the five English ships which he carried to Leith. This was the first blood to the Scots, a major sea victory of which they might well be proud.[15]

Henry VII, on the other hand, was far from pleased, for according to Lindsay he promptly offered £1,000 for the capture of Wood. His desire for reprisals had little immediate effect, however, as the English were now deeply involved in war on the Continent. It was not until the summer of 1490, when there was a lull in the international conflicts, that an English captain, Stephen Bull, decided he would try to win the reward ; and with this purpose sailed up the east coast to the mouth of the Forth with three ships. Like the English raiders of the preceding year Bull also came to blows with Wood's squadron which again gained the victory. James IV, however, because of the Englishman's valiant fight, and in order to keep in Henry's good books, permitted the raiders to return home.[16]

These battles and their favorable outcome seem to have whetted James' appetite for a larger navy. He was beginning to see more clearly than ever that if Scottish trade, and indeed Scottish national existence itself, were to be ensured, he must have sufficient ships to meet his realm's vital needs. On

December, 1489, after the first English attack, he had added to his navy a ship which he purchased from the Laird of Laight (Wigtownshire) for the sum of £130 and on which he spent a further £276 12s. for boards, timber, artillery, anchors, cables, and sailors' wages and food, in order to put her in a state of preparedness.[17] This vessel, perhaps "the king's little ship" for which a standard of blue was obtained in May, 1491, was no doubt placed, like the other two, under the command of Wood, now a trusted servant, and stationed off his barony of Largo on the north shore of the Forth, ready for action.[18]

If John Barton was still captain of the *Yellow Caravel* in 1489, it is probable that he, too, fought in the battles off Dunbar and the Bass Rock ; and, since by this time they were beginning to show some interest in a seaman's life, it is more than likely that at least one of his sons also took part.

That John had three sons, John, Robert, and Andrew, is quite certain, and this seems to be the order in which they came. Some writers have held that Andrew was the eldest, because of the three he was the most prominent as a searover during the first decade of the sixteenth century. Specific evidence, however, points in another direction. In a reissue of the letters of marque in 1506, the king referred to Andrew as "juniore filio Johannis Berton [sic]" and to Robert as "praecipue." Since John, junior, bore the name of his father, he was probably the eldest, while the description of Andrew would seem to emphasize that he was still a youth. These facts coupled with what we know of Andrew later on, as well as the reference to Robert as "the foremost"—neither eldest nor youngest—all point to the above order as the correct one. More than this one cannot say, for there are no legal records available to settle the matter. It would seem, however, that they were all born within a few years of each other for they all appeared on the scene about the same time, and later frequently participated in the same projects.[19]

That John Barton's family grew up in Leith would seem to be without question ; and one can easily imagine the impression which the life in that stirring little port made upon the three young boys. The continual arrival and departure of vessels from England, Holland, Denmark, France, and the Baltic, all laden with goods for trade, could not but have excited youthful interest and curiosity. As the lumber, the spices, the cloth, and other merchandise were unloaded at the port, one can picture a considerable group of teen-aged youths hovering around the ships much like the seagulls flying overhead, asking questions, peeking into bales and packages, and hoping that perhaps the sailors from foreign parts might give them some little momento of the countries they had visited. Added to this there would be the example of Barton senior, who was continually trading, and perhaps fighting, across the North Sea. His tales of bargains made, of storms defied, of police eluded, but above everything else of his maltreatment by the Portuguese, would all have their impact upon the boys' developing minds. Then too, if as has been surmised, Sir Andrew Wood were a close friend of John Barton, they would have heard much of his exploits as a seadog and no doubt have known him personally. All of these influences would help to fire their imaginations and turn their minds to a seafaring life.

What formal education they may have had is more difficult to determine. That they did have some is indicated by the fact that Robert could write and was also able later to fill efficiently the office of Comptroller of the Royal Household, revising its accounts and straightening out its finances. Owing to the hostility of Edinburgh to Leith at this time it is very doubtful, however, that they would have been permitted to attend school in the royal burgh. But that would probably have been unnecessary, as it is likely that the canons living in St. Anthony's Hospital conducted a school to provide an education for the local boys. It may be of significance in this connection that

St. Anthony's Church is the only church in which Robert ever seems to have had any interest.

Out of this milieu came the three Bartons, anticipating a life of excitement, hardship, and violence with relatively little chance for wealth in return. Although a successful man such as Sir Andrew Wood might commence his career as a sea captain and rise to be a friend of the king, there were dozens of others of the same type in and around Leith who merely eked out a living in the borderland between legitimate trade and piracy. Enterprising they had to be to survive, their enterprise at times being hardly distinguishable from open dishonesty. Such a background could not but mold the three young men who appear in Scottish history at the beginning of the 1490's.

The mist and fog which surround Robert's early years begin to lift, but only very slightly, around 1492. In a lawsuit of 1500, William Gray of Leith pursued before the Lords of the Council a certain Scot, John Chepman of Umflet (Honfleur?) who in 1492 had seized his ship, the *Bark of Liddale*, given to him by the king. As Robert Barton had become Chepman's surety for the ship which the latter refused to surrender, Gray demanded that Robert reimburse him for his loss. It is impossible to say when Robert had become surety in this case, but it may indicate that by 1492 he had sufficient knowledge of the port and those who visited it, to be prepared to go bail for a person such as Chepman, while at the same time his becoming surety seems to show that even at this early date he was a man of sufficient substance for his bond to be of some value.[20] As nothing further can be ascertained about him at this time the mist descends once again.

Before Robert reappears on the stage, other developments with a direct bearing on his next entrance must be noticed. As has already been pointed out, James IV had become interested in the idea of building up his navy. But in order to achieve this objective he needed both ships and well-trained sailors. Since

it was a common idea of the day that the best way to develop
a navy was to encourage fisheries, in 1492 the Scottish Estates
enacted a law requiring all royal and baronial burghs to build
vessels of twenty tons or more to participate in the industry.[21]
The success of this act was not overwhelming, but shipbuilding
and fishing were somewhat stimulated while the inhabitants of
the east coast ports seem to have been persuaded to take more
interest in venturing out onto the deep.[22]

James IV, however, was never a man to insist that others do
what he was not prepared to attempt himself. Although the
Yellow Caravel seems to have disappeared, probably because of
age, he still had the *Flower* and perhaps "the litill bote," to
which he had added some time earlier the *Douglas* and the
Christopher. This flotilla James now increased by a vessel built
especially for himself. It was small, and since it used oars
as its means of propulsion, was probably a galley. Sir George
Galbraith, Master of the Works, supervised its construction at
Dumbarton, making it one of the first Clydeside vessels on
record. Wood was obtained from the Highlands, Inch Calleach,
Sallach, Lus, and other areas, and perhaps the sixty Eastland
boards bought from Sir Andrew Wood went into its hull. For
the purpose of this study, however, the most important purchase was that of a cable from Robert Barton in 1494.[23] By this
time he seems to have been in business, dealing in naval stores,
but this is all we can say. The size of his business, the method
of its operation, and its other aspects are completely unknown.

Far more important than this minor transaction was another
event of the same year. On June 25 James IV issued to John and
Robert Barton letters of marque permitting them to capture
Portuguese ships, to recoup themselves for the losses their
father had suffered through the Portuguese act of piracy at
Sluis.[24] That the renewal of the letters of marque mentions
only John and Robert, and not Andrew, may indicate that the

latter was at this time uninterested in such things, either because of his youth, or because he had other matters on his mind. From this point on the family gradually emerges from darkness into the comparatively bright light of day. Henceforth it is possible to follow each member, particularly Robert, down to the end of his life.

Why the letters of marque were issued at this moment is impossible to say, but there would seem to be little doubt that the king gave them to Robert and John as a result of their influence with him, demonstrating that, although up till this time they do not appear very frequently in the records they had already established something of a reputation as seamen, and perhaps as merchants. Whenever, at later dates, the Bartons obtained renewal of the letters, they were usually high in royal favor and at the same time low in economic prosperity. They seem to have regarded the letters as a type of capital reserve upon which they could call whenever they found life boring or finances somewhat straitened.

Although John and Robert Barton obtained their coveted letters of marque in June of 1494, there is no evidence that they made any immediate use of them, but rather seem to have held them in reserve for an occasion of need. For the moment the brothers had other and bigger fish to catch. The Portuguese they had always with them, but more pressing business had to be attended to at once.

As far as Robert was concerned one matter of immediate importance was a lawsuit concerning some land in Leith. Although little is known of this property, including its location, it had been held by Robert's father John, at least since 1478. In that year Andrew Mowbray, burgess of Edinburgh, pursued John Barton and Alex Knichtson before the Lords of the Council for withholding from him an annual fee of 5 marks due from this land. Knichtson had apparently been the guarantor of the payment. What the nature of this annual fee was is hard to say, but it was possibly some sort of encumbrance granted by a former owner in return for a loan or gift. This is suggested by the Lord's decision that since the case involved questions relating to inheritance, they would refer the matter to the episcopal court, where apparently it was settled for there is no further mention of the suit.[25]

The next appearance of the property in the records seems to have been in July, 1494, when Robert, who had obtained title to it, probably from his father, likewise refused to pay the 5 marks owing Andrew Mowbray.[26] A complaint was therefore again made before a court, although which one is not stated, and judgement was given in favor of Mowbray. The victorious burgess thereupon had the Islay Herald go to Robert's "land and tenement" to "distrain" and "poynd" it for the amount owing. To this Robert quite naturally took exception, and physically ejected the representative of the law, thus being guilty not only of refusing to pay his just debt, but also of forcibly resisting a royal officer.[27]

As Mowbray, a prominent Edinburgh citizen, was unwilling to acquiesce in Robert's violence, on November 29, 1494, he appealed to the Lords Auditors of Causes and Complaints. The Lords responded promptly by handing down a judgement against the offender, ordering him to pay the sum currently due as well as that for the preceding year. The case of the Islay Herald against Robert they postponed to December 7, but as there is no further record of it the pursuer may have dropped it or settled it "out of court."[28] There is little doubt, however, that Robert had been beaten in this effort to avoid payment of what he seems to have regarded as an unjustified charge against his property.

Although not too much information is available on this law case, it does reveal some facts about Robert. For one thing, there is his attitude of defiance towards the law, a tendency which reappears time and time again throughout his life. His

summary treatment of the herald may have been sheer impulsive-
ness, or it may have been the result of a determination to have
his own way regardless of the risks or opposition. On a more
material level this case proves that by 1494 he had become a
landowner in Leith, from which one may conclude that he had
climbed at least a few rungs up the social and economic
ladder.[29]

He was, however, interested in more than the accumulation
of real estate. Those were exciting days that stimulated one of
his temperament to enterprise and action. As has been pointed
out in the first chapter, Scottish trade, despite all the hazards
involved, was beginning to expand. Consequently it is not surprising to find that the name of Robert Barton, along with those
of his two brothers, very soon made its appearance in contemporary commercial records.

One of the main streams of Scottish trade at the end of the
fifteenth century flowed towards the Netherlands and in particular the Zeeland area, where by 1490 the principal port of
entry for Scottish goods had been located at Middelburg on the
island of Walcheren. Situated on the North Sea, at about the
closest point in the Netherlands to Scotland, with a good
harbor formed by the upper reaches of the river Arne, this
city provided all that Scottish exporters needed in the way of
markets and trading facilities. An important step was taken in
1492 when a number of merchants, ecclesiastics, and others
who felt that it would be wise to have a permanent commercial
representative in Middelburg, arranged for a certain Andrew
Haliburton to hold that position. According to his ledger,
during the nineties he was the factor for a good many persons
on whose behalf he sold and bought goods throughout the
country.[30] At the same time other Scots were also trading
in Middelburg, in Veere, and in Bergen-op-Zoom on the
mainland.[31] Thus for the Scots most roads led to the Low
Countries.

How far Robert became involved in this trade by the middle of the decade is not easily determined, owing to the fact that there are neither customs records nor, apart from Haliburton's ledger, business documents which give any light on his activities. However, an entry in Haliburton's ledger in June, 1495, states that Andrew Barton brought over "a pok of brone woyll" in his ship for Andrew Mowbray junior, who may have been Robert's erstwhile pursuer in the courts. As this pok weighed 305 stone, the stone equaling either 16 pounds troy weight or 14 pounds avoirdupois,[32] this was obviously not the whole cargo, but only the part handled by Haliburton. Although Robert's name does not appear in the ledger during this period, it is logical to assume that he also was active in the North Sea trade.

But what form did the Bartons' participation take? Were they trading goods as merchants, or were they simply acting as carriers? Were they using their own ships or others which they had hired? It is of course possible that they were in the same position as James Wood who commanded the *Douglas* or John Irwin, master of the *Christopher*, both of whom paid the king rents between 1494 and 1498 for the privilege of using his ships as merchantmen.[33] On the other hand, it looks as though they had their own ships and, while carrying the goods of other merchants, also traded on their own accounts. Evidence in support of this hypothesis is forthcoming from an adventure which befell Robert in 1496, and which we must now consider.

In November of the preceding year King James had welcomed to his court a young man who claimed to be one of the sons of Edward IV of England. The pretender, Perkin Warbeck, represented the hopes of the exiled Yorkist faction who hoped to come to power through a "restoration" of the "Duke of York" by means of a Scottish invasion of England aided by a Yorkist uprising. As is well known, the whole plan fizzled out without accomplishing anything. James' expedition into

England obtained no support so that he returned disgusted with
the English and determined to rid himself of this now unwel-
come guest. Moreover, both French and Spanish representatives
were trying to obtain possession of the pretender in order to
use him as a pawn in the current game of international chess.

Warbeck, therefore, faced the necessity of leaving Scotland as
soon as possible. Although James would not hand the young
man over to Henry, he would be only too glad to see the last
of him. For this reason, Warbeck was persuaded that his best
chance of gaining the English throne would be to set up his
standard in Cornwall, the locale of a recent rebellion against
Henry's attempt to levy taxes. There he would find Englishmen
who would doubtless give him their wholehearted support.[34]
To this plan Warbeck agreed.

The willingness of Warbeck to depart, however, did not
immediately solve all difficulties. The next question was: how
could he be conveyed to Cornwall? James decided that the best
method would be to place him on board a ship which would
carry him directly to his destination. To this end he decided to
purchase a vessel called the *Cuckoo* hailing from Brittany and
owned by Guy Foulcart and Guillaume Pompton. The *Lord High
Treasurer's Accounts* contain under date of October 3, 1496, a
deleted item which states that he had paid £100 as part of the
price of the vessel. The deletion was made because on October
10 the shipowners were hailed into court on an unspecified
charge and five days later had paid back all the money received.
Since it might only have led to further English attacks if James
had sent the pretender to the English throne to Cornwall in one
of his own ships, it looks as though he decided that it would
be safer for everyone concerned if a foreign vessel were
employed.[35]

It is at this point that Robert and Andrew Barton became
involved in the operation. Although the available information is
somewhat sketchy, it would appear that James either persuaded

or forced Guy Foulcart, the restored master and owner of the *Cuckoo*, and a certain Henri de la Bar from St. Pol de Léon in Brittany, owner of another vessel, to transport Warbeck and his entourage to Cornwall. Although James later asserted that the Bretons had undertaken this responsibility gladly for adequate payment, Foulcart claimed that he had acted only under compulsion.[36] For neither claim is there offered any proof, but from the fact that Robert was commissioned to act as the escort of the two Bretons' vessels, and from the way in which he fulfilled his duties, it looks as though there may have been a certain amount of "persuasion" employed.

It has been stated in a number of accounts of this episode that the *Cuckoo* was Robert's ship and that he actually sailed with Warbeck, perhaps aided by his brother Andrew.[37] From what we know of later developments, however, such a reading of the evidence is mistaken. For one thing, it is certain that when Foulcart sailed with Warbeck on board, he still owned the *Cuckoo*. Furthermore, Andrew's connection with the venture was limited to the provision of 2,000 pieces of bread (cost £16) for the victualling of Warbeck's ships.[38] Robert on the other hand escorted the two Breton ships in his own unidentified vessel.[39]

In July, 1497, the squadron of three ships assembled in the harbor of Ayr, whither Warbeck came with his wife, his children, and a few supporters, and around the 20th they set sail. Some believe that, although the plan was for Warbeck to proceed directly to Cornwall, he decided at the last moment to try his fortunes in Ireland. On the other hand, word of an English flotilla lying in wait may have caused him to change his plan and put into Cork on July 26 in search of aid from the earls of Kildare and Desmond. They, however, convinced that he had no hope of success, endeavoured to arrest him, but he escaped inland where for over a month he eluded their forces, eventually coming down to Kinsale. There he found two

Biscayan or Spanish ships which he hired to carry him to Cornwall.[40]

Although the contemporary accounts of what happened after this are somewhat confusing, it would seem that Warbeck's ships were stopped by the English search squadron; but as the pretender had hidden himself in a cask he remained undiscovered, and shortly afterwards landed at the ancient port of St. Michael's Mount.[41] Despite his force of "eighty savage Irishmen," and support he received in Cornwall, he was very quickly outmaneuvred by Henry's forces and captured ; and with his imprisonment the last serious threat to Henry's throne disappeared.

What happened in the meantime to the others involved in this expedition ? It may have been at Cork or perhaps later at sea that the English seized both Foulcart's and de la Bar's ships for their part in this rather amateurish drama. The present writer feels that the capture probably took place when Warbeck sailed into the Irish port, for by the arrest of his vessels the local forces would feel that they had effectively cut him off from any possible means of escape. Moreover, the vessels' seizure would have been quite easy if Robert, having escorted them as far as the entrance to Cork harbor, had then left them to their fate. Naturally the Bretons were annoyed at such treatment, particularly as the expedition was apparently not of their seeking. When they returned home they complained bitterly to Anne of Brittany, but without much effect, for their suit for damages before the Scottish court was still pending six years later, and James and Anne were continuing to trade strong words over the way in which the Scots had treated the Breton shipowners.[42] Although Robert may have carried out his duties to James' satisfaction, it is quite certain that neither Warbeck nor the Bretons were favorably impressed.

As soon as he was free of Warbeck, Robert returned home. There he joined forces with his brother John, master of the

Crowney, who had been despoiled somewhat earlier by English raiders, and with a certain George Young. The three men then fitted out two ships to attack the English.[43]

The next thing one hears of them is that they had arrived off the coast of Brittany, west of St. Malo at Roscoff, the port of St. Pol de Léon. Their reasons for dropping anchor at this point were three. First, as it appears that Roscoff was one of the Breton ports most visited by Scottish merchants, indeed the usual port of call when one sailed from Dumbarton to France, Robert and his confreres would feel that they were among friends.[44] Secondly, the harbor was protected by the Ile de Batz and a line of jagged rocks, past which it would be difficult to navigate if one did not know the way, and so offering good protection to vessels lying within the reefs. Lastly, Roscoff was a very convenient location for any ship wishing to raid commerce passing through the Channel. Consequently, it is not surprising that the Scottish privateers looking for a safe base from which to operate, chose Roscoff, arriving there late in September or early in October of 1497.

Confident that they had nothing to fear, the ships having been made secure, the boats were lowered and a large part of the crews quickly covered the mile or so of water which separated them from the land. One can well imagine that after some weeks of living in a couple of small ships with poor food and even worse accommodation, the sailors were very glad to be ashore. From the information which can be gathered concerning the evening's jaunt, there seems to have been no trouble between the sailors and the local inhabitants. Everyone parted on friendly terms and the ships' crews returned to their quarters tired, but at peace with the world. In fact, they were so tired and so peaceful that they did not even set a watch, for they were sure that safe behind the reefs no enemy could attack them.

The friendly atmosphere of Roscoff was, however, deceptive.

4

The Scots had hardly returned to their ships when a certain
Hervé de Porzmoguer, Sieur de Villeneuve, a man who later
gained something of a reputation fighting the English, slipped
quietly from the shore with a number of accomplices, probably in fishing boats, across the narrow strip of water which
separated them from the unsuspecting Scots. Although part of
the force boarded the first vessel without giving the alarm, in
their attempt to take possession there was a scuffle and some
shouting. The stillness of the night carried this noise across the
water to the second ship. But its crew did not awake soon
enough. The other party of Bretons was already alongside.
Quickly they swarmed on to the deck where they overcame the
few wakeful crew members, and the second ship was taken.
They then towed their acquisitions into the harbor amidst the
rejoicings of the inhabitants, and the captured crews were lined
up and marched off to the prison in St. Pol de Léon.

The question which then had to be answered by both captors
and captives was : what would the Bretons do next? For
twenty days the Scots were kept in irons in the foul dungeons of
St. Pol where they were repeatedly threatened, as pirates, with
death. Robert and his confreres, however, seem at length to
have convinced the authorities that they should be freed. But
the Bretons did not return to the Bartons and Young all their
goods and possessions. Retaining one ship and both cargoes,
which probably indicates that some English prizes had already
been taken, they placed both crews in the other ship, and told
them to be gone. The expedition, which was to help recoup the
Bartons, their relatives and friends, returned to its home port,
not only without any profits but minus more than half its
assets.

The explanation for the Breton's behaviour which immediately comes to mind is that believing the two ships to be pirates,
they merely took the normal precaution of seizing them when
they had the opportunity. This does not seem probable, how-

ever, for piracy was usually an avocation of many whose normal vocations were those of the sailor or merchant. It looks, rather as though the folk of St. Pol and Roscoff had some definite objective in their attack, a surmise which receives support from the fact that Henry de la Bar, one of the merchants who conveyed Warbeck to Ireland, came from St. Pol. If word of his capture had reached home before the arrival of the Scottish expedition, or if the Bartons' sailors had talked of it in their cups, the Bretons may have felt they had the right to obtain compensation by arresting the ships. Indeed, they would be particularly certain of their moral justification if they realized that Barton had acted as de la Bar's escort.

Further evidence supports this hypothesis. For one thing, that the Bretons released the Scots while keeping one of their ships and both the cargoes may indicate they felt they were carrying out legitimate reprisals. Moreover, it would also explain why, when some years later de la Bar's complaint came up before the Scottish Lords of the Council, he did not press his suit. If he had done so, he would probably have been faced with countercharges by the Bartons or George Young, demanding compensation for their losses. Consequently, it looks as though Robert and his confreres suffered as the result of the Breton's involuntary participation in Warbeck's misadventure. On their return to Scotland they naturally raised a great outcry, but for the time being neither they nor the king were able to obtain any satisfaction.[45]

III

The Merchant Adventurer of Leith

The years of James IV's reign were some of the most interesting in the whole of the country's history. At this time the economy of Western Europe was beginning to recover from the depression of the earlier part of the fifteenth century. In 1492 Columbus discovered America and in 1497 da Gama rounded the Cape of Good Hope, leading to an extension of the European's world, which, accompanied by a mild inflation, stimulated economic development in the countries along the Continent's western seaboard. Denmark, Holland, England, and France were rising to new positions of importance as manufacturing and trading nations. It was only natural, therefore, that Scotland, too, would have a part in this advance which the other countries of the "North Sea Quadrilateral" were experiencing ; and in this economic upsurge Robert Barton soon found himself involved.

As has already been indicated in a previous chapter,[1] one of the Scots' best markets and customers was the Netherlands, in which, after Bruges' decline,[2] Middelburg and Veere became the principal entrepots. Middelburg in particular was so anxious to have them settle within its walls that it was prepared to make every possible concession.[3]

In 1498 the city fathers dispatched their official messenger with letters to the Scottish king and other important people in the country, setting forth the mutual benefits which would accrue if all wool merchants were obliged to trade exclusively in Middelburg. After 163 days' absence, the envoy returned having achieved no more than to persuade the Scots to send over an embassy to discuss matters. This may have been the same embassy that was still in Middelburg in 1500, but whether it was or not, during these years negotiations were carried on assiduously.[4] Their sole result, however, was the appointment of Andrew Haliburton, previously factor in the Netherlands for a number of Scottish merchants, to the official position of Conservator of Scottish Privileges. James IV requested the town authorities to recognize him as the Scottish representative and to see that all Scottish merchants, sailors, and captains obeyed him.[5] As Haliburton apparently favoured the idea of living in Middelburg he co-operated heartily with the local authorities in their attempts to gain a monopoly of the Scottish wool trade, receiving in return, as long as he stayed among them the sum of £20 gr. F. (great Flemish) a year. It was probably through his good offices that customs duties on iron exported to, and wool imported from, Scotland were reduced. Yet even this was not as important as the fact that the Scots now had an official representative in the Low Countries through whom they could act, giving them a feeling of security which heretofore they had not known. Therefore, although no staple for Scottish goods was set up formally at Middelburg, the result was much the same, since the merchants tended to concentrate in the city where the Conservator had his headquarters.

The Low Countries, however, were not the only area to which the Scots exported. With the opening of the Øresund stimulating a steady flow of the Dutch ships into the Baltic, it was only natural that the Scots also should take more interest in the north German ports.[7] From the middle of the last decade of the fifteenth century Scottish trade with the Eastland sea-coast town steadily increased. This is reflected in a comparison of the figures of the tolls paid by ships traversing the Øresund in 1497 and 1503. In the first year, out of 795 ships using the passage, 567 were Dutch, 202 German, 5 Danish, and 21 Scottish. Of the latter, 4 came from Aberdeen, 4 from St. Andrews, 7 from Dundee, and 5 from Leith, and one from an unnamed port. Six years later the total had increased to 1,222, of which 856 were Dutch, 21 English, 295 German, 5 Danish, and 43 Scottish. Thus the proportional increase of the Scottish ships was more than that of any other nationality. As for the numbers from the various Scottish ports, Leith led with 15, the second in order being Dundee, with 5, and all the others—St. Andrews, Cupar, Dysart, Inverkeithing, and Montrose—sending fewer. Thus it is not difficult to see that the merchants of Leith in particular, were intensely interested in the Baltic trade.[8] Many Scots, following this trend, migrated to towns such as Danzig where one could find on the burgess rolls such names as Skene, Forbes, Turner, Gordon, Burnett, and Fergusson. Scottish traders were going far afield in search of business.[9]

The "indwellers" of Leith, because of their enterprise in voyaging to distant points, faced no little opposition by the citizens of Edinburgh. As has already been pointed out, the relationships between the two places were never very friendly, and during the 1490's Edinburgh became even more over-bearing and restrictive. At the beginning of the decade the city authorities discovered that the indwellers of Leith were infringing their liberties by trading directly with foreign ships in the harbor. To stop this they determined to hold the "water court" in Leith backed by the full armed power of Edinburgh "that reformation and good rule may be had and brought in upon the enormous injuries and usurpation made and used by them in Leith upon the freedom of the town."[10] Furthermore, in 1496 they insisted that the entry of all ships to Leith should be reported at the Tolbooth in Edinburgh for the collection of local duties. Three years later, the council enacted a law which ruled that all ships had to be freighted under the eyes of "freightmen" or inspectors, appointed by the Edinburgh council, and that they, along with one of the baillies and the captain, were to determine the prices for which the goods exported were to be sold. The next year (1501) they ruled that all arrangements for the freighting of ships from Leith for Flanders had to be made in the Tolbooth.[11] To this was shortly added another regulation requiring all goods brought into Leith to be taken immediately to Edinburgh for sale, to prevent the Leith people from making any quick bargains. Indeed, the burgesses even attempted to stop Leith men from buying ships without their permission.[12]

In the light of Edinburgh's policy it is not difficult to see that Leith's commercial growth was certainly not due to the encouragement of the authorities of the larger city, for all profits or opportunities for profit were carefully reserved for those who had the good fortune to be Edinburgh burgesses. For the people of Leith not only sale and purchase were thus limited, but even the prices to be charged by the skippers in foreign markets were kept under rigid control. Here was ample cause for friction between the two towns ; and it is not surprising that this friction often developed into open conflict. That Edinburgh, the wealthier and more powerful of the two antagonists, was not able to keep Leith down completely was due largely to the support which the latter received from the king. Since James had on hand certain projects that necessitated the aid of the sailors of Leith, whether Edinburgh liked it or not, her wishes were not always acceptable to the government. The inhabitants of the port town, therefore, were for some time able to defy their neighbors around the Castle.

The most absorbing of James' interests at this time was the

building of his navy. Although the *Flower* was no longer in commission, he still had the *Douglas* and the *Christopher*, but they did not make Scotland a maritime power. Therefore, throughout the period from 1497 down to 1513, he worked steadily to increase the number of his ships. He could not build a navy, however, out of nothing. For one thing a large quantity of wood was needed. At first this was obtained from the shores of Loch Lomond, from Clydesdale, Borthwick, Saltoun, and Darnaway, but even these forests were not sufficient.[13] Consequently the king was continually on the lookout for timber being imported from abroad, as can be seen from the references to royal inquiries made in Kirkaldy and Montrose concerning timber ships which had arrived in those towns.[14] Likewise there was a constant demand for iron, most of which came from the Netherlands, 706 "duust yssers" being weighed out for the Scots on the scales of Middelburgh in 1500 alone.[15] Similarly the king found it necessary to bring in craftsmen : armorers, shipwrights, and smiths who could furnish the technical knowledge lacked by Scottish workmen.[16] Such interests and activity on the part of the monarch were bound to counter any limitations set by the narrow interests of Edinburgh on the kingdom's most important port.

There was, however, another, and in a sense a more personal reason which caused James to employ the sailors of Leith. Since he was planning to take unto himself a wife, Margaret, the daughter of Henry VII of England, he was anxious to make the most fitting preparations possible for the arrival of his bride. This meant large-scale purchases abroad. Through James Merchamston he bought in Flanders chairs of state and silverware, while for his own wearing apparel he imported quantities of materials, such as Holland cloth for shirts, as well as various items of clothing. The preparation of Holyrood for his bride was another considerable expense, involving the importation of tiles, boards, and joists as well as the employment of plasterers and other skilled artisans.[17] Here again the king's demands for goods and services exercised a restraining effect upon the over-bearing attitude of the Edinburgh burgesses, who could hardly object to his using Leith men to supply his needs.

It is against this background that one must view the activities of Robert Barton and his brothers. As shipowners and captains of Leith, they were bound to become involved in these projects of the king. Indeed, although we know that the Bartons were carrying on ventures of their own, most of our evidence concerning them during the period from 1497 to 1503 comes from the records of their services to the crown. Since there is no indication that they returned to privateering or piracy at this time it would appear that the hard blow suffered at St. Pol de Léon had made them realize that though profits might sometimes be high in that type of enterprise, the losses could also be very great. For the next few years, therefore, as long as the memory of the disaster was still green, and perhaps in order to recoup themselves, they devoted their lives to the less exciting but distinctly safer calling of the merchant.

During the last three years of the fifteenth century most of our information concerning the commercial activities of the Bartons centers around Andrew and John. Andrew is mentioned by Haliburton in November, 1497, as bringing over a "sek of skyns" for William Clerk and a "sek of vol" for Robert Rynd, the latter being sold in Berri for £17, while the former brought £28 from a man of Hertogenbosch. For each of these sacks Andrew received 30s. freightage. On the return trip in December he carried a pipe of exotic goods bought in Berri, containing 50 lb. of almonds, 50 lb. of rice, 24 lb. of pepper, and smaller quantities of ginger, mace, nutmeg, cloves, sandalwood, and saffron.[18] In February, April, and August of 1498 he was back in the Netherlands with cargoes of wool, but from this point on he disappears from the accounts.[19] His place seems to have been taken by his brother John, who was dealing

with Haliburton in April, 1499, and September, 1500. He may
also have been the John Barton who during the same years
exported from Dysart 30 barrels of salmon and 10 dakers or
100 hides and from Aberdeen 5 lasts (45 barrels) and 2 barrels
of salmon.[20] Although this does not by any means give us a
complete picture of how Andrew and John occupied themselves
during these years, it still indicates that they were active in the
carrying trade, if not actually in trading for themselves.

Despite the lack of information concerning Robert's
commercial interests before 1500, it is certain from the extant
meager evidence that he was engaged in the exchange of goods
with the Netherlands. Haliburton records that in October,
1498, he received out of Robert's ship a sack of Ettrick forest
wool and a sack of middlings. The freight charge for this item
was £3 1s. 2d. (gr. Fl.)[21] The next year by royal warrant
Robert received exemption from the payment of duty on 6 sacks
of wool, each weighing 18 stone, while the following year he
obtained the same privilege for 9 sacks of wool and 200 (or one
last) of hides.[22] The goods exported under these licenses may
represent the sum total of all his trade, but this is not likely. He
probably received these grants, as he did a payment of £6 at the
same time from the custumar of Edinburgh, for some specific
purpose or as a reward for some important service. If such were
the case, the exempt goods would represent only part of the
commodities in which he was dealing.

This interpretation is borne out by other information.
Thinking in terms of ever larger operations, some time prior
to February, 1500, he obtained the grant of the assize herring
of the "east sea." As a result of this privilege he could collect
the royal tax of herring caught off the east coast of Scotland
which amounted to about 3,000 fish a year.[23] He did not,
however, enjoy his profitable acquisition in peace, for Margaret
Spittale, widow of Thomas Crawford, entered a suit against him,
with the claim that she was the lawful lessee. The matter came

to trial before the Lords of the Council but owing to certain irregularities in Margaret's charter it was postponed, never appearing again in the records. The pursuer may have decided that her claims would not stand close investigation.[24] At any rate, that Robert continued to enjoy the profits of his concession may be indicated by the considerable quantities of herring which he exported during the next few years.

The acquisition of the assize of herring was significant also as an indication of Robert's increasing importance in the business world. He would have to pay a considerable sum for the assize, while the fact that although only a Leith indweller, he was able to purchase this right, indicates his growing economic importance.

Another sign of his progress was that at about the same time he began to expand his holdings of real estate. Early in 1501 he agreed to purchase from David Mailvin, son of the Edinburgh burgess of the same name, a property immediately to the east of his own holdings in Leith and bordering on the royal highway.[25] But as Mailvin seemed to be slow in completing the sale, in order to make sure of it, in September of that year Robert obtained from David Mailvin, senior, a piece of land situated on the north of the "king's street" in Edinburgh as a special warrandice or guarantee, to be returned when the deed of sale was made final.[26]

His great economic opportunity came when the king began to employ him as one of his agents. By this he acquired status abroad and immunity from Edinburgh's regulations at home. On February 21, 1501, he received a royal letter of protection for "his servandis, familiaris, factouris, procuratouris," to be in force from the time he left the country until forty days after his return.[27] No doubt he obtained this because he was going abroad on business for the king, and it may have been for the same reason that at this time he received from the custumar of Edinburgh the sum of £28 5s.[28] Two months later, on April 19, the treasurer paid him £109 12s. 6d. for $49\frac{1}{2}$ ells of "blew damas," and on December 19, 26s. 7d. for "twa bon-nets."[29]   But these were only part of his trade, for his customs exemptions in 1501 (£20 5s. 10d.) indicate that he handled practically all the herring and cod and more than one-quarter of all the salmon exported from the port of Leith.[30]

Throughout the year 1502 he continued his service to the crown. On February 10 he again received royal protection while traveling in France on royal business, and twelve days later, shortly before he sailed, he was paid £10 for 20 ells of small Holland cloth for the king's shirts. The records do not reveal the nature of his commission from the king, but the fact that by May 19 he had returned with naval stores such as "virgyne wax" would indicate that his main occupation had been the purchasing of supplies for James' embryo fleet. They were not, however, the only commodities which he imported. He had taken with him the servant of the king's French doctor, on whose advice he had bought £31 4s. worth of drugs.[31]

While serving the king Robert continued to care for his own interests, as is evidenced by his increased customs exemptions between August, 1502, and August 1503. During this period he shipped out free 16 sacks of wool, 6 sacks (or 2,880 lb.) more than the year before; 400 hides (2 lasts) as against 350 the preceding year; and 31 barrels of salmon, a fivefold increase. Only 1,200 cod and 14 barrels of herring showed a decrease from the 1501-1502 total. As a new venture he added to his list of goods 80 dozen woolen cloths.   The total value of these exemptions was more than £40, the actual worth of the goods prob-ably being double that of the preceding year.   These figures, of course, may or may not reveal very much since they refer only to Robert's exemptions from customs dues. If the grants were in return for specific goods or services which he provided they would tell little about his total trade. If, on the other hand, they represented a general remission of customs, it would appear that while his business doubled, his proportion of Leith's total export was less than the preceding year.³² It is impossible to be certain which interpretation is correct. All one can say is that his business appears to have been flourishing.

With his improving economic position, Robert seems to have felt that the time had arrived when he should take unto himself a spouse. That he did so in 1501 is indicated by the fact that among the people specified in the letter of protection issued to him in February of 1501 no mention is made of a wife, while that of 1502 refers to a certain Elizabeth. This was Elizabeth Jameson who became his bride in 1501, and probably was the mother of James, John, and Henry Barton, later referred to as Robert's sons. How long Elizabeth lived is unknown, but it is certain that she died before 1510.³³

It was at this point that Robert's interests became twofold. On the one hand he continued to be a merchant, but on the other he began to participate increasingly in the building up of the Scottish naval power. These two occupations were by no means mutually exclusive, for much of his work for the crown consisted in purchasing abroad naval supplies and materials ; and while he was busy in this work he also had sufficient time to trade on his own behalf. But before considering his activities as a seadog who helped both to build the king's ships and to use them against Scotland's enemies, it seems wise first to follow his career as a private merchant, always keeping in mind that this was only part of his interest.

Even as a merchant, Robert continued to serve the king. In mid-December of 1502 James IV's young illegitimate son Alexander Stewart, already Archdeacon of St. Andrews at the age of nine or ten years, came to Leith to take ship to the Continent. As the weather was very intemperate, the young man stayed for a week with Robert who outfitted him for this trip. His expedition, however, never took place, for as the storms did not abate it was decided to postpone the undertaking to a more convenient time.³⁴ While this incident was of no historic importance in that nothing particular came of it, one does see in it an indication of the trust reposed in Robert by the king, altogether apart from his work in connection with the building of the navy. Similarly in the spring of the next year Robert was commissioned to buy the king books in Paris as well as "a gret brown hors" probably from Normandy and six small feather beds.[35] This commission was followed in the autumn of the year, after James' marriage to Margaret Tudor, by another to purchase woolens and the like for the royal couple's winter wear, for which he also supplied buge (dressed lambskins) for the collar of a gown of "brochit satin" and for the lining of other articles of clothing.[36]

While acting as an agent for the king, however, Robert carried on his own trade, but since his account books are not extant it is very difficult to determine the volume of either his exports or imports. The most that one can do to estimate his economic importance is to take due note of his customs exemptions as recorded in the *Exchequer Rolls*, and to compare the amounts of his exemptions with those of other merchants, and the quantities of goods he exported duty free, with the total exports from Leith. When one makes such a study one finds that his exemptions are among the largest granted to anyone in the Edinburgh area, rising between 1501 and 1509 from £20 to £93. Likewise the quantities of goods increased over the years so that at times he seems to have held almost a monopoly of certain classes of goods leaving Leith. From 1509 on, his trade exemptions tended to fall which may indicate that owing to his preoccupation with other matters, he was not paying so much attention to trade. On the other hand, the appearance of Robert and Andrew in the fragment of William Adamson's *Introit Book* (1510) as exporting 31 and 33 barrels of herring respectively, perhaps shows that while his trade continued to grow he received fewer exemptions.[37]

What type of commodity was Robert handling in these

ventures ? As earlier, his exports were of the usual Scottish produce, wool forming the larger part both in quantity and value. Owing to the uncertainty of weights, it is a little difficult to estimate exactly how much wool was involved, but if as seems probable the last weighed approximately 4,500 lb., he was exporting some 10,000 to 12,000 lb. per annum at an average price of 2s. a pound. Along with the wool normally went salmon, herring, cod, and hides in varying quantities. Seldom did the cod drop below the 1,000 mark although salmon and herring might vary from 20 to 100 barrels, and the hides from 400 to 600. Between June, 1504, and 1505 he also dealt in some rather unusual items: 40 chalders of salt, 8 dozen woolen cloths, 4,050 lambskins, and 5 chests of sugar. It may be that difficulty arose over the export of some of these goods, as it is carefully recorded that the permits were given only on the authority of letters signed by the king himself.[38] The total value of all these goods is not ascertainable, but there would seem to be little doubt that they indicate a very considerable volume of trade for any one man.

Unfortunately, we have no statement of what Robert imported, except in the case of his purchases for the king. Wine, valued at £73 17s. 6d., was one item, while an image of gold for a bonnet, and a ring, together came to 47s. 10d. On April 1, 1505, the royal treasurer also paid him £21 for a coat which he had purchased in Flanders for a John Cowpans.[39] As will be seen later, most of his imports during these years apparently consisted of naval stores.

A question which also arises is: when was Robert able to carry on his business ? The answer would seem to be that whenever he went abroad on the king's affairs, he took trade goods with him in order to buy or sell as the opportunity offered. Traveling to Rouen, Dieppe, Bruges, and other Continental ports, he would have little difficulty in exchanging his cargoes for the valuable and exotic goods available in these entrepôts. For this reason, although occupied in building, buying, and equipping ships, he was always first and foremost a trader.

That he was able to carry on his commercial ventures while serving the king gives some indication of the destinations to which his exports traveled. No doubt most of them he disposed of in Dieppe or Rouen which seem to have been his principal ports of call at this time. A second place of business would seem to have been the Netherlands—Bruges, Middelburg, and Veere— whither he went occasionally on business for the king and where he had many friends. Some of his goods may also have traveled as far as the Baltic to which his brother John seems frequently to have sailed and which he himself visited at least once.[40] All told his trade seems to have been not merely quite large in volume, but also rather widespread in its distribution.

To carry on his business Robert needed ships. No doubt he often exported goods in foreign bottoms, but most of his goods seem to have gone either in one of the king's vessels or in his own. That he was either full or part owner of a vessel in the early days of his career seems to be indicated, but there is no certain information concerning this. However, by the middle of 1506 he had acquired the possession of a ship of about 300 tons, the *Lion*. Whether he built or purchased her is not stated, but at this point she was undoubtedly the joy of his heart. It may have been to show her off to the king that he carried James in her to St. Monan's Abbey on the Isle of May for a short holiday.[41] Three years later he may have been seeking to add to the *Lion* by having another ship constructed at Dieppe. In the hinterland of the city he purchased the necessary lumber, probably oak, which he had stored in a safe place provided by the Dieppe authorities. At this point, however, he experienced a set-back, for John Symon, who had been hired to act as shipwright, suddenly died. King James thereupon requested the city council to provide another master shipbuilder who would maintain the good reputation of the town. This may indicate that the king had a personal interest in the ship, although his added request for further information on shipbuilding in the area may show that he was also investigating the possibility of Dieppe's becoming a source of ships for the Scottish navy.[42]

At the beginning of the year 1504, Robert received a commission from the king somewhat different from that which he usually fulfilled. The Duke of Ross, James' younger brother, had received appointment in 1497 as commendator of the Archbishopric of St. Andrews, and although too young to be canonically consecrated to the metropolitan office, he enjoyed the archiepiscopal title along with all the revenues. The king, however, dissatisfied with this partial arrangement applied pressure at Rome, with such success that by the end of 1503 he had persuaded the Pope, despite Ross's youth, to grant him the bulls of appointment. These were transmitted to the banker, Jerome Frescobaldi, in Bruges who was to turn them over to the Scottish king's representative in return for the payment of the required fees.[43] To Robert Barton and Andrew Mathewson the king committed this responsibility, and sometime early in February, 1504, Robert who seems to have been in charge paid in Bruges the required 3,900 ducats or £1,007 2s. (Scots) in return for the coveted documents.

Although he had fulfilled his principal responsibility Robert did not immediately return home but waited a few days to turn over some money to the Scottish Lion King-at-Arms who was visiting in Flanders on royal business, and to buy the pin and ring mentioned above for the king's adornment. At the same time, he also purchased 2,104 feet of planks costing £32 12s., 1,575 lb. of wax at £23 2s. 6d., and two ships' tackles worth £6 or £7 each.[44] On this trip alone he carried with him some £3,000 in cash.[45] However, by the middle of the month he and Mathewson were once more in Scotland. The only difficulty was that before the Duke of Ross could be consecrated, he died.

It is in connection with this commercial activity that one first becomes conscious of a little anti-clericalism in Robert's attitude. On July 23, 1511, action was taken before the Lords of the Council against him and a number of his fellow Leith skippers, William Brounhill, Andrew Dawson, David Logan, and others, by Master Charles Fotheringham, chaplain of St. Ninian's Altar in the Carmelite Church at Bruges. He complained that they had refused to pay for the support of the altar the duties owed by each ship sailing from Scotland to the Netherlands, which amounted to one sack of wool from each ship containing 5 lasts, and one-third of a sack from each smaller cargo. The answer made to the chaplain's suit was that since the captains were on the king's service, they should not have to pay. For Robert Barton and William Brounhill this argument seems to have been effective, but as the others failed to have it accepted, on August 12 the Lords ordered them to meet their obligations. Although there is no question here of anything more than an unwillingness to provide the required dues to the church, it is worthy of note that, even though he does not appear in the final judgement rendered, Robert was involved.[46]

Besides his trading Robert seems also to have been developing another interest, that of money lending. He had already loaned money at times to the king for short periods, but now he seems to have gone into the business for the first time on a commercial basis. It would seem that prior to his death David Mowbray, Laird of Barnbougle and Baron of Inverkeithing, had been adjudged guilty of having illegally alienated some of his lands in Inverkeithing with the result that the king had taken possession of the barony. In 1508, James returned the estate to David's son and heir, John, but not before he himself had granted out some of the tenements, one being Balbugy and Castellan which he conferred upon Archibald Ramsay of Dunnune.

How much Ramsay paid as a composition is not stated, but the man who provided him with the required money was Robert Barton, who was to draw the rents until Ramsay liquidated the debt. In 1512 when Ramsay sued John Mowbray, son of David Mowbray, for illegally taking the rents of the lands Robert appeared, declaring that Ramsay still owed him 180 marks, the balance of the loan. The Lords Auditors, in attempting to give a fair judgement, examined the records, and to their surprise discovered that not only had Ramsay met all his obligations to the owner, but also that Robert had paid 1,600 marks more than required. They therefore ordered the Treasurer to return the 1,600 plus the 180 marks to Robert, and instructed Mowbray to infeft Ramsay immediately in his lands.[47]

A more exalted client than Ramsay was John Lindsay, Earl of Crawford, from whom in September, 1511, Robert received the lands and villages of Balhungy and Ardesty and half of the village of Donycan, in the barony of Downy lying between Dundee and Forfar. It would appear that Crawford, who like some of the other nobles was a spendthrift, had borrowed a considerable sum of money from Robert, to whom he gave these lands as collateral. Along with them he also put up the Barony of Kirkbuddo "in warrandice" in case the pledges were not of the full value of the loan.[48] Some two months later Robert also received possession, "under reversion," of the property of the late Robert Lauder, which lay on the south side of High Street in Edinburgh and immediately east of the land of St. Mary Magdalene. Apparently this was another case of his lending money only this time to a burgess, or his estate, in return for the property's rent of 4 marks a year until the debt was paid.[49] Thus it would appear that he had on hand a supply of ready cash, which he was prepared to lend on good security if he could be sure that he would receive a sufficiently large return. This was the beginning of what eventually became an important part of his business.

Of even more importance, however, was his use of his
wealth to obtain an entrance to the ranks of the landed gentry.
On March 1, 1508, James IV granted to his familiar Robert
Barton "pro bono servitio" the tower, castle, and lands of
Over Barnton which had escheated to the crown owing to its
alienation by William Dundas, the former owner. The property
lying to the northwest of Edinburgh in what is now Barnton was
of considerable value, for Robert paid a total £466 13s. 4d.,
the down payment being £188 8s. 4d., and on March 7 he
took possession of his newly acquired property.[50]

The purchase of Over Barnton made a radical change in
Robert's social and economic position. Up to this time he had
been a mere sea captain and merchant—trusted by the king, it
is true, but still nothing more. Now he had the standing of
the laird of a property near the capital which was bound to
put him on a different footing not only with his friends in
Leith, but also with the feudal nobility and the country's
governing class. He had progressed a long way in the fourteen
years since 1495, for he was not only able to pay a large sum
for this privilege but was also considered worthy of it.

Of equal importance with the actual content of the charter is
the information not recorded. Contrary to usual custom, no
mention is made in the grant of Robert's wife, which would
seem to indicate that by March 1, 1508, she was dead. In
a grant made by Robert on April 3, however, his son James
signed as a witness.[51]

It was around this time or perhaps a little later that Robert
remarried. The second Mrs. Barton was Elizabeth Crawford,
one of the six children of Thomas Crawford of Bonnington, a
local laird, and the widow of Gilbert Edmonston, a sea captain
of Leith. Elizabeth and her late husband, who had died sometime in 1507, had been close friends of the Bartons, for they
had stood as godparents for each other's children.[52] It is not
strange, therefore, that when both Robert and Elizabeth were

bereaved, probably at about the same time, they should decide to join forces, a decision which may have been put into effect shortly after Robert obtained possession of Over Barnton.[53]

When their son Robert was born is not indicated, but in October, 1511, Robert senior granted all his lands, including those obtained from the Earl of Crawford, to this small child. Elizabeth had apparently persuaded him to make over this land to her son in order to prevent the sons by the first marriage from inheriting his property. Robert probably favored this, for such a grant would ensure Elizabeth's economic security in case he met with some unexpected misfortune.[54]

On December 7, 1512, the king confirmed a grant to him of 24 mercates of land in Nether Barnton made by John Forester. This land he had probably bought, or acquired by means of a mortgage, to add to Over Barnton. Like his other property, this also he transferred to his son Robert.[55]

That Robert now possessed a considerable reputation in his own country would seem to be quite clear ; and there are indications that his name was becoming equally well known abroad. While much of his fame in all probability derived from his work for James IV, it would also seem clear that he was both known and respected as a merchant, the best proof of this being his participation in the new negotiations for the establishment of a Scottish staple on the Island of Walcheren. Although this is a rather complicated matter which has been treated fully in a number of monographs it is necessary to glance briefly at the problem if one is to understand the part that Robert played, at this time and later, in the negotiations.[56]

Middelburg commenced its campaign to have the Scottish staple set up within its borders with one distinct advantage: it was the home of Andrew Haliburton, the Conservator of Scottish Privileges in the Netherlands. But in the long run this had little effect, for August Caminade, the envoy whom the town authorities dispatched to Scotland early in 1507, accomplished little, as he died in Edinburgh during the negotiations. Meanwhile, to press the claims of Veere, Henry Van Borselen arrived with many gifts and urged his case with such effectiveness that, despite Middelburg's letters to various Scottish officials and magnates, by April 2, 1508, James decided that Veere should be the site of the compulsory Scottish staple.[57]

Although James made clear that this decision was final, the authorities of Middelburgh refused to take his pronouncement too seriously. The reason was that Robert Barton entered the picture in 1509 when he spent some time in Middelburg, at the house of John Simonson, the toll collector on the Dam. He was obviously regarded as an influential and honored guest, for the city council sent him as "one of the principal merchants of Scotland" three flagons of Rhenish wine. Such attention from the Middelburgers naturally inclined Robert to look with favor on his hosts' desire for the establishment of the staple in their municipality. Consequently when he returned home he may have been successful in persuading the king to reconsider his decision, for he wrote Simonson that it was not certain that the staple would stay at Veere unless the inhabitants of that town soon paid James what they had promised. He therefore urged Simonson to have his fellow citizens continue their efforts, despite James' professed determination to favor Veere.[58]

The response of Middelburg was immediate and direct. Letters were dispatched to Robert and the royal secretary, Patrick Panter, bespeaking their support in the attempt to break Veere's monopoly of Scottish trade. They requested Panter to co-operate with that "honest man" Robert Barton in pushing Middelburg's claims. The stress laid upon Robert's honesty would no doubt have been received with a certain scepticism in some quarters, but it undoubtedly won his support! To Robert they wrote, through Simonson, that if James were prepared to set up the staple in Middelburg for a period of fifteen to eighteen years, furnishing them with sufficient guarantees, they were prepared to pay 4,000 gulden in silver and gold. This is probably the letter referred to in the city council minutes of January 26, 1510, where it is stated that Peter de Cock of Opinen and Jan Janssone as councilors had been authorized to write secretly to an unnamed person in Scotland, offering 4,000 gulden for the establishment of the staple. The Council now agreed that if it should be necessary for the negotiators named to increase the sum offered by 1,000 or 2,000 gulden, they would be blameless. Since Robert was probably the unnamed person, it would seem that he was vigorously pressing the case for Middelburg.[59] At this point, however, the negotiations came to a stop, for other and more important matters were brewing both for Scotland and for Robert.

The Sea Dog of Leith

Trader, landowner, and financier that he was, Robert never ceased to be at the same time a sea captain and potential privateer. Indeed it was the combination of these two sides of his character and of his career that enabled him to rise not only economically but also in the king's favor during the years before James IV's death on Flodden Field.

He had already displayed a certain amount of interest in the more risky and less reputable aspects of seafaring in his escorting of Perkin Warbeck to Ireland and in his attempted privateering off the Brittany coast. His rather dismal failure on the latter occasion would hardly enhance his reputation with the king, but an opportunity to regain James' respect may have come when the latter dispatched his first naval squadron abroad.

The occasion of this Scottish venture was a rising of the Swedes against Hans of Denmark who in accordance with a treaty of 1499, called upon James to send him aid.[1] Nothing loth, James equipped a squadron of four ships which sailed for Sweden in June, 1502. The names of those who probably commanded two of the vessels, the *Douglas* and the *Christopher* are known, but the identities of the captains of the *Eagle* and the *Towaich* are unrecorded.[2] Since John Barton took a prominent part in the launching of the *Eagle*, a short time before the squadron left he may have been her master, and if this were the case Robert may have commanded the *Towaich*.[3] Andrew we know provided some supplies for the ships, and all three Bartons disappear from the records for the duration of the expedition.[4] Moreover, a few years later the brothers were on friendly terms with the Danish monarch, which might find its explanation in their introduction to him during this venture.[5] Thus although proof is lacking it seems that they may have taken part in the expedition which sailed again into the Firth of Forth at the beginning of August.

Once the squadron had returned, James seems to have devoted himself with even greater vigor to the expansion of his navy. While enlarging the docks at Leith, he scoured the country for lumber and qualified craftsmen who could build the ships and forge the necessary arms.[6] It soon became obvious, however, that Scotland had neither sufficient physical resources nor the "know-how" to enable her, unaided, to become a strong naval power. As a result the king was obliged increasingly to seek foreign assistance. This he obtained from the French, who for political reasons were only too ready to strengthen their "auld ally" that she might in time of war act as a continual threat to England. Consequently there appear many references in the treasurer's accounts to French wrights and armorers whom James imported to provide the skills necessary for the construction of a powerful fleet.[7]

In these plans the Bartons played an important role. While John was supervising the cutting of local lumber, Robert set sail for Dieppe in October, 1502, in search of both material and skilled artisans.[8] It was no doubt in the home of one of the Scottish expatriates on Rue d'Ecosse that Robert stayed while he carried out his mission for the king. Determined to be successful in what was apparently his first trip of this kind, he probably spent most of his time interviewing and bargaining with French shipwrights who may not have been overly anxious to leave home. Eventually he signed up a certain John Lorans, to whom he gave £10 with the promise of a further 10 French crowns (£7 Scots) a month. He also hired two armorers, Pasing and another Lorans, at the same salary. All three men were working in Scotland by the beginning of December.[9]

So successful had Robert been on his earlier venture that by January, 1503, the king had sent him back to Dieppe, this time for timber. To obtain exactly what he sought, he himself went into the woods of the hinterland with the cutters to supervise their work. Apparently he was again successful in his endeavour, for by January 16, 1503, he seems to have returned home, as on that date the treasurer reimbursed him for £13 16s. paid for the lumberman's wages. He may also have been the skipper who later in the month brought over fourteen more French armorers and an armor mill.[10]

After these two trips abroad, Robert remained in Scotland for a short time, occupied from about April 1 in supervising the cutting of timber. Before the end of May, however, he landed once again in Dieppe in search of more artisans and lumber. Instead of traveling in his own ship, it looks as though he used that of Alexander Makyson who was to carry home his purchases. On this occasion he made contact with a certain Jennen Diew, a shipwright whom he hired at the rate of £10 a month and expenses, amounting to a further £3 6s. 8d. Probably to persuade Diew's wife to agree, she received one month's salary in advance! Before sailing for Scotland, Diew and another shipwright, Jacat Tyrrell, spent most of June in the woods seeing to the cutting of trees, and in particular to the preparing of a ship's keel. It must have been a considerable disappointment as well as an expense when this piece, by some misadventure, was broken on the way down to Dieppe, and a new one had to

be prepared and shipped. By July 13 Robert was back in Leith
bringing Diew with him to work in the shipyards. As Diew was
lodged with David Melville, one of the Edinburgh custumars,
it is obvious that in the king's eyes Robert's work was of the
greatest important.[11]

Robert's work as a purchasing agent was not the only reason
for the king's notice. James had for some time been attempting
to bring law and order to his realm, a project in which he had
been only moderately successful. In 1503 he decided to accelerate the process of pacification by applying heavier pressure,
especially to the inhabitants of the Western Isles, who were
noted for their lawlessness. A grandson of the Lord of the Isles,
Donald Dhu, had been in prison for his crimes for some forty
years, but he escaped with the aid of the MacIans of Glencoe
who, along with the MacLeods of Lewis, in December, 1503,
helped him plunder Badenoch and give the town of Inverness to
the flames. James, roused to action by this attack, gathered his
forces at Dumbarton whence he dispatched an expedition
against the rebels. The Earl of Arran was commander, with Sir
Andrew Wood acting as his naval lieutenant.

Contrary to Tytler's statement, there is no evidence that
Robert was commander of the fleet,[12] although he did take part
in the operation. One of the rebels' principal strongholds was
Cairnburg, the most northerly of the Treshnish Isles, lying some
two miles west of the Isle of Mull. A solid block of granite
rising sheer from the sea and protected by strong, treacherous
currents, it was almost impregnable. James, however, was
determined to reduce the fortress and ordered it blockaded.
Some time after the commencement of the siege, on May 6 to
be exact, Robert and Hans "the gunner," either a German or a
Dane, were paid £4 4s. to go to Cairnburg. What part they
played in the ensuing action is unknown, but the fact that the
fort fell shortly afterwards may indicate that Hans' cannon
achieved the desired result.[13] Robert probably commanded the

ship which carried the gunner to the scene of action, and perhaps helped to bring about the fortress' surrender.

How long he remained with the Earl of Arran's expeditionary force is not indicated, but he also served under the Earl of Huntly the next year on a similar police action. Tytler tries to make out that John was the commander of the fleet under Huntly, but there is no evidence that up to this point either he or his brother Robert had done more than command individual ships, either their own or the king's.[14]

It may have been that in the Cairnburg expedition Robert was in charge of a small vessel called the *Columb*, for in early June, shortly after his return from the siege, he conveyed the king in her to the mouth of the Firth of Forth to hear mass at the monastery of St. Monans on the Isle of May. That Robert was owner as well as captain of the vessel the wording of the accounts leaves quite indefinite, but he did receive £10 13s. for this service.[15]

Having successfully carried out these various commissions, Robert now received new orders. King James was in the process of building what was so far his largest ship, later named in honor of the queen the *Margaret*, which by February, 1504, although far from complete, had already cost some £1,200. As he needed further supplies for her which he could obtain only in France or the Netherlands, he again dispatched Robert to the Continent.

Very shortly after the trip to the Isle of May, Robert set out in the *Columb* for Dieppe whence he had returned by July 15 with 3,317 feet of great planks, 2,477 of second-grade planks, 1,369 of third-grade, and 14 dozen smaller boards. Along with these he brought Hamburg nails, four-wheeled carts, harness, saws, gimlets, and a keel for a ship to be constructed in Leith. He received £108 17s. 6d. "for the litill bark callit the *Columb* hir vittalis and mennis hires furth of Deip," which was about the usual cost of hiring a crew and of supplying its food for the round trip. The view of the editors of the *Treasurer's Accounts* that this sum included the sale price of the *Columb* is hardly warranted, as the vessel would undoubtedly have cost more than the small amount mentioned. If the king eventually acquired possession of her, he must have done so later.[16] But even if the *Columb* did change hands at this time, the captain remained the same, for on July 26 Robert brought down lumber in her from Alloa, and shortly afterwards sailed her around the north of Scotland to Dumbarton. There he left her, John Merchamston, who may have been his lieutenant, assuming command.[17]

One other project in which Robert participated during these months was the building of New Haven. This was a dockyard and harbor lying a little to the west of Leith not far from Robert's own property, and projected by King James to facilitate the building of his war vessels. From the treasurer's accounts, it would seem that the timber brought down from Alloa by Robert was for the purpose of making bulwarks in these shipyards. The day after he was reimbursed for transporting the wood he received another payment, this time for giving money to the sailors setting up the bulwarks.[18] But he did not spend much time at this work, for more important matters were demanding attention.

James IV was trying to accelerate the construction of his ships. In October, 1504, Jacat Tyrrell, the French shipwright, returned to France, apparently in search of more wood and artificers. Others, both Scots and foreigners, were importing in ever-increasing quantities oak planks from Normandy, brass fittings from Flanders, masts from England, and armorers for the artillery from France.[19] Simultaneously the shipbuilding facilities were being enlarged. Not only was New Haven put to good use, but even a priest's yard at Dumbarton was fitted out as one of the first Clydeside shipyards.[20]

Most important of all, however, was the activity centered

around the completion of the *Margaret*, and it looks as though Robert, during the autumn of 1504, was in charge of the work. We know that at the end of January, 1505, he was responsible for taking her off the stocks, while his entertaining of the king at dinner on board a week or so later would seem to indicate that he was also responsible for preparing her for sea.[21]

Meanwhile, in the summer of 1504 James had contracted with Martin le Nault, a Breton from Le Conquet a little to the west of Brest, to build him a ship, 100 French crowns (£70 Scots) being paid immediately, and a further 100 crowns promised for October. Apparently the construction proceeded with rapidity, for late in March or early in April 1505, Robert, who went to Le Conquet no doubt to inspect the new vessel, made payment of a further 100 crowns. He was present when the mast was stepped, and distributed drinksilver both to the sailors and to the smith who performed the operation. It was not until February, 1506, however, that the *Treasurer*, as the ship was called, neared completion. At that time Andrew Barton made further payments to the shipbuilders, and at length in September the new addition to the Scots' navy sailed proudly into Leith.[22]

Perhaps it was while visiting Le Conquet in 1505 that Robert remembered some unfinished business which he had with the folk at St. Pol de Léon and Roscoff not far away. Up to this time no reparation had been made for the losses which they had inflicted upon him in 1498. On his return to Scotland therefore, he requested the king to send a letter to Louis XII of France, demanding compensation. James, only too willing to aid such a faithful servant, dispatched a strongly worded communication, outlining the whole case and seeking the French monarch's support for Robert's demands.[23]

At this point, apparently having little confidence in such negotiations, Andrew also decided to take a hand in the game.

Late in March or early in April of 1505 somewhere on the high seas he attacked and captured the *St. Mary* of St. Malo, from which he took part of its cargo: 10 whole great packs, 2 broken great packs, and 21 small packs of goods, as well as 92 rolls of sail canvas, all valued at first at 2,200 French crowns or £1,540 (Scots). He then set sail for home, stopping on the way to sell some of the goods to the merchants of York.[24]

When he arrived in Scotland Robert was not pleased, for Andrew's misjudged venture would certainly jeopardize the hopes of obtaining compensation from the Bretons. Moreover, Andrew's victims now appeared on the scene to take legal action to recover their goods. At first Andrew adopted an attitude of complete indifference to their complaints, ignoring even the court's summons to appear to defend his action. Robert, however, intervened, making himself responsible for his brother's defense. The result was a long trial which finally ended in the Lords of the Council finding Andrew guilty of stealing altogether 15 great packs of canvas and other goods which they valued at 9,600 French crowns, or £6,720 (Scots), a tidy sum.

The Lords appointed Robert trustee of the goods ordering Andrew to turn over to him the loot still in his possession and to recover from the purchasers what he had sold. As Henry VIII had seized the goods bought by the men of York, Robert was ordered to repossess them by reimbursing the Englishmen for the 260 angel nobles they had paid Andrew. In the meantime, until the Bretons received full compensation all Andrew's goods and real property were to be held as security.[25]

Andrew's action must have caused no little trouble to both the Bretons and Robert who was held responsible for regaining possession of Andrew's loot in order that it might be restored to its owners, a thankless and difficult duty. On more than one occasion Robert had to take legal action against purchasers who did not wish to part with their goods, or who having used them,

did not wish to pay for them again. All this took time so that
he was not clear of the matter until March, 1506.[26]

It may have been, however, that Andrew's attack upon the
Bretons brought results, for in the records of the Chancery of
Brittany, under the date of June 9, 1506, there is a "mandement
de justice," concerning the earlier robbery by the people of St.
Pol. The royal judges by this document were instructed to
summon Hervé de Porzmoguer and others to Nantes and place
them under arrest until they should recompense John and
Robert Barton and George Young for the damages which they
had suffered. Although action had been slow, James IV's plea,
perhaps coupled with Andrew's action, had brought some
good results in France, even though Andrew had garnered only
trouble in Scotland.[27]

While Robert was busy defending his brother he was also
occupied with other matters. For one thing, on May 16, 1506,
he received £60 from the king's treasurer in payment for
timber for "the schip," presumably the *Margaret*. It would also
appear that at about this time he participated in the purchase
made by James Makyson, probably in France, of a ship called the
Jacat. This was a somewhat peculiar transaction performed
perhaps on the king's behalf, but with Robert's and Makyson's
own funds, although the king himself provided the cables and
tackle at a cost of £232 7s. The vessel was home before May
26, and the following day the king inspected it with Robert
who gave the captain, William Merrymonth, called "King of the
Sea," 14s. probably for extra drinks. In September the king
bought out Makyson's share for £80 and in November that of
Robert for £150. It may have been that the two seamen had
really lent the money to the king who repaid them by buying
out their shares in the vessel, doubtless at more than cost.[28]

During the last half of 1505 Robert seems to have devoted
himself almost entirely to the *Margaret*. By November 9 he had
paid out considerable sums of money for completing her fitting,

for stepping her mast, and for preparing her for the sea. This project completed, however, he immediately found himself involved in something more momentous.

The most ambitious of James' naval schemes had now begun to take shape. He planned to build the biggest ship afloat, believing that this would put him in the forefront as a powerful and influential ruler. A great project, demanding large quantities of equipment and material, it necessitated the acquisition of ever-increasing amounts of timber, as was demonstrated by his purchase in February, 1506, of 52 trees in Dysart and a few months later, when the weather had improved, by his laying plans to obtain more from the north of Scotland. In April, Alexander Makyson was sent to Caithness to cut trees for the king's ship, and in the following months a Dutch ship, the *Raven*, was employed to bring that which was cut from Caithness, Ross, and the Isle of Lewis. William Brounhill of Leith also transported timber in his ship from the northland.[29] Thus even the most distant points of the country were laid under contribution.

Robert's part in this project was that of purchasing supplies in France. Throughout the year accompanied by George Corntoun he seems to have spent most of his time shuttling between Scotland and the ports of Normandy in search of timber, which he obtained by the grace of the French king and the Cardinal of Amboise.[30] In June he paid out £100 and in September 1,300 francs for planks.[31] On this last trip he also turned over 320 francs—£60 (Scots) as the final installment on the *Treasurer* built at Le Conquet. Along with the timber he brought back for the king two images of gold and "ane margreit" set with stones, worth £19 5s. 10½d., 16 pieces of taffeta of various colours, and 10 pounds 6¾ ounces of sewing silk for which he paid £83. Besides these items he obtained an anchor for the *Raven*, arranged the transport of the French Mountjoy Herald to Scotland, and performed a multitude of other duties.[32]

6

We can picture Robert setting out from Leith in the *Lion*, and some days later sailing into the mouth of the Seine and the port of Rouen. Here, it may be in the ancestor of the present-day L'Auberge du Canard on Rue d'Ecosse, or in the home of one of his compatriots, he would take up his residence while fulfilling the king's commissions. In the warm Norman summer sun or in the not-so-warm spring and autumn rains, he would hurry along the cobbled streets calling on city officials, scouring the port for shipwrights, and visiting important lumbermen who could provide him with boards, planks, and squared timber. Then in his spare time he might make a hasty trip to Paris to buy taffeta, golden images, and a "margreit" for the king and his lady. He had become an important royal servant, always in haste on the king's business.

Patrick Tytler has described the position of the Bartons at about this time in the following terms :

> The family of the Bartons, which for two generations had been prolific of naval commanders, were intrusted by this monarch [James IV] with the principal authority in all maritime and commercial matters : they purchased vessels for him on the continent, they invited into his kingdom the most skilful ship-wrights ; they sold some of their own ships to the king, and vindicated the honour of their flag whenever it was insulted, with a readiness and severity of retaliation which inspired respect and terror.[33]

Although this description is primarily true of Robert, from whose actions Tytler generalizes to the whole family, it applies also to a certain extent to Andrew, who at this point takes the center of the stage "to vindicate the honour of their flag."

Up to this time, although no doubt busy, Andrew had not been prominent in the king's service. He had performed a few acts of piracy, usually with unfortunate results, and had done some trading. He may also have participated in the royal shipbuilding program, but there is no record of this until

February, 1506, when perhaps as Robert's agent he paid £50 to some Bretons, presumably those building the ship at Le Conquet. Sometime that year he also sold 5 ells of Rissilis brown cloth to the king.[34] By September, however, he was definitely in royal employ, for he paid the wages of the sailors in "the great ship" the *Margaret*, at the Pool of Airth, on the Forth above Leith. This he continued to do until the end of January, which may indicate not only that he was in charge of preparing her for sea, but that when she was ready to sail he would be her captain.[35]

That this was the plan soon became clear, for once the *Margaret* was fully rigged and supplied, the king turned her over to Andrew for a piece of work which fitted in well with his natural proclivities. Dutch and Flemish pirates who were plentiful on the North Sea had been preying on Scottish shipping, probably along the approaches to the coast of the Low Countries. James, highly incensed at their depredations, and having a large war vessel now at his disposal, decided to take summary action against the robbers, by ordering Andrew to clear the seas.

Such a command was sweet music in the ears of the youngest Barton, for it not only gave him the opportunity to attack his country's enemies, but it also opened up a larger vista. Capturing pirates would no doubt be a profitable as well as an exciting occupation, but he now bethought himself of the old grudge his family bore the Portuguese. Why not have the letters of marque renewed at the same time ? After all, it would be a pity if he should encounter some Portuguese vessels and not have the authority to obtain reparations. At any rate, on November 6, 1506, he received the coveted charter under authority of the secret seal and sign manual.

That the letters were reissued just as Andrew was setting forth in the *Margaret* explains a number of other matters. Even if the letters granted to Robert and John in 1497 were still in force, Andrew had not been a party to them, no doubt because as a younger son of John Barton he had been either too young or too busy with other matters at that date to have shown much interest. Now, however, with everything in his favor he wished to try his hand at making the Portuguese give satisfaction. Thus it was that although Robert and John both appear in the grant, the person who actually received it was Andrew.[36] The vindication of his country's honor and his own profit could in this way be made suitably to coincide.

Sailing from Leith in the late autumn, he soon encountered the pirates and attacked them with considerable success, probably despoiling and scuttling the ships, as was the custom of the day. To his conquests he added, however, a special touch. Having slaughtered the crews of the pirate vessels, he had them decapitated and their heads packed in a barrel which he shipped back to Scotland as a proof of the vigor with which he was carrying out his commission.[37] His mission having been accomplished, he then returned home. It was this performance which gave Andrew an immediate and great reputation among his "brither Scots," a reputation which he has never quite lost.

Meanwhile the shipbuilding program had gone steadily forward, the vessel under construction at Dumbarton being the next on the list for launching. Robert, in March, 1507, supplied some 35 stone of nails and 136 stone of resin to Sir William Melville, who was supervising Martin le Nault, the Breton responsible for the completion of the fitting.[38] On July 17 Robert and Andrew sent eight seamen to Dumbarton to step the mast, and within six weeks the ship was about ready for its trial run. In that month Andrew received from the royal treasurer £106 13s. 4d. for supplies for the new vessel, and for herring which were to be its first cargo, to pay for wine in Bordeaux. Within a month the fish were ready for shipment, but whether Andrew commanded on the voyage to France is not stated. That he disappears from the records for the weeks subsequent to his furnishing of both the supplies and the trade-goods may indicate that he had temporarily taken up the unexciting business of importing French claret.[39]

Robert in the meantime had continued to import materials for the *Great St. Michael* and to supervise her construction, for on one or more voyages to France he brought home several French shipwrights from Dieppe along with 2,200 feet of planks and two "barrottis" for the great ship.

The summer of 1507 marked a turning point in the history of all three Barton brothers. The greatest change came, however, in the career of Robert. While he had been working hard at building the king's ships he had also been busy carrying on trade with the Continental ports of Rouen, Dieppe, Antwerp, Bruges, Veere, and Middelburg. Despite all this by the middle of 1507 he may well have been suffering a certain boredom. The ships under construction for the navy were progressing satisfactorily and his trade was bringing adequate returns. But it was all rather dull. What is more, the Portuguese traffic in spices and sugar to French and Netherland ports was growing by leaps and bounds. Here was an opportunity for excitement, profit, and revenge.

Although there are references to the granting to the Bartons of the letters of marque there are few clear statements available regarding their suspension—which seems to have taken place frequently. It was probably sometime early in 1507, at the earnest request of John and Robert, that James had reissued the letters, which stated that the Bartons were to have the right to seize up to 3,000 French crowns worth of goods from all Portuguese, with the exception of those subjects of the King of Portugal who had received James' special protection. Although the Bartons might well feel pleased that they were now in a position to recoup their father's losses to the Portuguese, James almost immediately forbade the letters' use until he had once more called upon the Portuguese authorities to reimburse his subjects; and to this end he dispatched the Rothsay Herald to Portugal.[40] The Bartons would have to wait.

While John as commander of the *Treasurer* was occupied with various errands for the king, Robert apparently now held the post of captain of the *Margaret*. On November 3 he provided a chalder of coals for the ship, while four days later "ane cheld" was paid 2s. to carry the king's writings to Robert in Leith. Neither of these facts proves that he was the commander, but there is further evidence in the story of Robert's activities during the following few months. We know that the *Margaret* was kept at the Pool of Airth from November to the end of January, 1508, but she disappears from the records just about the time Robert sailed to the Continent at the beginning of March. Shortly afterwards he is mentioned as being in charge of taking down her tackle and of having her caulked.[41] Such responsibilities were usually those of the commanding officer.

That this was his position would seem to be confirmed by the fact that his trip in January and February to the Continent was for the purpose of carrying out various duties assigned to him by the king. Although his itinerary is nowhere outlined, it looks as though he sailed for Spain where he visited the shrine of Santiago de Compostella, offering on behalf of his royal master a silver vessel weighing 31.5 ounces and valued at £33 18d. He also gave £7 7s. to the priests by royal order. James seems to have been much interested in this shrine, one of the most important in western Europe, hoping perhaps that through this offering he might obtain certain benefits, especially a son.[42] From Spain, Robert may then have sailed north to Nantes to appear as the plaintiff in the case against Hervé de Porzmoguer and his accomplices. His charges were proven and the raiders declared guilty, but the judges awarded Robert very light damages, amounting to what he claimed to be only about one-tenth of the value of the goods lost and less than one-half the costs of the suit. It was perfectly obvious that Robert would not be satisfied with this judgement particularly as he had to await payment by those who were guilty.[43] However, as he could do nothing more about the matter, he had to be content for the moment.

Setting sail from Nantes he then headed for Dieppe where he arranged for some £250 worth of lumber to be shipped by James Wilson and William Cristell to Scotland, along with armor, a barrel of Hamburg glasses, and various other commodities ordered by the king, and a horse for himself. Most important of all, however, he brought back with him the Bishop of Ross and Anthony D'Arcy, Sieur de la Bastie, a French envoy to Scotland, when sometime before March 1 he landed in Leith.

That Robert had carried out his duties to the king's entire satisfaction, but not to his own, is clear from the fact that shortly after his return James wrote strongly worded letters to both the Parliament of Brittany and Louis of France. He pointed out how dissatisfied Robert was with the judgement of the Council of Brittany, and threatened that if nothing more were done Robert might well take the law into his own hands. What came of these communications one cannot say, but the council found that even the comparatively mild punishment it had inflicted was difficult to enforce. On February 7, 1509, the Chancellor of Brittany granted de Porzmogeur the right to compel his accomplices to pay *pro rata* towards the Bartons' demands. He was not successful in doing this, however, the result being that whatever was paid in the way of compensation came from his pocket alone.[44] This was the end of the case, and the Bartons and George Young were obliged to be content with what they could obtain.

In the autumn of 1508, the Bartons' letters of marque again came into force, as the Rothesay Herald, during the summer, returned from Portugal without having achieved anything. The only course of action now left to the king was to give the Bartons their freedom to seek reparations at the sword's point, which he did, probably in August or September.

There is no account of Robert's and John's immediate reaction, but it is clear that before very long they availed themselves of the liberty they now possessed. By October, Robert had seized at least one Portuguese ship, probably carrying it into Veere for sale. Subjects of the King of Portugal, however, were not inclined to take such high-handed treatment without protest, so they promptly instituted proceedings in Veere against him for piracy and had him thrown into jail. By the beginning of November the trial had taken place and Robert, being found guilty, had been sentenced to compensate the Portuguese owner for his losses. Although he gave pledges to obey the court's order he was kept in the Dutch prison, apparently until he paid, which probably irked him considerably. Perhaps an attempt to slip away from Veere had convinced the authorities that jail was the best guarantee of his meeting his bills. The Lord of Veere, Sir Henry Van Borselen, attempted to intervene on his behalf at this point, but without avail. The prisoner did not suffer such treatment passively, for not long after the judgement had been rendered he appealed for aid to his king. To this plea James responded by writing a vigorous defense of Robert to Margaret of Savoy, Regent of the Netherlands, and to the Emperor Maximilian. Since Robert's attack on Portuguese merchants was quite in accord with the law of nations, the Scottish monarch demanded that he be freed. Along with these communications James may have included a transcript of the letters of marque made by the Burgh Council of Edinburgh who had officially registered them two days earlier.[45] The royal protests, unfortunately, had little effect, for Robert was still in prison the following months with apparently no hope of release in the near future.[46]

Meanwhile John also was having his troubles. In Robert's absence he took command of the *Lion* in which he put to sea with the letters of marque tucked firmly in his pocket. Where he went is unknown, but that he met with success is shown by the fact that he soon returned with a Portuguese prize. The only difficulty was that the ship's cargo seems to have belonged to English, Flemish, and French merchants. At least that was the tenor of the complaint made by the owners of the arrested goods on December 17 to the Lord High Admiral. To prove their claims, the complainants were given time to obtain evidence of citizenship from Bruges, Middelburg, Rouen, and La Rochelle, but nothing further is heard of this case.[47]

Nor was this the end of the letters of marque, for Robert, freed from his Dutch prison sometime after the middle of January, 1509, once more went into action, only to have misfortune follow him. A Portuguese ship he had taken went ashore on the coast of the County of Eu, where the local authorities who had seized it refused to make restitution. Robert thereupon appealed to the King of France who ordered the Countess of Nevers to see that her people gave satisfaction. As this communication had no effect, on May 1 James of Scotland wrote the countess warning her that she had better meet Robert's demands or he would report her to her liege lord.[48] There is no evidence, however, that Robert ever regained possession of his prize.

Meanwhile, John and Andrew had continued their privateering. Probably during the same month in which Robert lost his ship to the Countess of Nevers, another woman, Margaret of Savoy, wrote King James complaining that these two Barton brothers had plundered her subjects Andrew Marvex, Arent de Bladel, and Eurax Brachorst. The Scottish king, never one to forsake his friends, replied somewhat indignantly that John had not been at sea when her subjects claimed to have been robbed, while Andrew had assured him that he had never seen them.[49] Although one cannot help but admire the king's loyalty to his captains, it is impossible not to doubt the reliability of such a reply, particularly when one considers that just about this time Andrew illegally seized the *Fasterinsevin* of Antwerp which he would not surrender until ordered to do so by the king himself. Andrew, as charged by Margaret of Savoy, had apparently slipped over the rather thin line separating legitimate privateering from piracy. While Robert and John did not commit this error, the impetuous Andrew was building a piratical practice which, if not restrained, would provide a good excuse for those who might be looking for an opportunity to do away with him.

In the light of Andrew's activities, it is a little ironical to find James in October writing again to the king of Portugal in a tone of great indignation. The latter had granted letters of reprisal to a Portuguese merchant whose ship had been seized by the Scots. As the merchant had never taken his case to court in Scotland, this was clearly illegal, and James demanded that the letters be recalled.[50] From this grant of letters of reprisal and also from complaints which were at that time on the way to James from Portugal, there is little doubt that even if the Bartons were not accumulating very much wealth from their privateering, they were at least stirring up the Portuguese and others by making themselves thorough nuisances. Their successful attacks on the Portuguese along the western coasts of the Iberian Peninsula infuriated and frustrated their victims. "Nather culd the King of Portugal be counsel," says Bishop Leslie, "nather his subjects of Portugal be strength or force evir hinder the Bartons fra spoilzie and reife."[51] From this one would gather that all was going so well with the Bartons' ventures that they would soon be able to reckon themselves reimbursed for their father's losses.

How many prizes the Bartons actually seized is not indicated, but there are records concerning two. During the summer of 1509 John Barton commanding Robert's *Lion* picked up a Portuguese vessel out of Madeira carrying the goods of an

Englishman, Edmund Floure. Although the supercargo protested this action since the goods were English, John, declaring
that he could not read the bill of lading, apparently threw it
away and appropriated the cargo of sugar along with any of the
passengers' and crews' goods he fancied. Probably it was on
the same expedition that he also captured the *Lady of Perle*, laden
with sugar and other goods worth £50 belonging to a Frenchman
and a Fleming. All three victims carried the matter to the Lords
of the Council in 1510, demanding restitution, as the seized
goods were not Portuguese. To this the Bartons replied that
according to precedent in the English courts the nationality of
the ship determined that of the goods, and moreover the
pursuers, though not Portuguese subjects, were Portuguese
residents as was indicated by a receipted bill for the Flemings'
rental of a house in Madeira, which the defendants submitted to
the court. At this point the cases were postponed until the
pursuers could obtain further evidence to support their suits.[52]

Robert and John, however, apparently carried away by the
enthusiasm of the moment, were not content to attack only
Portuguese vessels but took the further step of seizing the cargo
of the ship of Hans Koyner, "Dutchman," perhaps a Hansa
merchant, of Beroun (Bergen?), consisting mainly of 70 lasts of
stock fish. Although Hans appealed to the Scottish courts there
is no evidence that he ever obtained compensation.[53]

It was probably as a result of these lawsuits and the trouble
caused generally by the Barton brothers' use and abuse of their
privileges of reprisal that King James at this juncture stepped in
to suspend the letters of marque for one year. By doing so he
hoped to persuade the Portuguese to give justice and so end the
unfortunate conflict which had developed.[54] In this, however,
he was not successful. The suspension did turn the Bartons'
attention temporarily in other directions, but once the letters
were renewed they were back at their old game, a game which
for them was to end the next time in tragedy.

V

The Enemy of England

The last four years of James IV's reign (1509-13) were for Robert some of the busiest and perhaps the most exciting of his whole life. It was during this period that he became better known as a sailor and privateer, especially as one who possessed a violent dislike for England. This apparently sudden hostility to Scotland's "auld enemy" had its ultimate source in the Barton family's relations with Denmark, so it is necessary to look first at Denmark's problems during the first decade of the sixteenth century.

The victory of the Danes over the Swedes in 1503 had by no means brought the conflict to an end. The Hanseatic League, particularly Lübeck, were angry with King Hans who was attempting to free the trade of the Baltic from their control, and this led them to support the Swedes in any rebellion they might attempt. The result was that from 1505 on, Sweden was always in a state of revolt or semi-revolt against Danish rule. Because of this state of affairs King Hans repeatedly appealed to both the French and the Scots for help. The former showed complete indifference but the latter, because of personal and dynastic connections, were much more sympathetic. James IV on more than one occasion sent embassies to the Baltic to help arrange peace treaties, and by so doing did help to modify the conflicts to a certain extent.

Truces, however, were of no use. Either the Hansa had to regain control of the Øresund in order to maintain a monopoly of Baltic trade, or it had to face total collapse. King Hans' realization of this necessity made him determine that he must now administer a knockout blow to his adversaries. He therefore renewed his pleas to James for ships and troops. The Scottish king replied by dispatching Andrew Barton who sailed on April 9, 1509. He may have been the Scottish skipper who during the summer captured a pepper-laden Lübeck "hulk," but there is no evidence that he accomplished anything more. It was obvious that such assistance was not enough. Hans, therefore, appealed to James to provide him with 2,000 men equipped with ships and arms, and in November added the demand that the Scottish king seize all Lübeck vessels in Scottish ports. To gain the support of private interests in Scotland, he also promised any Scots attacking and despoiling Lübeckers permission to keep their prizes. This promise was soon extended by an offer of general letters of marque to any sea captain who waged war on the Lübeckers or their allies in the Baltic or North seas, with the added privilege of trading prize goods in Copenhagen free of tolls, on condition that they give him one-quarter of their booty. Finally, on December 28 he sent another pressing letter to the Scottish king requesting the loan of the *Margaret* along with three other ships, and permission for Andrew and Robert Barton to serve him with their own vessels.[1]

The Bartons naturally welcomed such an invitation. Once the sailing weather had improved, Andrew was again at sea, picking up a German ship, laden with pepper valued at £933 (Scots), off the coast of England. At about the same time he came under attack as a pirate, perhaps in the Danish or Scottish courts, for his capture of the Lübeck vessel the preceding summer. King Hans met this charge by certifying that the Scottish captain had not committed piracy, since he was acting under his royal orders.[2] With such support Andrew appears to have felt that he could do much as he pleased on the high seas, for about this time he also seized a Breton vessel laden with the goods of some Antwerp merchants. Such actions were bound to lead to trouble internationally as well as personally, for when complaints were made against him in the Scottish courts, the latter do not seem to have taken any effective action.[3]

Robert went to sea somewhat later, in the middle of May (1510), but unlike Andrew he enjoyed James' protection and blessing. Although there is no record of his operations, when he returned to Scotland in September King Hans gave him a letter patent stating that whatever damage he had inflicted during the summer on the enemies of Denmark by taking their merchandise and ships, he had done by royal authority. At the same time, by the hand of Robert, the Danish king sent a message to James explaining that a force of Germans from Lübeck, Rostock, Stralsund, Luneborg, and Wismar had attacked Sweden, forcing her to come into the war; and for this reason a large number of troops as well as a fleet would be needed from Scotland by next Easter. By a second letter, also delivered by Robert, he asked James to try to gain the emperor Maximilian's support for him against Lübeck.[4] From comments in the letters concerning Robert's reliability, it is clear he had so won the Danish king's confidence that Hans believed him an eminently suitable go-between for the two kings.

James' reaction to these letters was apparently favorable although owing to the lateness of the season he could do nothing for the moment. When, however, he received from Hans another letter early in 1511 requesting him to send Andrew Barton again to his help, and if this were impossible, at least to send his ship, he immediately agreed. Andrew with the *Bark*, called variously the *Bark of Scotland* or the *Jenny Pirwin*, and Robert's ship the *Lion*, left sometime around April 24 and by May 11 he was in action, having captured a Danzig ship that he brought into Copenhagen for examination. It looks as though he had picked up this prize on the way over to Denmark, for King Hans disavowed any responsibility for the ship's arrest. He also informed the Danzigers who protested, that he had ordered the ship released but could not say what happened to it thereafter. The sharp tone of the king's letter would seem to indicate that he was none too pleased with Andrew's action; and it may have been because of further unauthorized seizures that about two months later he paid off the Scottish adventurer who left Denmark in the *Lion*, taking with him the *Jenny Pirwin*.[5]

For Andrew it was fortunate that he was free of obligations to the Danish king just at this moment, since the year of suspension of his letters of marque against the Portuguese was now at an end.[6] What actually happened at this time, however, is not quite clear. There is no evidence that Andrew returned to Scotland from Denmark. It is probable, rather that he headed directly along the French seaboard, with the intention of intercepting Portuguese ships coming north. In any case he was successful, for he picked up a considerable number of prizes, the cargoes of which he sold in French ports such as Dieppe. His only mistake was that he did not confine his attacks to Portuguese vessels, but seized some English merchantmen also, a dangerous proceeding.[7]

As one can well imagine, Henry VIII was not inclined to tolerate this kind of treatment, so when the Portuguese urged him to take action against the Scottish sea rover, he needed little encouragement. He ordered Sir Edward Howard, later Lord Admiral, with a couple of ships to arrest Andrew, who was now heading for Scotland. The result was a battle on July 25 which has come down to us not only in the accounts of such historians as Hall and Leslie, but even in ballad literature.[8]

According to *The Ballad of Sir Andrew Barton*, the *Lion* carried
36 guns and the *Bark* 180 men and 30 guns. Furthermore the
Lion was equipped with weighted beams attached to the topcastle, so that when Andrew closed in to board, they could be
dropped upon the deck of the enemy ship in the hope of
punching a hole not only in the deck but also in the hull.
Therefore, when the English grappled with the *Lion*, Howard
warned of this device by a merchant who had been a prisoner of
Andrew, employed his longbowman to shoot down those who
attempted to release the beams. After losing a number of his
men to the English marksman Andrew in his suit of armor
climbed to the topcastle where he tried to free the beams himself, in order to sink the enemy. Horseley the bowman, with
his last arrow, struck him under the arm, knocking him to the
deck.

> " Fight on, my men," Sir Andrew sayes,
> "A little Ime hurt, but yett not slaine;
> Ile but lye downe, and bleede a while,
> And then Ile rise and fight againe.
> Fight on, my men," Sir Andrew sayes,
> "And never flinche before the foe;
> And stand fast by St. Andrewes crosse
> Until you hear my whistle blowe."

But all was in vain, for Andrew was fatally wounded, and when
the English overcame the *Lion*'s crew, they found many of
them dying or dead by the side of their captain. The 360 men
who survived they took prisoner.[9]

According to the ballad, Howard's cannon sank the *Jenny
Pirwin* at the commencement of the engagement, but from Hall,
corroborated by other evidence, we learn that the English
captured her intact along with the *Lion*, carrying both ships into
the Thames as prizes. In this way Henry VIII received two useful
additions to his fleet at very little cost. The crews of the ships
he turned over to the Archbishop of York who sent them back

to Scotland after they had acknowledged the error of their ways.[10]

One of the Bartons had thus come to his end, beginning the breakup of what had become a famous, or notorious, triumvirate. The reaction in Scotland was violent. James was very much angered at what he considered an unwarranted English attack, which had not only deprived him of two ships, but also of a favorite and able sea captain. Moreover, he felt wronged since just about the time that Andrew was killed, he had once again recalled the letters of marque.[11]

Henry, on the other hand, not only boasted publicly of the achievement of his captains, but also refused to give any compensation, and incorporated both the captured ships into his fleet. This became the cause of an acrimonious dispute between the rulers of the two countries, although it would seem to have been of less moment than many historians think. Andrew's death took place in August, 1511, and James did not go to war with England until almost two years later. The importance of the event lies in its giving the Scottish king a further reason for annoyance at his brother-in-law, while at the same time it turned Robert, who had considerable influence with his sovereign, violently anti-English. Both these factors, although they did not actually precipitate it, did help to prepare the way for the eventual conflict.

It was this year that the pope organized the Holy League consisting of Venice, Spain, and the Papal States with which he hoped to drive the French from Italy, and, in order to make as certain of this as possible, he desired to add England and the Holy Roman Empire to the alliance. Although neither Henry VIII nor the emperor seems to have worried much over the pope's problems, they were attracted by an opportunity to attack France. To ward off such a combination Louis XII had only two possible allies—Denmark and Scotland—neither of whom was anxious to participate in the conflict. As the former had obtained no aid from France in her battle with the Swedes and the Hansa, she bluntly refused to help. James of Scotland, desiring to organize a crusade against the Turks, hoped to see established in the west a permanent peace. Louis apparently wrote Denmark off his books immediately, but was prepared to make every possible effort to bring the Scots into the war on his side. In this he was aided considerably by Henry of England who not only rejected all James' demands for compensation for Andrew Barton's death, but also treated James in a patronizing manner which increased the latter's annoyance.[12] Consequently, it was not too difficult to forecast James' eventual alignment with France.

Although about the middle of 1512 James renewed "the auld alliance" with Louis, he still seems to have been hesitant about making any overt move against England, at least until his navy was ready for action.[13] Despite repeated calls from Louis, it was not until May, 1513, that he finally decided to participate actively in the war.

During the two years between Andrew Barton's death and the Scottish declaration of war, James had steadily pressed the work of bringing his fleet to completion by both the purchase and the construction of ships. If war did come he believed that it was on the sea that he would make his power felt. Throughout the fourth volume of the *Accounts of the Lord High Treasurer* there are frequent references to the king's attempts to collect taxes, to enforce payment of feudal dues, and to make his debtors pay him the money which they owed, in order to buy the material and supplies required for the new ships. From all over western Europe, Scots such as Peter Brewhous, William Brounhill, and James Simson of Edinburgh, and foreigners such as Kasper Lepus, Jacat Tyrrell, Anthony Gervaise, and Andrew Jensen were importing cordage, tar, spars, boards, guns, gun stones, copper, tin, nails, and the like. If one glances through the accounts of expenditures, he will quickly realize that as far as the king's limited resources permitted, he was doing everything possible to create an efficient and well-supplied naval force.[14]

Sometime before April, 1511, the *Clofars* was bought from William Wood, and in October the *James* was purchased for the navy by John Forman and John Mowbray from Wood's executors. Another ship was acquired about the same time, the *Pansy*, and a little later on references are made to the *Gabriel*, a prize taken from the English.[15] Most important of all, however, was the addition made by Scotland's own shipwrights. In past years they had built vessels, such as the *Margaret* now under John Barton's command, which were of average size.[16] It was, therefore, a proud day when the Scots launched probably the largest ship afloat, the *Great St. Michael*. For five years she had been under construction and her builders boasted that she would outfight any other vessel. According to Lindsay of Pitscottie, the hull measured 240 feet in length, 36 feet in breadth, with sides above the waterline 10 feet thick. She could carry 290 sailors, 120 gunners, and 1,000 fighting men, while her armament consisted of 34 large guns along with some 300 small pieces. The total cost was something over £30,000. The man who supervised the construction of this vessel, Sir Andrew Wood of Largo, became her quarter-master or principal captain, while Robert received the post of master. Just what responsibilities these positions entailed is not quite clear, but it may have been that both Wood's and Robert's ranks were primarily honorary, as neither of them ever seems to have fulfilled any duties on board ship.

Here was an instrument of war which when once ready to go to sea would be an important factor in any international conflict. It is therefore easy to understand why both Louis XII and Henry VIII quickly realized that they must neutralize the *Michael*'s effectiveness, if they could not make use of her themselves.[17]

Although Robert does not seem to have been directly involved in the launching or fitting of the *St. Michael*, by the very

early months of 1512 he was once again in James' employ.
Between January and April, accompanied by his nephew
Alexander, Andrew's son, he sailed to the Continent on royal
business, and although no evidence is available to show what
he was doing, it may have been that he was again buying naval
stores for the king. As his official duties would not occupy all
his attention, however, it would seem reasonable to believe
that while in Honfleur on the king's business, he also made
arrangements for the building of a new *Lion*, to take the place of
that now flying the Tudor ensign.[18]

Meanwhile events had been moving rapidly on the international scene. England and Spain were preparing to launch an
invasion of French soil. To meet this threat Louis had been
sending embassy after embassy to Scotland with great promises
and loud pleas for help. Peter Cordier, Sieur de la Motte, and the
Bishop of Ross both appeared in Edinburgh appealing to James to
launch an immediate attack on the northern English counties.[19]

While James listened to the French propaganda he continued
to work on the construction of his navy. During February, 1512,
he obtained from Duncan Stewart of Lorne some "big Ersche
schippis," while he also had a galley built at Dumbarton.[20] At
the same time his scouring of western Europe for skilled shipwrights resulted in Danes, Spaniards, and Frenchmen working
side by side with Scots building or readying other vessels for
service. From Dieppe, Veere, Middelburg, Copenhagen,
and Norway as well as from the north of Scotland James brought
ropes, tar, canvas, boards, compasses, night glasses, cannon,
gunpowder, and the like in the hope that the navy, his pride and
joy, would soon be ready to sail the high seas.[21] Yet with all his
urging and encouragement, the work must have gone forward
very very slowly. The Scots, never used to continual pressure,
were not taking too kindly to it now. Only gradually was the
navy taking shape, and until it was ready, James was not prepared to go to war.

As usual, the two remaining Bartons were deeply involved in these preparations. Apparently as James' financial representative abroad, Robert had by May 25 paid George Halkerstone a total of £2,642 18s. 4d. for the latter's purchase of naval supplies. At the same time he, himself, spent £943 6d. 8d. for metal, timber, and other materials. Similarly, his brother John, along with John Balzarde and William Cristell of Dieppe, in January was appointed factor to purchase in French ports by license of Louis XII, ships, arms, and food. It was, no doubt, while carrying on these duties that on February 22 John was paid £40 "to furnish the king's half of his ship" in victuals and wages. Two months later he was in Dieppe buying cables which were shipped back home on the vessel of Gillieam Gilgot, and on May 25, £500 was delivered to him by George Halkerstone's factors in Dieppe, for the purchase of more cordage.[22]

During these months James continued to demand from Henry compensation for Andrew Barton's death. The English king, although not anxious to accede to the Scottish claims, but feeling that it might be well to make a pretense of negotiating, in reply dispatched Lord Dacre and Dr. West to Scotland. Bishop Leslie reports that these two envoys promised payment of damages, on condition that Robert and his confreres should be kept at home. That the English promises were worth anything is doubtful, however, for it looks as though Henry was merely trying to keep the Scots out of the Anglo-French conflict. Be this as it may, as a result of the Anglo-Scottish talks James, notwithstanding his alliance with France, seems to have become even more dubious about the advisability of going to war.[23]

Robert, for his part, regardless of the king's attitude, had by this time made up his mind to attack the English whenever and wherever possible. During the early part of the year 1512, despite his involvement in both his own and the king's affairs, he had taken service as a sea captain with the King of France. This gave him the right under French letters of marque to

attack the English without restraint. Probably it was to Robert
that Henry VIII referred in July, when he stated that Scots
attacking the English were always French privateers, but if
captured they always turned out to be subjects of James of
Scotland.[24] That Henry's objections had some basis is evidenced
by the Scottish Lord High Treasurer's payment to Robert of
£96 12s. (Scots), equaling £23 sterling, for the ransom of
certain Englishmen whom he had captured. And this was not
the end, for during the following month or so Robert, according
to Bishop Leslie, captured 13 English vessels, a success which
gave even James some qualms of conscience. The Scottish
king, however, was unable to restrain his subject, for he was
in French service. All he could do was continue the policy of
trying to ransom Robert's English captives, while at the same
time forbidding David Falconer of Leith and others suspected
of being Robert's accomplices to attack the English.[25]

As a result of Robert's depredations James found himself
in a very awkward position, for as long as he was unsuccessful
in obtaining compensation for Andrew's death, he could hardly
restrain Robert too definitely. On the other hand, he wanted
to keep the peace with Henry. Besides this he did not dare
offend Louis of France by refusing to recognize the latter's
letters of marque to Robert. In all of this, Robert alone seems
to have profited.

In the meantime the international situation had been steadily
deteriorating. Helped on, no doubt, by Robert's activities,
relations between England and France were worsening so
rapidly that a formal declaration of war seemed imminent.
Therefore the French king, at the end of May, dispatched
Sieur de la Motte and James Ogilvy, Abbot of Dryburgh, to
Scotland with a final draft of the proposed Franco-Scottish
treaty of mutual aid, in hope that the Scots would support
their "auld allies." The embassy did not lighten James' burden
for on the way over from France its escorts, according to

Bishop Leslie, seized some ten English vessels which they brought to Scotland as prizes.[26] This, coupled with Robert's privateering, removed the possibility of peace to a greater distance. Consequently, unless James were prepared to break completely with France, an action which would have put him in England's pocket, there was little that he could do but agree to the alliance. By July, 1512, he had signed the fateful treaty.

The English, as one might expect, were not prepared to take all this without instituting countermeasures. They stationed a fleet in the north, probably at Berwick, in the hope of intercepting de la Motte on his voyage back to France. To offset this move, when de la Motte and Ogilvy set sail on July 11, James sent along an escort consisting of ships commanded by Scotland's most redoubtable captains. Robert Brounhill, James Wallace, David Falconer, and Robert Barton who had perhaps come from France with de la Motte, all took part, and since one of the ships was the *Margaret*, John Barton was no doubt also present.[27] But even this display of strength did not deter the Englishmen. Under the command of Sir Robert Candysshe, and apparently with overwhelming power, they attacked the Scottish squadron, sinking David Falconer's ship, capturing Falconer himself, and forcing the remainder of the convoy to "lascher" to Denmark for safety.[28]

When news of this misadventure reached the Scottish court about the middle of July the king wrote a sharp note to Dacre, the English Warden of the Marches, complaining of the English seizure of Scottish merchants, and in particular the capture of Davy, who had been merely escorting the French ambassadors home. In the light of the same ambassadors' performance on their way to Scotland, one cannot but admire the boldness and brazen attitude that now enabled James to demand compensation. Dacre, unimpressed by this outburst, informed Henry that he would require the restoration of all the English goods taken by de la Motte, Barton, and Falconer, before giving satisfaction. He advised his master not to execute Falconer as a pirate too quickly, since musterings were going on in Scotland, the inference being that the sea captain might make a good pawn in case of difficult negotiations. Henry replied by writing James that the deeds of David Falconer and "Hob [Rob] of Barton" show "what they be," and by assuring Dacre that he would keep Falconer safe in jail until he should see the nature of James' plans.

The Scottish king, however, having by this time taken another breath, decided that since his principal captains were out of the country and his fleet unprepared, he had better return a soft answer. He therefore promised redress for Robert's activities "because he was within our realm," although actually in the French king's service.[29] For the time being this seems to have pacified the English.

Meanwhile, what had happened to Robert? He apparently did not stay long in Denmark, but sailed south to Veere in Walcheren, where he endeavoured to purchase a galley. For whom he was making the purchase is not stated, but it was probably to be an addition to the Scots' navy. Word of his arrival in the Low Countries spread rapidly, so that on July 27, perhaps as a result of English representations, Margaret of Savoy, the regent, issued orders to the Rentmeister of the Wester Scheldt to arrest him and all other Scottish pirates entering Zeeland, because they had robbed English merchants. But to Robert this was not a very serious threat, for in Veere he had many friends who would no doubt protect him from the zeal of the imperial authorities.[30]

By September 11 he had returned home, although whether he brought back a galley is not certain. His reception on this occasion was very cool, for he and the other captains had been guilty of running away in a fight and of allowing one of their fellow sailors to be captured. Robert endeavored to prove his innocence of any misconduct by laying the blame on Brounhill, while the latter returned the compliment by leveling the same charges at him.[31] The king could not permit a quarrel between his leading captains, however, so he received them all back into favor and concentrated upon obtaining Falconer's release and on preparing his fleet for action.

That James would be glad to see Brounhill and the Bartons back is made clear by the condition of the navy itself. Despite all his efforts and activity, he had not succeeded in preparing it for war. In fact the English were probably more ready in August, 1512, than were the Scots. On the 7th of the month Lord Dacre reported to Henry VIII that the King of Scots could do little for he had not 20 ships of his own. There were the *Great St. Michael*, the *Margaret*, the *James*, and a new vessel of about 300 tons, two or three of around 100 tons, and the remainder of not more than 80 tons each. Even by September 11 the situation had not improved noticeably for John Ainslow told the Bishop of Durham that James could raise only some 16 vessels "with toppes."[32] Thus despite all his expenditure of treasure and energy, James had not achieved his ambition to build an overwhelming naval force.

Meanwhile fighting had again broken out between the French and English navies, which caused Louis to send further representations to Scotland. James, who was anxious to help the French monarch, in turn sent envoys to Denmark asking for assistance in the form of ships but without any effect. Consequently, as Louis later admitted, if the French and Scots were to accomplish anything it would have to be by themselves without any foreign aid.[33]

While these international negotiations were going on, the two Bartons had, as usual, been busy. John, if he had commanded the *Margaret* in de la Motte's escort, had returned by August, during which month he worked hard to obtain supplies for the king. On the 7th the treasurer reimbursed him for 300 rough spars which he had imported, while in September, probably in Dieppe, George Halkerstone delivered cordage to him for the *Trinity*. Robert on his return from Holland at the end of August would seem to have been occupied with similar duties.[34]

Sometime around the middle of November, 1512, James sent John to France, probably for supplies, and about the same time ordered Robert who was apparently commanding the *Gabriel* to ready himself for the same voyage. Robert's instructions, however, were countermanded before he could sail. Not until December 10 did he and his nephew Alexander receive, under privy seal, respite from all suits from that date until 40 days after their return to Scotland.[35] Once again Robert was going to sea in the king's service.

Robert's and Alexander's departure was a sign of what was about to take place. Tension was mounting on both sides of the Channel as the two nations prepared for full-scale war. At the same time, each of the would-be belligerents began to put increased pressure on Scotland in the hope that the highly praised Scottish fleet might be theirs in the coming hostilities. Whichever side obtained possession of the Scottish naval forces would undoubtedly have command of the seas.[36] Henry, in hopes that a soft answer would guarantee at least Scottish neutrality, began to talk about negotiating certain points at issue between his and James' subjects, a concession which was a little late. At the same time Louis was sending messages to James asking him to send his fleet to France as quickly as possible. Though James had no intention of deserting his ally, he replied to all the French communications that he was preparing for action and also awaiting the arrival of a fleet he had requested from the King of Denmark. Despite his apparent hesitancy it was clear by April, 1513, that Scotland was committed to war with England, although when or where he would take action James had by no means decided.[37]

Whether Robert and Alexander returned with the *Gabriel* is

unknown. According to Spinelly, while on a visit to Honfleur to spy on the French naval preparations he encountered Robert who boasted that his new vessel which was of 300 tons' burden would be capable of as good performance as the first *Lion*. Spinelly added that although the French arrested him he regained his freedom through Robert's intercession. Pierdux, another of Henry's informers, also reported having discussed the new ship with Robert.[38] From these accounts one receives the impression that the latter was a rather typical sailor, full of energy and very proud of what he was doing, but, as shown by his help to Spinelly, bearing no malice. Perhaps one might call him in modern psychological terms something of an extrovert who took a great delight in doing things, quick to anger, but not spiteful.

By Easter of 1513 the *Lion* was off the stocks and by the end of May she was ready for sea. Robert meanwhile may have devoted some of his spare time to privateering that was very close to actual piracy. It is not unlikely that during the spring while commanding the *Gabriel* he participated in some of the enterprises which caused the Hansa to make numerous complaints to James that their vessels were being taken by Scottish freebooters.[39] He may also have been devoting his attention again to the English, for at the beginning of April Dr. West wrote Henry VIII from Edinburgh that he had raised the matter of Robert's attacks on the English, and had demanded that James make a general abolition of all letters of marque. To this the Scottish king had responded that if the English had given Robert redress for Andrew's slaughter, he would not be causing them trouble now.[40]

In the same letter Dr. West informed Henry that Jok (John) à Barton and the Unicorn Herald who had sailed from France on March 20, had arrived in Scotland bearing news of the pope's death, and more to the point, bringing a large cargo of wheat, gun stones, and powder. Despite this aid, James, it appears had

not yet made up his mind as to what part he would play in the
coming conflict, but went ahead with the equipping of his fleet,
so that by April 13, according to West, the smaller Scottish
ships were in fighting trim.[41] Even then, however, James still
does not seem to have been anxious to take action, as can be
seen from his letter of condolence to Henry VIII on the death
of Sir Edward Howard, killed when the English fleet came to
blows with the French at Brest on April 25.[42] The Scottish
king was still hesitating on the edge of the precipice when de la
Motte arrived to help him make up his mind.

In his instructions (May 8) to James Ogilvy, who accompanied
de la Motte to Scotland, Louis XII stated that he desired James
to send over his fleet immediately along with such Danish ships
as had arrived. The two fleets would there link up with the
French naval forces and together with seven more galleys sail
back to Scotland for James' use. That Louis would return the
ships once they were in France seems hardly credible, especially
since he was apparently unwilling to try conclusions again with
the English until he had the backing of his ally's fleet.[43] Although
Ogilvy and de la Motte were persuasive, they were not entirely
successful in convincing James of the necessity of sending his
naval forces to France and of preparing for an invasion of England.
After some discussion they returned to France, but without full
assurance of James' aid.[44]

This embassy had hardly reached home when Louis dispatched
another. Probably because the first envoys felt that James
needed further convincing, the new persuader was Robert
Barton. He left Honfleur around May 25 or 26 in his new ship
the *Lion* manned by a crew of 300.[45] He was a natural choice
for such a mission, representing, as he did, probably the most
violent of the anti-English element. Moreover as a favorite of
the Scottish king he was bound to carry much weight in the
country's councils. Although direct evidence is lacking to
determine the extent of Robert's influence, it is significant

that shortly after his arrival James reached his fateful decision. He would send the fleet to France. The die was cast! On July 26 he dispatched the Lion King-at-Arms to Henry's camp at Terouenne in France, to demand that he cease his attack on the French, and the next day he ordered the Earl of Arran to sail with the fleet, now consisting of 16 ships with tops and ten smaller craft, to a rendezvous with Louis' forces. Shortly after this he summoned the army to meet him on the Burrow Muir of Edinburgh in the third week of August.[46] This was his opportunity to overthrow the Tudor king.

At this point, everything went wrong. Arran, instead of obeying his orders, sailed to Ireland where he raided Carrickfergus, returning to the town of Ayr with his booty. James, extremely annoyed at this turn of events, thereupon dispatched Sir Andrew Wood to take command of the fleet, but before the latter could reach Ayr, Arran, apparently informed of his coming, sailed for France. The army was in a somewhat similar state, for although it may have numbered around 100,000 when mobilized, morale was low. From lip to lip were passing reports of omens of disaster, the most important warning of future catastrophe being a defeat suffered by Lord Home who had just made a preliminary raid across the border.[47]

Despite all indications of impending doom, James was determined to fight. He therefore led his forces across the border on August 22 and on September 12 he faced the Earl of Surrey at Flodden Field. Knowing little about strategy, and caring even less, he paid no attention to the advice of his ablest military leaders, but threw his army headlong against the well-placed enemy. The resulting defeat left James and the flower of his nobility dead on the field.[48] The promise of a brilliant reign had ended in disaster.

Before Arran's fleet left Leith, Robert had returned to France, but he may not have remained there long. According to a charge leveled against him by Felix Hannolt, agent of

James Fogner of Augsberg, he seized one of the latter's ships
off the coast of Norway in July. Robert denied the charge
vigorously, but the fact that he lied by claiming the *Lion* was not
at the time off the stocks would seem to favor the suspicion
that he was guilty.[49] He may have returned to Scotland by
August, as at that time he was paid £53 6s. 6d. by the Lord
High Treasurer for his overpayment of the composition for part
of the barony of Inverkeithing the preceding year. Since the
treasurer, on the other hand, could have made this payment in
Robert's absence, it is possible that throughout this period he
was at sea, serving the King of France as a privateer, a suggestion
which finds support in the fact that on August 24 he was once
again in Honfleur revictualing his vessel in preparation for
another two months' fighting. Indeed he may even have been
present to welcome the Scottish fleet when it arrived in the
mouth of the Seine.[50] If this were so he would, no doubt,
have seen his brother John who was in command of the
Margaret; and one can well imagine the annoyance of the two
brothers at the stupid actions of the Earl of Arran. This was
probably the last time the two men met in this life. Louis de
Rouville, who was placed in command of the Franco-Scottish
fleet, failed miserably to stop Henry's return to England in
October, nor did he achieve anything else. Consequently within
a few weeks the French king disbanded the fleet, keeping some
of the largest ships in France while sending the rest home.
In the *Margaret*, John sailed up the west coast to Kirkcudbright
where he landed, a very sick man, some think from sheer
heartbreak over the turn of events. How long he lived and
whether he ever returned to Leith is not known, but by
November 13 he was dead.[51] Robert was now the only remaining member of the triumvirate which had made such a name for
itself during the preceding fifteen years.

VI

First Political Activities

Scotland after the disaster of Flodden Field, with her king and most of her nobility slaughtered, and the enemy still strong and powerful on her borders, faced a desperate situation. Lacking an effective government because of the extreme youth of the new monarch, James V, resistance to England was hopeless. Had Henry of England at this point ordered his forces to march on Edinburgh, they could have done so without difficulty. He preferred, however, to disband his army, confident that the Scots would now be unable to endanger any of his plans. Yet, while he made no direct attack upon the distressed country, he made no attempt to bring peace. Dacre, his Warden of the Marches, continually intrigued with various Scottish nobles, notably the Douglases, in an attempt to stir up trouble for any government that might try to rule. As a result, most of the normal activities of the country were restricted. Merchants were afraid to put to sea because of threats of an English attack, marauders roamed the Highlands ravaging as they pleased, and what government there was, was set at nought on every hand.[1]

It was in this crisis that the Scots began to divide into English and French factions. Those bribed by English gold or fearful of an English invasion supported Archibald Douglas, sixth Earl of Angus, and other magnates in their recognition of Queen Margaret's right to be regent. Those, on the other hand, who had reason to fear English domination favoured as regent a cousin of James IV and next in line to the throne, John Stewart, Duke of Albany, who had spent all his life in France. For the moment, however, a general council named Margaret head of the state, in order to establish some semblance of a government.²

Meanwhile what of Scotland's foreign relations? As soon as word of the disaster of Flodden reached France, Louis dispatched an envoy to Denmark asking the recently crowned king, Christian II, to send assistance to the Scots. To this request Christian paid little or no attention. Nor did the French king do more. Apart from returning some Scottish ships, his only constructive act was to send along with Arran, who arrived in Scotland early in November of 1513, the Sieur de la Bastie. A number of nobles who feared English predominance had appealed to Albany for help, and it would look as though de la Bastie was to find out if the country as a whole favored their plea.³

Surprisingly enough it apparently did, for after considerable discussion, sometime early in 1514 the Lords of the Council decided, perhaps with Margaret's concurrence, to send Mr. James Ogilvy to France, bearing a request that Albany come to Scotland. The person appointed to provide transportation for the envoy was Robert Barton, now seemingly one of those who strongly favored Albany in order to restrain the Douglas faction. To avoid English cruisers he sailed in the *Lion* from Dumbarton, probably for Brittany, but a storm in the Bay of Biscay forced him into La Corunna, in the north of Spain. As Spain and France were at this point at war, the Spaniards promptly imprisoned Robert and his passenger in Madrid, where they were kept until the enemies agreed to a truce. Consequently, although he had left Scotland early in the year, probably January or February, the envoy reached Paris only at the beginning of June.[4]

The French king did not react very favorably to the Scots' request for Albany. Having suffered a number of military reverses, he had hopes of obtaining a peace with England at an early date, and any attempt to aid the Scots might only hinder his plans. Probably because of this the duke, himself, did not give any satisfactory answer to the Scottish representations. After expressing his thanks for their invitations, he went on to point out that as a treaty of universal peace was being discussed at the time, there might be no need for him in Scotland. This, however, he hastened to add, did not indicate any lack of French concern over Scottish affairs. Indeed King Louis was so interested that he was planning to dispatch another embassy to Denmark with a request that the Danes send over some 6,000 troops to help the Scots. At the same time, Albany urged his countrymen to refrain, if at all possible, from provoking the English.[5] No doubt Margaret and Angus felt great relief at this answer, for it meant that Albany would not, at least in the near future, interfere with their plans. In the meantime he had given his blessing to the idea of maintaining the peace with England. To the Anglophiles everything seemed once more on an even keel, for French treachery was playing right into their hands.

This became even more obvious shortly after Ogilvy's return, presumably in the *Lion*, with Albany's letter. On August 7, 1514, the representatives of England and France signed a treaty of peace, which although ostensibly including Scotland, left that country completely at England's mercy. Only very reluctantly did the Scots agree on September 18 to their inclusion in the treaty, while at the same time they demanded that both Albany and the remaining units of the fleet be sent to Scotland immediately. They had come to the conclusion that if they were to maintain their independence they would have to do so by their own strength.[6] Their only encouragement was a

8

message from Christian II of Denmark that he was prepared to give a subsidy to help Scotland resist the English incursions. Once the peace treaty was signed, however, Scotland was not in nearly such great danger from external attack as she was from internal chaos.[7]

The cause of this chaos was the impetuous queen mother. Having concluded that she needed a man to fight her battles, on August 6, 1514, she married the Earl of Angus. The result was immediate conflict among the leaders of the country. Those bound to the Douglases by family or feudal bonds favored the move as it would put them in power. Bishop Gavin Douglas, for instance, having become chancellor in September, promptly attempted to obtain the vacant archbishopric of St. Andrews. This in itself was enough to cause trouble, and when one adds the fact that many of the nobles feared any type of Douglas domination, one can easily see the possible outcome. Lord Home, the chamberlain; the Earl of Arran, next in line to the throne after Albany; and Archbishop Beaton of Glasgow, all seeing immediate threats to their positions, joined forces to oppose Angus' attempts to rule the country, even going so far as to seize the queen mother herself.[8] Yet, it was soon recognized that the combination of Margaret and Angus, backed by English money, was practically invincible. The only hope of over-throwing the Douglases lay in Albany, who, by reviving French influence, might perhaps restore the balance of power.

While this conflict was going on a solid substratum of Scots of all classes desired peace and quietness in which to carry on their ordinary vocations. Prominent in this element was the trading middle class. Thus it is not surprising that the call to Albany was supported by this group, one of whom was Robert Barton.[9] He presumably had brought back the ambassador carrying Albany's letter to the Scottish Lords. Then shortly afterwards, when the Lords revoked the sentence of forfeiture against Albany's father, and turned over Dunbar castle to the duke's representatives, Robert assumed the responsibility of provisioning the stronghold. These facts make it clear that from the first he was one of Albany's supporters, no doubt in the hope that the latter would be able to give some political stability to the country.[10]

Early in the new year Robert was again in France. On January 1, 1515, Louis XII had died to be succeeded by Francis I, who was inclined to be somewhat more interested in helping the Scots and who, to this end, agreed to send over the Duke of Albany. It may have been to provision the convoy for Albany that Robert had supplied 110 salted "beasts" and 110 pigs to the king's ships at Dunbar. But even if these items had no connection with Albany's coming, it is certain that Robert was in Honfleur by March to help escort the duke, then waiting to embark at Rouen. The original idea had been to return the remaining ships of the Scottish fleet with Albany, but the French suddenly changed their plans, suspending all action for the moment.[11] It may have been because of this suspension that Robert went to Paris to press Scotland's case, or perhaps he went to arrange for the sale of the *St. Michael* to the French. But whichever it was, the French relented and dispatched the fleet carrying Albany, who landed at Dumbarton on May 18.[12]

It would be outside the purpose of this study to enter into any long discussion or description of Albany's first regency, which lasted from the time of his arrival until June 7, 1517. Suffice it to say that he not only represented the French interest, but he also did his best to bring peace to the country. In this latter endeavor he found his greatest hindrance to be the underhanded dealings of the English king, who used the queen mother and Angus as his agents. Under these circumstances the duke believed it necessary to take vigorous action against Margaret and her faction, forcing them to flee to England. There Margaret bore a daughter to the Earl of Angus, but at the same time by her haughty and overbearing attitude alienated most of her supporters, including her husband. Consequently Angus, Home, and the other pro-English magnates soon returned to Scotland where they and the governor were reconciled. For his desertion Margaret never forgave Angus. But as far as Albany was concerned peace could now be restored.[13]

Although Robert's trail disappears for a time while these events were taking place, he comes into view once again in March, 1515, in connection with the inheritance of his ward and nephew Alexander, Andrew's elder son. Prior to Andrew's fatal expedition against the Portuguese he had acquired the manor of Ballinbreich from the king who held it as security for a debt of the Earl of Rothes. Since by July, 1513, the Earl of Rothes had repaid James IV the money he owed, thereby obtaining restitution of his property, he had immediately begun to collect from his lands in Fife, including those of Alexander's manor of Ballinbreich, rents which amounted to 12 bolls of wheat, 24 bolls of bere, 2 chalders of meal, and 3 dozen fowl. Despite Robert's objections, parliament in March, 1515, ratified the restitution. On July 25 Robert appeared before the Lords of the Council with the demand that the lands be adjudged to Alexander and the revenues restored. In answer to Robert's action the earl claimed that the land had really been returned to him in 1510, but as he produce no evidence in support of his defense the Lords ordered him to restore the rents of the lands to Alexander, whose they actually were.[14] Although there was some further disputing over the amount of the rents, Robert succeeded in vindicating his nephew's rights to the ownership of the estate left by the unfortunate Andrew.

While helping to defend his nephew's lands against the encroachments of one of the kingdom's great nobles, Robert also had to take action on his own behalf. A certain woman, Malkin Duchir, in the name of John Lyndsay, natural son of herself and the late Earl of Crawford, had brought suit against the Countess of Crawford and a number of others for occupying and using the lands of the manors of Downy, Dunfyndy, and Corlingy, in Forfarshire, which belonged to her son by grant of his father. Apparently taking advantage of the lawlessness of the years following the defeat of Flodden, the accused had simply refused to pay their rents. It was at this point that Robert entered the picture.[15] As we have already seen, in September, 1511, he had purchased from the Earl of Crawford certain lands lying in the manor of Downy which was involved in this lawsuit. He therefore protested on December 3 that this case did not concern him.

His protest was of little avail. As the purported owner of Malhungy and Ardesty in the manor of Downy, he was responsible for "misappropriating" young Lyndsay's rents. Malkin Duchir, therefore, sued him along with the others. In answer Robert produced his infeftment with its clause of warrandice and had the Earl of Crawford called as a witness to the authenticity of the document. His defense was unassailable, for on February 26, 1516, although Malkin was pursuing other people, Robert's name had disappeared from the suit.[16] He continued to hold the lands for some years longer.

As there were other lawsuits at the same time plaguing Robert, and since apart from them we have little information about him during this period, it seems worth while to seek any light which they might throw upon his activities.

The first suit was a charge of horse-stealing instituted by Campbell of Ard Kinglass, who had discovered a gray horse stolen from him the preceding Easter, in Robert's stables at Over Barnton. Robert replied that he had received the beast as a present from Sir Donald MacDonald of the Isles. As the latter was notorious in the Highlands as a riever and a rebel one can well imagine that he may have stolen Campbell's horse, but why he should have given it to Robert is left vague. Likewise the ultimate outcome of the case is not revealed in the records.[17]

Another lawsuit involving not only Robert but also his

nephew Alexander was instituted by Felix Hannolt, a German of Antwerp and factor for James Fogner of Augsburg, on charges of two acts of piracy committed against his employer. He accused the late Andrew Barton of having taken from the ship *Mary of Bertanze* (Brittany) in March, 1510, some twenty bales of pepper worth £933 (Scots), and Robert of having spoiled in July, 1513, off the coast of Norway, a ship of Hoorn in Holland of five bales of copper worth some £810 (Scots). Alexander flatly denied that his father had ever stolen any pepper; and with regard to the seizing of the copper, Robert claimed that this was impossible since, on the date of the alleged piracy, his ship was still on the stocks in Honfleur. To prove this Mr. Robert Galbraith, attorney for the Bartons, then asked for instruments which would give the date of *spuilze* of the copper, an important point. In the face of these statements the Lords deferred the case until the end of August.[18] Throughout the month of August further evidence was collected and finally on September 7 the Lords cleared Robert of all complicity in the attack on the ship of Hoorn.[19]

Although everything had apparently been thus settled in his favor, on September 11 Robert was back in court acting as surety for an Allane Dais, a George Wallace, and a James Wilson whom Hannolt accused of having in their possession some of the copper in question. As the defendants refused to surrender the goods, claiming that they were the true owners, Master Gavin Dunbar, canon of Aberdeen, and Master Thomas Hay were appointed to go at 8 A.M. to the New Kirk in Leith, to inspect the disputed copper, 220 pieces in the hands of Dais, 14 in those of Wilson, and 118 in those of Wallace, to see if they bore Fogner's sign. They were then to return the copper to Wallace and Wilson since Robert Barton had guaranteed that the copper would be produced whenever called for. Since Dais was not included in this latter provision, Robert may not have been prepared to be his surety.[20] Even this did not bring the matter to a conclusion, for on February 12, 1516, the Lords ordered Robert to produce before them one of the pieces of copper claimed by Hannolt as they themselves desired to examine the mark in order to give justice. At this point Hannolt stated that this copper had been taken in July, 1514, off the coast of Norway, from the ship of Vibrand Skiphernis of Hindloepen, Holland, by *John Bertounis Berk* under the command of George Wallace, which was a new story. Not until May 17 was the case finally settled, but on that date the Lords ordered the defendants, Dais, Wilson, George and James Wallace, and Helen Dudingston, John Barton's widow, to restore the copper marked with Fogner's sign as described by the authorities of Antwerp and Amsterdam, and as identified by Gavin Dunbar and Thomas Hay. The end of this case must have come to Robert as a great relief, for as he was the executor of his brother John's will he had been occupied with the matter ever since the latter's death.[21]

He was now finished with the Hannolt suit, but he was by no means free of problems which arose out of piracy or privateering, not on his part it is true, but on the part of some of his friends. As a result of the conflict between Hans of Denmark and the Hanseatic League, the Scots became the foe of the German Baltic cities. The result was that wherever Scottish skippers had the opportunity they would pounce upon a German vessel, carrying it into a Dutch or Scottish port as a prize. In pursuance of this policy, during the late summer or autumn of 1515 a certain David Logan along with some other indwellers in Leith arrived home with two ships of Hamburg in tow; and about the same time a William Scott of Montrose captured another vessel from the same port. The owners of these prizes, having discovered what had happened, instituted proceedings before the Lords of the Council. Robert, who appeared as the representative of the defendants, claimed that they were quite within their rights as they were merely seeking compensation for past

losses to the Germans. However, he promised to guarantee the
return of the ships and cargoes if they proved to be unlawfully
held.[22] The outcome of the suit is unknown, but Robert's
interest in it may be evidence that he had some financial stake
in the Scottish vessels and their ventures, or it may be that he
was continuing to fight the Hansa by proxy. But one thing is
certain, his fellow skippers regarded him as being sufficiently
influential to seek his help when they were in trouble.

One of the reasons for Robert's influence was his growing
wealth, which he may have been increasing less by trade or the
acquisition of real estate than by money lending. For example,
about this time the crown confiscated the lands of Bavillan, part
of the property of John Forester of Nudry who had alienated
them without royal consent. The penalty for this infringement
of the royal prerogative was set at £200, and Robert, probably
in collusion with Forester, paid the sum involved receiving
possession of the land. By March 6, however, Forester had
reimbursed him for the £200 and again took over the property.[23]
How much Robert made by this transaction one cannot ascertain, although there is little doubt that he received some
recompense. In all probability he was carrying on a good many
such business transactions which could not but result in a rapid
accumulation of wealth.

Influential as he might be, however, Robert did not have
everything his own way. For instance, as a landlord he had his
difficulties with tenants such as Elizabeth Arbuthnot of East
Broughty.[24] But even more important at this time was his
coming into conflict with the Burgh of Edinburgh. Now that
James IV was dead, the burgh authorities felt that they could
enforce their control over Leith by demanding that all the
goods of those infringing their monopoly should escheat to the
town. Although this was opposed by the governor as being
unwarranted,[25] still, anybody who opposed Edinburgh could
now expect trouble.

In July, 1514, the burgh council had fined Walter Ker of Leith for selling goods to a Frenchman. Then in the spring of 1516 the city fathers sued Antoine a merchant of Rouen for purchasing from the same Walter Ker and from Robert Barton four lasts and from George Corntoun one last of hides. As the vendors were indwellers of Leith and not citizens of Edinburgh they had by this transaction broken the law. Therefore, the provost and baillies declared the goods escheated to the town, a judgement in which Antoine acquiesced.[26] Although Robert and his friends found themselves obliged to accept the judgement their submission was only temporary. This was but the first battle in a prolonged campaign which the Leith merchants and sea captains were to wage against Edinburgh for the right to carry on their business in freedom. For the time being Robert and his confreres had been obliged to retreat, but it was only to gain strength for the struggle.

This renewal of strength was ultimately to come from Robert's growing interest and activity in the political conflicts plaguing Scotland. He now seems to have thrown his full weight and influence behind the Duke of Albany. The latter, having again come to blows with the Earl of Angus and his party, in September decided to seize the Angus strongholds; and to supervise the transportation of supplies for the expeditions, he employed both Robert and his friend David Falconer. On September 27 a certain Captain Jonet Bousket, a Frenchman and commissioner of artillery, received from the treasurer £38 5s. 2d. which he had paid to Robert and David to go by the governor's command with mariners on certain errands to Tantallon Castle, one of Angus' fortresses. Two days later the treasurer paid Falconer a further £62 13s. for carrying food and munitions from Leith to Dunbar, Fastcastle, Castle Douglas, and Tantallon.[27] Robert and his friends were clearly becoming known as members of the anti-English party.

An obscure reference in the *Acts of the Lords of the Council* points not only to this, but also to another facet of his pro-Albany activities. On January 10, 1516, the prior of St. Andrews, John Hepburn, asked instrument "that he renuncit the obligacions maid to Robert Barton for the furing of my lord of Arane to Fraunce as his part."[28] From this it would appear that Hepburn had hired Robert to carry Arran to France as a representative of Albany, but that he now wished to back out of the agreement. Robert refused to submit to such treatment, insisting that Hepburn keep his word. Whether Hepburn did or not is unknown, but the next month in a violent storm along the coast of Holland three or four Scottish ships went down, the sole survivor being the vessel carrying an ambassador to the court of Francis I. To avoid interception by the English the captain had apparently crossed the North Sea to the Dutch coast, whence he could sail south to a French port.[29] It is likely that this ship which succeeded eventually in bringing the official safely to his journey's end was Robert's *Lion*.

But if Robert was responsible for the ambassador's transportation, he was also active in opposing the collection of taxes to pay the ambassadorial expenses. Although early in January a number of royal burghs had been taxed to meet the ambassador's needs, many had either ignored the regent's demand or had refused to pay. As a result, on January 18 letters patent were issued canceling the freedom of Glasgow, Linlithgow, Stirling, Rutherglen, Renfrew, Paisley, and Dumbarton and ordering the goods of their baillies seized. The following month similar letters were issued against other towns.[30] No doubt these latter, none of which were royal burghs, felt that it was up to those enjoying special privileges to foot the bill; and among these non-royal burghs was Leith.

To this town Robert Hart, one of the Lord High Treasurer's officers, went on February 26 to distrain the baillies for the tax. In this he was entirely unsuccessful, the baillies probably threatening his life if he attempted to carry out his orders. The

next day he was back again, but this time with witnesses, that
evidence of Leith's recalcitrance might be taken. Even this
achieved little, for on the 29th James Nesbit, a macer, and
three officers were dispatched to seize the Leith baillies' goods.
When matters had reached this stage Patrick, Lord Lindsay, and
Robert appeared before the Lords of the Council on behalf of
Robert Logan, Laird of Restalrig. They protested that although
Logan, the feudal lord of Leith, was prepared to meet the
demands of the king and the regent for taxes so far as he was
able, he insisted that his town of Leith should not pay anything
more.[31] Apparently the protest was effective for the matter
seems to have been dropped. Robert's participation in this
action is significant since it shows both that he was on intimate
terms with his feudal overlord, and also stood as one of the
leaders in the civic affairs of Leith.

Meanwhile, the Duke of Albany had lost most of his friends;
English gold and intrigue as well as Scottish jealousy had ranged
many of the would-be leaders of the country in opposition to
him. Consequently there were few people whom he could
trust, except some of the middle class. Not insensible to the
state of affairs, Albany apparently endeavoured to guarantee
their support by gifts and favors. This was probably the reason
why on January 31 in Edinburgh he granted, "of the King's free
grace," to Robert Barton of Over Barnton, the wardship of all
the lands and rents of the late James Fothryngham of Powry,
including the marriage of James' brother Thomas, a gift which
would eventually be worth a considerable amount.[32]

Perhaps an even better indication of the governor's confidence
in Robert is given in his appointment as one of the commissioners responsible for the renting of royal lands in Fife
(January 2, 1516), and in Strathearn (February 23). These lands
were one of the principal sources of the king's revenues, and
since there was no distinction between the royal private income
and that of the state, if the government was to administer the

country adequately, it had to keep the returns at the highest possible level. During the period following James IV's death, the commissioners in charge of letting out the lands had very often rented them dishonestly or at low rates to their friends. The Duke of Albany was now trying to remedy the situation by appointing a few loyal and hard-headed businessmen to the commissions which dealt with these matters. Robert by virtue of his administrative and business ability was becoming useful to the government in its attempt to solve Scotland's most pressing problem, that of finance.[33] The renting of crown lands was, however, only a step to higher office. Albany apparently felt that Robert should be given even greater responsibilities and powers in order that he might use his talents for the benefit of the government. Therefore late in July, 1516, the duke named Robert Comptroller of the Royal Household and Custumar of the city of Edinburgh.[34] With these two appointments, he stepped from the role of a private citizen, albeit an important one, into one of the most crucial administrative positions in the country, becoming both the government's chief financial officer and also the man in control of the export of goods from Edinburgh. This meant power and influence far beyond anything which he had ever held before.

VII

Recouping the Royal Finances, 1516–1518

In order to grasp the meaning of Robert's appointment to the office of comptroller, it will be necessary to glance for a moment at the office itself. According to the editor of the first volume of the *Accounts of the Lord High Treasurer*, James I was the ruler responsible for setting up a dual system of financial control under the treasurer and comptroller. The former was to receive and disburse the occasional feudal dues received from vassals, fines and issues of courts, returns from stewards of feudal properties, and special taxes and contributions, while the latter received the fixed revenues accruing from the rents of crown lands, the burgh mails or taxes, and the customs duties. The treasurer's expenditures were for miscellaneous royal charges: livery for the king's retinue, gifts, houses and their furniture, mercenary soldiers, royal castles and dwellings, alms, fees and bullion for coinage. The comptroller on the other hand met the recurring charges for food, wages, and the like.[1]

The only difficulty with this explanation is that it is too well defined and logical. When one goes to the actual accounts themselves, the receipts and disbursements of the two officials

frequently overlap, although in principle the distinction holds
true, particularly in the matter of income. The fixed revenues
of the comptroller were obtained in one of two ways. Either
they were leased, as was frequently done in the case of the
customs of some small burghs; or they were collected by local
officials. When the Audit of the Exchequer took place, those
responsible for the collection of the monies would come up to
Edinburgh where, before the Lords Auditors, they would
present either the revenues received or receipts for payments
which they had made. In the case of those paying to the comptroller, many of their receipts would be for payments made on
the instructions of the king himself. These might include gifts,
pensions, alms, or reimbursements of a servant for expenses
incurred on royal errands. Although this system may look somewhat haphazard to modern man it seems to have worked with
moderate efficiency throughout the fifteenth century.[2]

It was during the first quarter of the sixteenth century that
the breakdown of the system began to manifest itself. All over
western Europe, for various reasons, government costs were
rising while royal revenues not only remained stationary but
were collected so slowly that in order to exist from day to day,
the government had to seek loans at exorbitant rates of interest
from bankers and merchants. To this rule the administration of
James IV of Scotland had been no exception. Moreover, since
he was not only endeavouring to maintain his government's
operations, but was also trying to build a large navy, he was in
continual difficulties. For 1512–1513 alone the treasurer's
deficit was £1,965 17s. 7½d., equivalent to about one-third of
the total income, which gives some idea of the situation. Therefore, when the government fell to pieces after the defeat of
Flodden Field, the result was financial chaos.[3]

The extent of this chaos is indicated by the fact that there was
no treasurer from September, 1513, until June 25, 1515, when
the Bishop of Moray took over the office. From the time of

Flodden until June 1, 1515, nobody seems to have acted as comptroller either, and even on that date Patrick Hamilton of Kincavil and James Kincragy, Dean of Aberdeen appear merely as "Receivers of the King's Property." They, however, were really comptrollers although they acted only until November of the same year. By that time they had incurred a deficit of £1,062 3d. Their revenues had amounted to £2,982 4s. 5d., but with Albany's household expenses alone coming to £3,403 17s. 10d. (the king's were only £69 2s. 5d.) they had very little chance of achieving a balance. The following March, Sir Alexander Jardine of Applegarth took over as comptroller with slightly greater success, reducing the deficit to £1,035, as the governor's expenses leveled off at £3,349. He, however, was replaced in office at the beginning of August by Robert Barton.[4]

Why did Robert take over Jardine's duties? The editors of the *Exchequer Rolls* believe that it was because Jardine had defrauded the crown by giving himself a long tack, or lease, of the English customs at a very low price. Although this, of course, may have had some influence, it would not seem to be the ultimate reason. The fact is, as shall be seen later, that despite the crown's ownership of considerable property throughout the country it was receiving very small returns. Most of the stewards or baillies were simply appropriating the income for themselves as were also the custumars in the various towns. What the country needed was a hard-headed, strong-armed comptroller who would force the payment of all monies owing to the crown. In Robert Barton, the Duke of Albany found such a man.

That Robert was appointed to the position of comptroller for the prime purpose of reforming the whole financial administration is obvious, not only from the state of the finances at the time, but also from the conditions on which he accepted office. Apparently he would act only if he could have the widest powers.

Therefore Albany assigned "the hale properte to him for the sustentacioun of the kingis frends and my lord gouvernor, and dischargit (forbade) all custumars of intrometting (interferring) with our soverane lordis custumis that he myt sett and dispone (dispose) therupon to the kingis maist avale (greatest profit)."[5] But, although the grant of such powers meant that Robert had the right to put the crown's finances on a sound basis, he would still have to fight many a battle before he achieved success.

The first problem he faced in attempting to bring order and light into Scotland's chaotic financial situation was that of forcing those officials and magnates who owed the crown money to pay their debts. Therefore, almost immediately after his appointment he turned to the Lords of the Council before whom he arraigned many of the defaulters, including some of the council members themselves.

As a result of his investigations Robert discovered that the custumars of the northern shires had been making no returns of customs since the day of Flodden Field. Therefore on December 1, 1516, he began a series of suits against the defaulting officials of the burghs of Forres, Elgin, and Aberdeen and of the counties of Ross, Ardmanach, Caithness, and Sutherland which included all of Scotland north of Moray Firth. The amount of money owing he set at close to £600 and threatened that if the officials did not produce itemized accounts he would demand that the Lords accept his estimate.[6] This heavy-handed policy quickly showed results, for when the delinquents saw that he had the support of the Lords, they began to pay what they had taken.[7]

With Gilbert Menzies, custumar of Aberdeen, Robert had a little more trouble. Menzies, member of an important family of burgesses who also held considerable land in the neighborhood, had apparently failed to present his cocket book for inspection. For this reason Robert, since he had been appointed to clean up the finances with full authority to take action, removed him from the office of custumar. To such treatment Menzies did not take kindly, for he appealed to the Lords for reinstatement on the grounds that he had been appointed to his position by James IV, which apparently meant that whether efficient or not, he had the right to occupy the office as long as he desired. Robert replied that he had the right to discharge custumars as he pleased. The Lords, apparently not willing to take action in the case, postponed it until the following February. Robert thereupon appointed a George Congillon as custumar, but he was unable to fulfill his duties as Menzies and his friends continued for the time being to lift the customs.[8]

Up to this time Robert seems to have been pursuing only burghs and burgesses who were delinquent in their financial relations with the crown. By the middle of February, however, he had begun to widen his scope of inquiry. Not only was he interested in the question of customs, there was also that of wardships. These were of considerable value since the king had the right to draw the revenues of the property and to arrange for the marriage of the minor heirs or heiresses of all deceased tenants who held land from him. With the high rate of sudden death common in Scotland at the time, this should have been profitable, but since the nobles were doing very much as they pleased in their own districts, it was often hard to collect the monies owing to the royal treasury. Robert therefore took steps to obtain these revenues, by instituting proceedings against various offenders, the first being the Earl of Athol who had for three years appropriated the income of the Earldom of Buchan. The latter's wardship had been in the hands of James IV at the time of his death, and Athol had simply taken the money without giving any account to the crown. The Lords decreed that he should pay forthwith, but it was some time before he met his obligations.[9] This was but one case and others were to follow.

Meanwhile a third type of attack was being made on the government deficit. As much of the royal income came from the revenues of lands, the comptroller was interested in keeping the rents at as high a level as possible. To this end he persuaded the Lords of the Council in the early days of his term of office to appoint a commission consisting of the Lord Chancellor, the Bishop of Galloway, the Archdeacon of St. Andrews, the Dean of Aberdeen, and himself to rent and supervise all the king's lands in his lordships of Galloway, Fife, Strathearn, Kinclevin, and elsewhere. A quorum of three or four of this body was sufficient to deal with its business, but the comptroller always had to be present. The latter provision indicates that Robert was determined that the lands should not be rented merely to friends of the commission's members and that they should produce as much as he could obtain. The commission commenced operations the following January, and during the winter and spring of 1517 worked steadily on the problem of the royal properties scattered throughout Scotland.[10] In all of this Robert was unceasingly active, no doubt hoping that he might be able to increase the revenues which were so badly needed if Albany were to govern the country as he should. Even these measures, however, do not seem to have satisfied him that the king was receiving all that he required.

It was probably on his advice, therefore, that about this time the governor and his councilors decided to levy a tax throughout the country, not only on the nobles, but also on the clergy and the burghs. But as might have been expected, it was not very successful, for although the Lords repeatedly sent out letters demanding the tax, they had little effect.[11]

As the country's leaders obviously did not favor this approach, Robert had to rely primarily on the old methods, and it was for this reason that on March 16 he took action against the Earl of Argyle and John Ogilvy, heir of Strathearn. He charged Argyle with having taken revenues of the crown lands in South and North Kintyre, Cowell, and Rosneath, and of having failed for three years and one term to turn them over to the comptroller.

Ogilvy he accused of appropriating for the preceding three years the rents of the land of Petty Broughty and Strathearn, and the customs of Banff. The Lords, after hearing the witnesses and examining Robert's evidence, ordered the Earl of Argyle to pay in accordance with his father's commission for the collection of the rents of the lands of Knapdale. Similarly they instructed Ogilvy to account for the land rents which he had received, while the question of the Banff customs they postponed for a week until Robert could show their value. Argyle made no attempt to pay until 1522.[12]

Government finance, however, was not Robert's sole preoccupation; the administration required his help in other fields also. When the governor attempted to bring peace by suppressing the lawless highland chieftains, Sir Donald MacDonald of the Isles, who had given or sold Robert a gray horse somewhat earlier, and his two brothers attempted to lead a revolt, but were arrested and brought to trial. The duke thereupon appointed a commission of temporal lords to decide what action the government should take. Unfortunately, the commissioners disagreed; the earls of Huntly and Lennox, the lords of Drummond, Ogilvy, Balwery, and Kers, most of them northern nobles, wished to avoid any decision by placing the responsibility for a verdict on the shoulders of the regent. The earls of Cassillis and Argyle, the lords Erskin, Borthwick, Lus, and Kincavil, the captain of Edinburgh Castle, Robert Barton, and Adam Otterburn, the king's advocate, on the other hand, recommended that they "be justified according to their merits," letting the law take its course. Robert, despite any possible friendship with Sir Donald, took his stand on the side of law and order, while at the same time desiring to relieve the regent of the onus of making what might be in the Western Isles a very unpopular decision.[13]

As one might expect, under the pressure of his official duties Robert seems to have had little opportunity to attend to his own private business interests. There are virtually no references to his trading activities during this period, although one may surmise that the absence of certain records may be the cause of the lack of information. It is well to note, however, that even the *Exchequer Rolls* and the *Treasurer's Accounts* contain no reference to any commercial activities on his part. Most of the extant information concerning his private affairs is contained in certain lawsuits in which he was either defending himself or seeking to make people pay their debts.

One of the first suits against which he had to defend himself was that brought on December 5 by Demetrius de Costa on behalf of Philip Gualterot an Italian living in Flanders, for having taken from the latter's ship a cargo of pepper. The Lords of the Council desired to make sure that justice was given, but Robert claimed that this question should come before the Earl of Bothwell, Lord High Admiral, who was, however, a minor. In this exception taken by Robert he received the support of John Hepburn, Prior of St. Andrews, tutor of the earl. Although the Lords wished to take a hand in the proceedings they were so occupied with other matters that they allowed Hepburn to appoint an admiral-depute, Patrick Barron of Edinburgh, who after examining the evidence declared Robert "not guilty." This decision did not satisfy de Costa since he felt there was collusion between judge and defendant. However, his appeal to the Lords was no more successful, for Robert produced a notarial document to show that he had taken the goods from a Portuguese ship off the south coast of Portugal. De Costa declared the instrument a forgery but did not pursue the case further.[14] That Robert had acquired the pepper while serving the King of France is likely, but as no dates are given for his depredations it is impossible to say when or where he acquired this "hot" pepper.

Two other suits in which he figured during February, 1517, he himself instituted. In one he took action to force the Earl of Crawford to guarantee him in the possession of Kirkbuddo,

Malhunghy, and Ardesty which he proved had been deeded to him on October 11, 1511. In the other he sued Sir Duncan Forester of Gardene for £26, the balance of £41 which the latter owed him for spice purchased on behalf of James IV. As Sir Duncan did not appear, the Lords found him guilty and ordered him to pay not only the principal sum, but—an unusual item in the *Acts*—also the court expenses. In order that his bill of costs should not be too large, however, the Lords added that on March 20 they would review the amount charged.[15]

In the records of this court case there is an indication that Robert was rising socially in the community. He had now achieved the position of being referred to as "of that Ilk." It is also noteworthy that he was regarded by John Forestar of Nudry as being of sufficient importance and prestige to be employed at this time in a lawsuit before the Lords of the Council as an advocate.[16]

Yet while receiving honor and deference in certain quarters, he was not growing in popularity with the Edinburgh burgesses. The reason for thinking this is that late in April or early in May, Robert and the burgh's authorities came to blows over the question of the latter's control of trade in Leith. A Dutch ship commanded by Hendrik Cordson had arrived in Leith harbor with a cargo of timber which, when unloaded, the treasurer of Edinburgh examined and priced in order that he might make a common bargain in the name of the burgesses. Before he could complete arrangements, however, Robert appeared on the scene supported by a group of his neighbors of Leith, and seized the cargo, giving the reason that, as comptroller, he had the right of first purchase for the king of any goods coming into the country. Although the city treasurer had resisted what he considered to be an illegal act, he succeeded only in rousing the Leith men's ire. What happened to the timber is not disclosed, but it is reasonable to suspect that it went to Leith, thus depriving the Edinburgh burgesses of the profit which they would have derived from retailing it to those who had made the seizure.

Naturally such high-handed action on the part of one whom many may have come to regard as an upstart would not pass unnoticed or unavenged. Suit was brought against the comptroller. The Laird of Restalrig thereupon intervened, protesting that any action of the Edinburgh authorities should not derogate from his rights as feudal lord of Leith, while similarly the king's advocate, no doubt on Robert's orders, protested that whatever was done in this case should not limit the king's privilege of first purchase. The Lords, obviously not wishing to offend either Robert or the burgh when they gave judgement, contented themselves with merely issuing an order that when foreign ships came into the "raid of Leith," the royal treasurer and the comptroller had prior rights of purchase for the king's household. After that, the Edinburgh council could buy the goods they desired. There is no record that any further action was taken to punish Robert for his act, but R. K. Hannay believes that this leniency resulted in a riot in Edinburgh against the chamberlain and chancellor.[17] Edinburgh was determined to maintain its privileges come what might, and in so doing, the town authorities soon realized that Robert Barton was one of their chief enemies. It looks as though he was becoming completely out of patience with Edinburgh's outmoded privileges which attempted to keep himself and his neighbors from carrying on their business according to their own wishes. The new commercial opportunities were destroying the antiquated medieval trade restrictions and regulations.

While these conflicts had been going on, Robert had reached an amicable arrangement with the Earl of Rothes concerning the lands of Hall Tacis on behalf of his ward, Alexander Barton. Andrew Barton had obtained these lands along with the manor of Ballinbreich which the king had confiscated from the Earl of Rothes for debt. Although he and his son had received them in

life-rent, the Earl of Rothes, son of the debtor, no doubt
financially solvent owing to his marriage to Margaret Crichton,
the widow of an Edinburgh merchant, now came forward with
an offer to redeem the lands. As Robert was apparently on
friendly terms with the earl, he agreed on condition that the
original purchase price of £1,605 plus another 200 marks was
forthcoming. The countess, therefore, paid the money,
parliament ratified the abrogation of the infeftment to Andrew,
and Robert and Alexander agreed never to attempt to regain
possession of the property. This was a good business arrangement as Andrew or his son had drawn the rents of the lands
since 1510, and the son now sold them for the original price
plus about an 8 per cent profit.[18]

While personal matters naturally occupied a part of his attention Robert still continued to struggle with the government's
economic problems. As the time for the Audit of the Exchequer
came around he no doubt waited anxiously to see if his financial
strategems had brought him a balanced budget. On July 3 the
Lords Auditors including the chancellor, the Archbishop of
Glasgow; Gavin Douglas, Bishop of Dunkeld; Andrew Forman,
Archbishop of St. Andrews; and others were present in the
Tolbooth to receive the accounts submitted by the sheriffs, the
chamberlains of the royal lands, baillies of burghs, baillies of
other properties, and custumars. Each one presented his receipts
and expenditures, and paid to the crown any balance which remained. For instance Robert Moncrief, tutor of John Wood a
ward of the crown, remitted to the comptroller £53 18s. 4d.
for the revenues of the fief of Fethirkern and Abirluthnot. John,
Lord Drummond, chamberlain of Strathearn and maternal
grandfather of the Earl of Angus, reported that after meeting
all expenses he held a balance of £407 11s. 8d. Of this he
turned over £200 to Robert, keeping the remainder as compensation for the time that he was custodian of the king and
governor of Stirling Castle. Robert in his own accounts as

custumar of Edinburgh allowed himself £13 12s. for the purchase of coal for the Castle of Dunbar, and £40 for Mr. John
Chisholm "pro suis laboribus," along with a number of other
payments, all of which were deducted from his total receipts
of £1,655 9s. 3d.[19]

One can, perhaps, picture Robert sitting in the Tolbooth
with the other officials backed by a number of clerks who were
keeping careful tally of the accounts as they came in. The big
question uppermost in the minds of all, but especially in that
of the comptroller, would be: will the accounts balance? Or
will there be another large deficit? This was the first real test of
the effectiveness and value of the new policy of trying to force
payments from the reluctant hands of the officials and of the
feudal nobles. Therefore, on September 3, when the accounts
were finally all cast up, it must have been something of a
disappointment to Robert to find that he had not entirely
solved the financial problem.

Yet while he had not succeeded in placing the government
financially on its feet, he had materially improved its position.
Jardine of Applegarth who had been comptroller from March
1, 1516, to September 26, 1516, had ended his seven months'
tenure of office with a deficit of £1,035 having received a total of
£4,428 along with victuals, hides, and other produce worth
£105. Except for receipts from the sheriffs and the burghs
all the items in Robert's statement for the period, October 12,
1516, to September 3, 1517, showed an increase more than
proportional to the amount collected during his predecessor's
seven month term of office. His customs returns had risen from
£1,545 to £2,056, his rentals from royal lands from £1,982 to
£3,875, and his "extras" including produce from £696 to
£1,650. These figures demonstrate very clearly that he had
succeeded in forcing a good many men, who since 1513 had
been avoiding making proper payments, to meet their responsibilities. The result was that when the financial year ended

he had narrowed the gap between receipts and expenditures, his deficit amounting to only £522 16s. 4d.[20] Perhaps by the next audit he would be able to balance the budget.

One aid to the stabilizing of Robert's accounts had been the departure for France on June 7, 1517, of the regent, whose rather lavish household had cost between £3,000 and £4,000 annually. As early as January, Albany had vainly endeavored to extend the truce with England from November, 1517, to June, 1518, in the hope that once peace was attained he could go back to France which was his true home. The Scots had not been too happy about any suggestion of his departure, but when, in May, they were considering the possibility of inducing France to renew the "auld alliance" formally, Albany saw his opportunity. On May 25, therefore, after considerable persuasion, he finally obtained the council's permission to return to France for a period of four months with the object of ascertaining Francis I's plans. The Scots demanded that the French king should state plainly whether he wished to continue the Franco-Scottish friendship, and also whether he was willing to give James V one of his daughters to wife.[21] With these instructions Albany left early in June.

No sooner had the regent departed, than trouble raised its head. Queen Margaret, who had steadily refused to return as long as he held power, now appeared in Scotland where she and her husband, whom she hated bitterly, were temporarily reconciled. Still this did not give them control of the government, for Albany had left a council of regency made up of the archbishops of St. Andrews and Glasgow, and the earls of Huntly, Argyle, Angus, and Arran, with de la Bastie, his right-hand man, filling the office of his deputy. Not long after he had left, the Homes, in revenge for the duke's execution of Lord Home, ambushed and killed de la Bastie; and as many suspected Angus of being a party to this deed, the council seized his main henchmen and threw them into prison. At the

same time Margaret, once more alienated by Angus' insolence
and unfaithfulness, against her brother Henry's wishes instituted
proceedings at the papal court for a divorce.[22] The outcome of
all these maneuvers meant but one thing: chaos, and in this
chaos the crown's finances suffered sorely, to the distress and
frustration of the comptroller.

Yet even while these troubles were brewing, Robert continued steadily on his course making every effort to collect the
royal revenues. On September 5 he had the Lords of the Council
forfeit the royal lands of the Forest of Corriemuklow and
Glenschira in the lordship of Strathearn which were held in
feu-farm by William Murray, heir of Sir William Murray of
Tullibardine, who had failed to pay his rents.[23] As a good
many of the king's properties had experienced the same treatment at the hands of the nobles in the preceding years, this was
a warning to defaulters that they would now have to pay the
crown the money they had been pocketing. In this connection
another technique which Robert employed for making sure
that the king received everything that was his due was that of
having sub-tenants pay their rents directly into his hands. This
appears in a dispute (Mar. 1, 1518) of David Lindsay of Dunrod
and his wife, Isabel Elphinstone, with the Earl of Eglinton,
steward of the royal lands of Stewarton. Whether some of the
revenues stuck to Eglinton's fingers is not stated, but eventually
Robert issued to him a precept under his signet and signature
"to charge all the tenentis . . . of ye lands and myln contenit in
our letters of assedatioun undir the prive sele, to answer to
us zerly and termly of the malis firmes and dewties therof and
to none utheris."[24]

Three days after this was settled, Robert took action to
obtain other monies owing to the crown. Hay of Ardendracht
had been banished for the murder of Alexander Bannerman, his
goods being declared forfeited. These the crown sold to the
Earl of Huntly for a large sum of which he paid only part. The

earl then took over the escheated property, with the intention of keeping it for himself without making further composition. Robert, however, brought the matter before the Lords who thereupon ordered Huntly to pay the balance immediately, in order that it might be used to defray the expences of Dunbar Castle.[25] The earl agreed and the money was duly remitted to the comptroller.

The great lords were not, however, the only objects of Robert's concern. In July, 1518, he haled the monks of Dryburgh before the council for failing to honor a purchase of grain for the royal household which he had made from the abbey's commendator. Apparently the monks objected to the transaction because the commendator was to receive the money. Following this he went on to sue the authorities of Haddington for permitting the export of wool, hides, and fleeces free of duty, and those of Dysart for allowing the free export of salt. Last of all he took action against the burghs of Nairn and Kintore for failing, since 1510, to pay their burgh mails amounting to £70 and £48, respectively. In all of these cases he was successful in obtaining judgements against the delinquents.[26]

That Robert was not the only one who was pressing the council to make sure the crown received its due is shown by the protest in July of the treasurer, John Campbell of Lundy. He pointed out to that body that there were a good many individuals, even among the Lords themselves, who owed money to the crown for wardships and the like but who would not pay their debts. He had borrowed as much money as he could, and it was now the Lords' responsibility to force the delinquents to meet their obligations.[27] This did not go down very well with some of the council, but it was the only logical course of action to adopt.

Although both the treasurer and the comptroller possessed a certain amount of independent authority which they could employ to force the payment of their debts, there was one who was not only dependent on the royal revenues, but who had no power to collect that which was owing to her, namely the queen mother. While absent from the country she had received nothing from her properties, except a few sums of money which Albany had collected and forwarded to her. As to the rest of her lands, either the tenants had simply omitted to pay or some of the great nobles had appropriated the revenues to their own uses.[28] The manors of the East and West Barns of Dunbar are cases in point. Soon after her return to Scotland, Margaret appeared before the Lords demanding that they take some concrete action to ensure that these two holdings produce adequate revenues. The Lords thereupon asked for time to straighten out the situation. They acknowledged that the Archbishop of St. Andrews and de la Bastie, whom the Homes had recently murdered, had taken over the preceding year's returns, but more than that they could not say. They promised, however, that the archbishop would account for every penny, and in the meantime they informed her that they had given orders to the treasurer and comptroller, for the future to pay all the dues of the Barns of Dunbar, commencing with those of the current Martinmas Term, to her directly.[29] By this means they hoped to meet, at least temporarily, the queen's need.

The Lords' decision, while undoubtedly fair and considerate, was not economically sound. As they were at this moment planning an attack upon the Homes for the murder of de la Bastie, they needed an army to send into the Marches. Armies, however, cost money, so on March 4 they instructed Robert to coin 80 ounces of gold into unicorns, at eight to the ounce. At this the treasurer protested that four days earlier the Lords had ordered him to pay over the equivalent of the mails of Dunbar to the queen which he had done, but only at the cost of emptying the treasury. If they wished to pay for an army, they would have to provide him with the necessary funds.

Whether he received the money or not is not stated; but the army did march south under the Earl of Arran and the Homes submitted.[30] It may have been that wealthy merchants loaned money for the expedition, and of their number no doubt Robert would be one. The importance of this incident is its indicating another responsibility of the comptroller, namely that of coining money, and at the same time it also demonstrates, despite all attempts to increase the royal revenues, the hand-to-mouth financial expedients to which the officers of the crown were reduced.

It was probably because of such monetary difficulties that neither the council nor Margaret took any action to oust Robert from his position, despite the fact that he was an Albany appointee. Gavin Douglas some years later used as an argument to discredit Albany that he had made the "pirate" Robert Barton, comptroller, but it is evident that even when the Douglases were trying to strengthen the finances of the crown for their own use, they were only too glad to leave him in office.[31]

With the audit of his accounts which commenced on August 27, 1518, the second year of Robert's work as comptroller had come to an end. On that date he appeared before the Lords to present along with the government's accounts, his expenses of office. These latter included £23 for "fals plakkis" which he had negligently accepted. Although it was his own fault that he had taken this bad money, the Lords exonerated and reimbursed him for his loss. Apparently they felt that since the accounts were generally so well kept they could not be too hard on him. Another bill which he presented was for £170 10s. covering the wages of five servants who cost £73 6s. and for the hire of six horses at 1s. a day.[32] This was the staff with which Robert was attempting to untangle the kingdom's finances, and his methods are perhaps revealed by the fact that he paid hire for the horses for 321 days. Continual traveling through the country to inspect accounts seems to have been his plan for making sure that the officials paid to the crown all the funds which were its due.

That Robert's tactics bore fruit was abundantly clear when the returns from the whole country were in and the accounts were finally completed. As one glances over the various items in Robert's financial statement, one can gain some idea of the improvement which had been wrought, despite all the political uncertainty, in the short space of twelve months. The returns of the sheriffs had increased from £34 to £75, those of the baillies of burghs from £100 to £149, those of custumars from £2,056 to £2,631, and those of the baillies *ad extra*, from £3,875 to £4,367. Altogether there had been a total increase in revenue from £7,833 to £8,936, while at the same time, owing to the absence of Albany, expenses had been cut so that the year's operations were finally brought to a close with a balance on hand of £1,816 4s. 9d., one of the first surpluses obtained by the government in many a year.[33] The comptroller's policy had brought good results which anyone could appreciate. The only question was, would they continue?

Although such success had been achieved by dint of concentrated effort Robert had by no means ignored his own affairs during his two years in office. About the time of the audit he brought to fruition a plan which he and John Mowbray of Barnbougle had concocted somewhat earlier, before the latter's death. As the Barton property of Over Barnton and the Mowbray properties of Barnbougle and Dunmany were contiguous, it was only natural that these two landowners should have been on friendly terms. This apparently led to an agreement for the alliance of the two families by the marriage of Barbara, only child of John Mowbray, to Robert, the son of Robert Barton by his wife Elizabeth Crawford, on condition that Robert, junior, should take the name Mowbray. Therefore, when Mowbray died, probably in 1517, and the fief came into the hands of the king owing to the fact that Barbara was a minor, Robert saw his plans in danger of frustration. Indeed it would seem from a comment in 1522 by Gavin Douglas that Angus or one of his followers was casting covetous eyes upon the property. To prevent this possibility, Robert now requested the wardship of Barnbougle which he received by grant under the Privy Seal on June 27, 1518, for the sum of £1,333 6s. 8d.[34] This put him in a position to carry out his design of marrying his son into one of the landed families of the district, while at the same time he would make a profit on the money he had invested in the wardship.

Profits also came his way from other directions. For one thing he seems to have been increasing his purely financial activities. On August 25 he had appeared before the Lords to become surety for £120 to Margaret Crichton, Countess of Rothes. She had received the £120 as the redemption price of certain rents which her former husband, the late George Halkerstone, had at one time held in Edinburgh, and which came to her, probably as part of her marriage portion. She had promised the Provost of Crichton who was the tutor of Halkerstone's son and heir and presumably also her son, that she would use the money to purchase other lands to provide her with a life-rent, which on her decease would go to his young charge. If she died before the £120 was invested in rents, Robert was to pay it immediately to the tutor, on the guarantee of the Earl of Rothes that he would be reimbursed for his expenditure.[35]

How Robert came to be involved in this affair is not quite clear, although his interest in it undoubtedly came from the fact that he was a friend of the Earl of Rothes and had been a friend of Halkerstone whom James IV had employed in the purchase of supplies for the navy. There are two possible explanations of the part he was playing at this time. One is that as a friend of the deceased he was acting, perhaps for a price, as the backer of

Margaret's promissory note to the Provost of Crichton. On the other hand, it is also possible that he was fulfilling a somewhat more important function. Margaret may have turned over to him the £120 to invest in real estate, which he had not yet done, and he was simply guaranteeing to the provost that the money would be properly employed. If this latter explanation is correct, it would indicate that Robert was also dabbling in a primitive form of investment jobbing.

This latter interpretation would seem to be borne out by the fact that Robert may have acted on more than one occasion as the agent of the Earl of Rothes and his wife. Some two years later the earl redeemed, as he had previously done in the case of Hall Tacis, certain lands which by virtue of the debts of his father, the late earl, had come into the hands of John Melville of Grantown. The man designated to carry out the payment of the 300 marks involved and to receive delivery of the land on Rothes' behalf was Robert Barton, who again appears as the earl's representative.[36] How much of this type of business Robert was doing it is impossible to say, but this one example does show that he was extending his sphere of business activity, becoming particularly interested in the profits he could derive by acting as a financial middleman.

Most important of all, however, although not reflected in the official records, his interest in trade seems never to have waned. Indeed, if anything he seems to have expanded his business to the point where he was becoming the principal magnate of the Edinburgh area. The evidence for this is contained in a complaint made by the burgh authorities against him to the Lords of the Council. According to this body he had gained monopolies of all wool south of the Forth and all tallow throughout the entire region. As wool was the country's principal export while tallow, used for candles and as a lubricant or preservative, was also extremely valuable, Robert was thus well on his way to becoming extremely wealthy. Coupled with this he was also accused of buying up large quantities of hides, cloth, skins, wine, fish, and victuals most of which he exported. Moreover, as he had these goods illegally "pakked and peeled" in Leith and sent them abroad, without first allowing the Edinburgh authorities to fix their prices, he probably undersold his Edinburgh competitors on the foreign market. To climax these sins, the Edinburgh authorities said, he was guilty of purchasing goods directly from foreign ships anchored in the Firth of Forth without awaiting the prior setting of prices by Edinburgh's treasurer, which meant that he was able to obtain foreign goods more cheaply than his competitors in Scotland.[37]

No doubt those making these charges exaggerated them as much as they dared, but their statements do reveal certain things. One is that Robert was impatient with the medieval restraints which both the church and Edinburgh attempted to impose on his commercial activities. If risks were taken, large profits also could be made, and he was prepared for the one if he could obtain the other. By Edinburgh's testimony, Robert had come so to dominate the export trade of southeast Scotland that its burgh authorities simply could not keep him under control.

Thus by the autumn of 1518 Robert was in a position of power and influence to which few Scottish merchants had ever attained. He had so increased in wealth that even his bitterest rivals were obliged to recognize that he was surpassing them, and at the same time he had successfully balanced the government's accounts—an achievement not known in Scotland for many a year. Even if his enemies did not, he had good reason to be pleased with his accomplishments.

The Struggle to Maintain the Government's Solvency

Robert's unpopularity with the burgesses of Edinburgh, although partially the result of his business success, was no doubt increased by his holding the positions of Comptroller of the Royal Household and Custumar of Edinburgh, particularly as he was still rated only as an "indweller" of Leith. It would be a galling experience for the high and mighty inhabitants of the Cowgate to be obliged to appear before this upstart to have their goods inspected and customed before they could send them abroad. Likewise it must have been extremely humiliating to the Edinburgh city fathers to have to appear in their own Tolbooth, or some other Edinburgh house before the sharp-eyed comptroller from Leith who would take a grim delight in finding discrepancies in their accounts. That there was considerable grumbling about Robert and his ways would seem to have been only natural.

This undercover complaining and whispering seems eventually to have come to Robert's ears. He was not the man to permit it to continue without taking direct action to force the grumblers to come out in the open, state their case, and prove their accusations. Therefore, in the autumn of 1518 he demanded before the Lords of the Council that the Provost and Council of Edinburgh should cease their whispering about him and substantiate the rumors that they were spreading around the country. To this demand they responded on November 16, by appearing in court where they set forth their grievances, thus recording for history the description of his economic activities to which reference was made at the end of the last chapter. To the Edinburgh authorities, however, of even more significance than his actual business dealings was his obvious unwillingness to be bound by Edinburgh's outmoded right to dominate the trade of the area and his continual commission of the three sins regarded as most heinous in the medieval catalogue of economic vices. The city fathers charged him with engrossing (cornering the market), forestalling (buying from the producer before he brought the goods to the open market), and regrating (selling at a higher than the just price)—all of which were officially never, or at least hardly ever, permitted.

The climax of his evil ways, according to the complainants, was his exercise of authority as Custumar of Edinburgh. He was guilty of refusing to custom the goods of merchants exporting in ships other than his own, until his own vessel was fully laden. He was thus attempting to use his office to force exporters to employ him as a carrier, in order to increase his own returns from freight charges. Although Robert strongly denied these accusations, that he was telling the truth is something which one cannot determine seeing that evidence is completely lacking. The only thing one can say is that as long as he kept the accounts there are practically no references to his own exports in the documents. How far this might indicate misuse of his office for his own profit is impossible to ascertain. And, of course, any attempt to force exporters to employ his ships would be entirely a matter of verbal persuasion which no one could ever verify except by the presence of witnesses.

It is perhaps important to notice that one accusation which the Edinburgh authorities did not make against Robert was that he exported his own goods without paying customs duty. Of course, since the "great customs" belonged to the crown they were probably not interested, but in the light of their obvious desire to convict him on any or all counts, one would think that they would have employed this charge if at all possible. It may be, therefore, that the paucity of references in the records to his trading ventures indicated that he was not obtaining exemptions like those granted him during the reign of James IV.

For the council members to make any decision in this case must have been very difficult since they were being asked to condemn a man who was admittedly one of the wealthiest merchants in the country and also one who had just balanced the country's budget. Since it would be dangerous to be too hard on him, it is not surprising that their reaction to the Burgh of Edinburgh's charges was rather mild. They reiterated Robert's right, on the king's behalf, to the prior purchase of imported goods, although at a determined price, but at the same time farbade him to contravene the liberties of Edinburgh. They took no evidence to verify the charges, but simply contented themselves with the declaration that the law must be observed. The Edinburgh burgesses had obviously lost this round to the "indweller" of Leith.[1]

Robert was not quite so successful in his defence in another suit two days later. James Dundas of that Ilk protested to the council that James III had given his grandfather a charter promising him the lands of Dundas and Echlyn in the barony of Dunmany, Linlithgowshire, whenever they should happen to fall into the crown's hands by reason of wardship. As Robert had now obtained the wardship of the lands of the late John Mowbray of Barnbougle whose property included Dunmany, he had been attempting to make the tenants of Dundas and Echlyn pay their rents to him, contrary to Dundas' charter. Although Robert defended his action vigorously, the Lords, accepting the validity of Dundas' claims, ordered him to desist from troubling the tenants.[2] On much the same grounds a little later (March, 1519) he also lost the Mains of Barnbougle to John Mowbray's widow, now the wife of Robert Douglas. Despite his reminding the council that he had paid a high price for the wardship and his assertion that the claimant's charter was invalid, the Lords turned over the lands to her with the proviso that they were not passing judgement on her charter. Apparently this settled the case.[3]

While fighting to retain his hold on Barnbougle, Robert was also continuing to have difficulties in connection with the lands of Malhungy and Ardesty obtained from the Crawford estate, his main problem being that the earls were dying so rapidly that he was unable to have them appear in court in support of his defense against the claims of Malkin Duchir. He seems to have succeeded, however, in June, 1519, for he had no further trouble with her from that time on.[4]

Yet Robert's worries did not end here, for Scotland itself was to give him many headaches. Ever since Albany's departure and the return of Queen Margaret and Angus to power, the country had been suffering from gradually spreading chaos. Like Israel of old, "every man did what was right in his own eyes." One result of this state of affairs was that the queen mother had never regained possession of her revenues which the nobles and others had appropriated for themselves. For instance, she claimed the customs of New Haven on the Firth of Forth, but the Abbot of Holyrood insisted that they were his. This matter was before the Lords in July, 1518. But what was worse, the lands which she held as her marriage portion were still not producing the returns they should, despite the recent Anglo-Scottish truce in which it had been promised on England's insistence that she should receive all her revenues. She therefore made request to the Lords that they place her lands, except those in Stirlingshire or Linlithgowshire, along with those of the king, in the hands of the comptroller and that he pay "of the rediast of the kingis properte" the amounts owing to her. To this the Lords agreed, ordering that the provision be included in the next treaty made with the King of England.

As a result of the queen's protest also, the Earl of Angus agreed to renounce his right as her husband to control the property in question, indicating that he had been one of those responsible for her lack of income. The English Warden of the Marches, Lord Dacre, who had apparently persuaded Angus to make the renunciation, appointed Gavin Dunbar, Archdeacon of St. Andrews; Robert Barton, the comptroller; Sir Thomas Halkerstone, Provost of Creighton; James Wishart of Pettarvie; and Mr. Adam Otterburn, king's advocate, as substitutes for the earl. These men were to receive her revenues, hold courts for her vassals, and generally to administer her property, that she might have sufficient money to live in a manner befitting her station. By this arrangement Robert found himself in a position to keep a close check on the queen's finances, and to reimburse the household accounts for what he paid from the king's lands, according to the earlier instructions of the Lords of the Council.[5]

At this point, Robert was suddenly faced with much larger responsibilities, for western Europe was dividing into two armed camps: England and Spain against France who hoped to obtain the support of Denmark and Scotland. French hopes, however, were destined to disappointment. The Danish monarch had his eyes fixed firmly on the Swedes whom he was attempting to subdue, while the Scottish authorities had all they could do to keep the political volcano under their feet from erupting. Consequently neither country was willing to do anything for France, and when Christian of Denmark sent to Scotland asking for help against the Swedes in 1515, 1517, and 1518, the

Scottish authorities took the same ground as they had with their "auld ally"; they were powerless to do anything owing to the chaotic state of their own country.[6]

It may have been in the light of this state of Scottish affairs that on January 12, 1519, Christian II dispatched Alexander Kinghorn "the lang doctor" to Scotland with the plea that since he had been forced to retire into his own kingdom of Denmark because of the Swedes' rebellion, James should now send immediate help. Christian needed by Easter 2,000 mercenaries with food and pay for four months, after which he would be responsible for their wages and provisions. To help in recruiting this army Kinghorn pointed out that since about 1,000 people in Scotland had been sentenced to banishment for crimes, he would be glad to take any of these who might be interested in volunteering, while at the same time he hoped to persuade magnates such as the earls of Arran, Argyle, Angus, and Huntly, who maintained private armies, to send over some of their men.[7]

The king, Albany who was still in France, and the great nobles all replied to Kinghorn's solicitations by explaining that although they would very much like to help, under the circumstances they could give no assistance.[8] The Lords of the Council, on the other hand, perhaps influenced by Robert, took a different view of the situation, for Christian's suggestion that banished criminals might be used was to them an excellent idea. They therefore decreed that all men under sentence of banishment, except those involved in the murder of de la Bastie, would receive remission of their sentences if they would appear before Kinghorn or Robert Barton and agree to go to the help of the Danish king. The two representatives were then to inform the Lords of what was needed in the way of equipment by the "volunteers," which if lawful they would grant. To make doubly certain that the rules would be carried out, the Lords ordered that they be inscribed in an act, and letters containing them be issued under the Privy Seal. Probably feeling that he had fulfilled his mission, Kinghorn now sailed for France with some Scottish representatives to try to persuade Albany to return. The forces for Denmark, however, did not leave as soon as he expected, for Angus and his followers, in league with some of the inhabitants of the Western Isles, were causing trouble, so that the authorities could not implement their decision until May 3. On that date the Lords of the Council reiterated their plan to allow banished men to leave the country, this time appointing Mr. John Campbell of Thornton, the treasurer, to take Kinghorn's place as one of the two certifying agents. Campbell and Robert were to issue certificates of remission to the volunteers, Robert being responsible to keep copies of the "signatouris" until he was certain that each man had arrived in Denmark.[9] The Lords, while anxious to help Denmark, also wished to be certain that these undesirable characters were well out of the country.

With Kinghorn away in France, the responsibility for the Danish operations fell principally on Robert's shoulders. To transport the forces, he had apparently agreed to sell the Danes his ship the *Lion*, which he now fitted out at the cost of £1,894 16s., provided, presumably in the first instance, from his own pocket. On May 28 the expedition made up of the *Lion* and a number of other ships sailed with James Stuart of Ardgowen, Albany's representative, in charge.[10] A few days later Robert dispatched another ship, smaller than the *Lion* loaded with merchandise, iron-tipped lances, halberds, and hand bombards, as well as the remainder of the volunteers. He requested Christian to see that the Danish navy did not molest this ship, and that he return it along with its trade goods as soon as possible.[11]

Robert had good reason for fearing the loss of his ship, for while the Scots were readying their expedition to aid Christian, the Swedes had captured a Leith vessel off Stralsund, and although the Danes recaptured it they did not restore it to its owners. The Scottish government entered a strong protest and demanded that the owners be compensated, but the ultimate fate of this ship and its cargo is unknown.[12] Robert now received similar cavalier treatment for by September 22 he was complaining that he had not been paid for his goods and services. He wrote Christian pointing out that there was still a balance owing to him for the *Lion* as well as for the other ship which one of Christian's captains had taken over. While he added that of course such matters were superseded by Christians' present needs, obviously he was rather anxious to be reimbursed for the material which he had supplied to the Danish army.[13] It must also have been a very sore point that this expedition had upset his nicely balanced household accounts, so that once again he would have to battle with a deficit. Whatever his feelings, however, he had worked hard and had been of no little help to the Danish King.

Meanwhile the factional strife at home was continuing. By October the nobility had divided into two camps. The queen and Angus, enjoying a temporary, tenuous reconciliation, supported by the Archbishop of St. Andrews, the bishops of Dunkeld, Orkney, Dunblane, Aberdeen, and Moray, the earls of Huntly, Argyle, Morton, Glencairn, Errol, Crawford, and Marischal, and the lords Ruthven, Glamis, Hay, and Gray were holding Edinburgh and Stirling. Albany's faction, made up of the Archbishop of Glasgow, the bishops of Argyle and Galloway, the earls of Arran, Cassillis, and Lennox, and lords Fleming, Maxwell, Ross, and Sempill, held Glasgow. Ready to fly at each other's throats over the question of who should rule the country, they permitted no peace to any man. Even the lieutenant-general, Arran, could not obtain admission to Edinburgh to exercise his office, nor could the regents make their authority effective.[14]

Under these circumstances, Queen Margaret still found it

somewhat difficult to obtain payment of rents and mails owing to her. On July 4 she complained to Lord Dacre about the hardships she had endured since coming to Scotland. Even though Albany was now out of the country the situation had not improved, for the nobles had taken her lands into their own hands, refusing to let her have the revenues which were her due. Moreover, because of her needs, she found herself obliged to do exactly what these men required, which was humiliating and contrary to English interests. Indeed had it not been for Robert Barton, the comptroller, who had helped her out, she would not even have been able to pay her household expenses, and, she added, "I am sobar as can be."

By the end of the month Margaret's position had become so difficult that in opposition to Henry VIII and Angus she had swung over to Albany's side in order to prevent the country from falling into total anarchy, and to obtain some money for herself, for she had no more than £500 which Robert had given her as a loan. Fifteen months later she reported to Dacre that she had pawned all her jewels and dismissed all her servants, for she had obtained no more than £500 from her lands and had it not been for Robert's loan out of his own pocket, she would have been destitute.[15] To the queen mother at least, Robert was the very keystone of the country's finance being both able and willing to supply her with funds in her need.

Although proof is lacking it is possible that it was because of these loans to Margaret, that when a little later (February, 1520) David, Lord Drummond was served heir to his grandfather, he was turned over as a ward of the crown to Robert for safekeeping. He may have been a type of collateral by which the queen mother guaranteed the eventual repayment of her debt. Whether or not it was ever repaid is impossible to say for it may have been combined later with other obligations of the crown to Robert. One thing is certain, however, the Douglases did not approve, for the late Lord Drummond was Angus' maternal grandfather and had been an opponent of Albany. Now the property was in the hands of an Albany supporter.[16]

As a result of continual complaining Margaret finally persuaded the Lords of the Council on October 27, 1519, to do something to provide for her necessities. She pointed out to them that although she had the right to £2,000 sterling annually, a sum which they had guaranteed to her in a "band" with her brother, she had received practically nothing. Whether it was her reference to their agreement with Henry VIII or her destitute condition which stimulated them to action is not clear, but at any rate the Lords now decreed that Robert, as comptroller, was to advance her the money she needed for her expenses, until December 25. This money was then to be refunded, presumably because in the meantime her rents would have come in. It was probably at this time that the Archbishop of Glasgow, who was also Chamberlain of Fife, paid to the queen mother on Robert's instructions £200 from the returns of Largo. That she received more than this is not indicated, but there is little doubt that she would need everything she could obtain.[17]

Queen Margaret's situation was symptomatic of the upset condition of the country. King Chaos was practically absolute in his rule. Many of the nobles were fighting among themselves and those few Scots who desired to live peacefully, carrying on their business according to their opportunities, found life difficult. At length the conflicts came to a head when, in April, 1520, the Hamiltons and the Douglases fought out their differences along Edinburgh's High Street, in what was known as "Cleanse the Causeway." The Douglases were victorious, which meant that Margaret now had to keep on the right side of her husband, despite her desire for Albany's return.[18]

That the queen mother was not alone in her attitude to Albany soon became apparent when the council sent word to

France that unless the duke returned immediately they would make peace with Henry. This had little effect. Francis I soon met the English king at the Field of the Cloth of Gold where he promised that Albany would not go back, a decision which he then communicated to the Scots. Yet while France had sold them out to the English, they did not give up hope that the governor would reassume his duties.[19] It may have been to help him acquiesce to their importunities that in August of 1520 Robert dispatched the *Black Barque*, owned jointly by himself and his nephew Alexander (who incidentally, was now a burgess of Edinburgh), to France, with some 500 marks which the regents were apparently sending to the duke as a pledge of their loyalty. Unfortunately the vessel while sailing south along the east coast of England anchored off Yarmouth where she was attacked by a Spanish captain, who forced the crew ashore and departed with the *Barque* and its cargo as a prize. Although complaints were made repeatedly to the Spanish authorities, nothing came of them, and thus what may have been an attempt to bribe Albany failed miserably.

Robert's only compensation for his losses was an allowance for 500 marks in his accounts at the Audit of the Exchequer in 1522.[20] The reason for the two years' delay in reimbursement was that although the Lords may have attempted to hold exchequer audits between 1518 and 1522 apparently they were unable to do so. Administrative disintegration had reached such a point that it was impossible to force the individuals responsible to appear with their accounts. Therefore, although Robert continued with his assistants to keep the rolls of the royal household, he had no opportunity of really casting up his accounts, for he was unable to obtain payment of all the money owing to the king.

His hopes of maintaining the royal finances, however, never seem to have died, for while carrying on his frustrating duties as comptroller, he was also active in the renting of crown lands. On February 1, 1519, he was dealing with the leases in Cuttiswra; on March 28, 1520, with those of Mylnebank, Galloway; on August 6, with those of Stewarton; and a few months later with those of Blacklaw, Fife, and Strathearn.[21] He was endeavouring to obtain what he could from every available source.

That such diligence was necessary is underlined by the continuing financial difficulties of the queen. Because of her support of the movement for Albany's return she had found herself in greater straits than ever before. In reprisal Angus seized the lands which she had received as a marriage settlement from James IV, depriving her of any revenues they might produce. To add to her troubles Robert, who had loaned her some £600, had now come to the conclusion that this was his limit. Consequently he flatly refused any further advances of funds and the queen mother, to put it plainly was "broke."[22] She was not the only one, however, who was having trouble obtaining money, for Robert himself was finding that the fulfillment of his responsibilities as comptroller was becoming increasingly difficult as appears from certain indications in his accounts for 1518-1520. During this two-year period the records show that only one sheriff, the sheriff of Ayr, remitted his dues which amounted to £65 13s. 4d. Likewise few burghs paid what they owed, the names of only seven appearing in the accounts, and they all of small towns situated around Edinburgh or Glasgow. Since none of the big cities such as Edinburgh or Aberdeen met their obligations, apparently Robert was able to persuade only those which were small and not far distant to make payment. With the collection of customs he was somewhat more successful, obtaining returns from twelve different officials located all over the country from the southeast to the northwest. It is noticeable again, however, that the custumars in the big cities are missing from these accounts.[23] Owing to the lack of a strong central government, it was difficult to force those responsible for the collection and transmission of royal revenues to fulfill their duties.

While the condition of the country, as revealed by the accounts, was becoming worse and worse, the international situation had been changing. Francis, having now turned away from his friendship with England, decided that it would be to his interest to send Albany back to Scotland. On November 21, 1521, the duke arrived in Stirling to take over the reins of government.[24] For many in Scotland this was a great day. It meant that some sort of stable government might be restored, for with Albany in control the traitorous Angus and his master, the English king, would find a restraint placed upon their scheming.

Albany's return meant, above everything else, Angus' downfall. Charged with treason he was obliged to leave the country, eventually arriving in France where he was imprisoned. The queen, on the other hand, at least outwardly turned completely over to Albany's side, welcoming him gladly; in fact rumor had it that her welcome went a little too far. Whether this was true or not, it is impossible to say, but there is little doubt that most people hoped stability would once more characterise the Scottish administration. To this end the duke immediately set out to win over any whose loyalty might be uncertain. It was probably with this in mind that he ordered Robert, as comptroller, to pay the queen £6,408 1s. 4d. in compensation for the rent of her lands which she had not received for the past three years.[25] How that would affect the household accounts it is hard to say, but there is little doubt that it would make their balancing a somewhat difficult matter.

At the same time that the duke was trying to gain support in Scotland, he was also doing his utmost to persuade foreign powers to help him against English intrigue. Still all his hopes came to nought, for nobody was ready to do anything. Francis was more interested in his own ventures in Italy, while Christian of Denmark had all the trouble he wanted right at home, having alienated the Swedes, the church, the nobility, and the Hanseatic League. Indeed, he seems to have made even Robert a somewhat uncertain friend for very soon after Albany returned to Scotland, Robert approached the governor with a request that something be done to reimburse him for the *Lion* in which he had sent troops to Denmark some years earlier. The duke on April 1, 1522, wrote Christian, reminding him of his obligation to Robert and pointing out that it would be good policy, if nothing else, to pay what remained of the debt. Nothing came of this request.[26] Christian was not the type who worried about such minor matters, and even if he did, he could have accomplished little, for it was not long before he, himself, was in exile.

The only person who seems to have been ready to attempt anything at this time was Henry of England. During the same month in which Albany wrote Christian, he sent seven ships to raid the Scottish coast, where they attacked Tantallon Castle but were driven off. They then turned their attention to the mouth of the Forth shooting at Leith and some other towns, but again without very much effect. Apparently there were but two ships in the roadstead at the time, one belonging to Falconer and the other to Robert, neither of which the invaders were willing to attack.[27] Finally they sailed off home having accomplished nothing.

In the meantime with a modicum of peace restored to the country plans were laid for the Audit of the Exchequer, the first in four years. By May 31, 1522, all the returns were in, and some evaluation of the country's economic condition was possible, but the result did not rejoice the heart of the comptroller. It is true that the past two years had seen a vast improvement in the collection of the royal income. Five more sheriffs had made payment of a total of £108 9s. 8d., while at the same

time nine more burghs appear on the list of those paying
£323 3s. 4d. for burgh mails. But what is probably even more
important than the mere number is that Aberdeen, Inverness,
Dundee, and Edinburgh were now meeting their obligations.
Similarly the custumars had reported for most of the larger
centers including Aberdeen and Edinburgh which paid £760 and
£7,094 respectively, to the royal coffers. During the period
1518-1522 customs brought in some £9,387 19s. 6½d.,
which when added to the other revenues including £12,000
from the rental of royal lands gave a total of £28,931 10s. 11½d.
and considerable amounts of produce. As far as receipts were
concerned, Robert's work, coupled with improving political
conditions, had done much to restore the government's
financial stability.

The only difficulty was that while revenues had risen, costs
had climbed even more sharply. Yet this was not owing to
increased expenditures for the royal household, for they had
remained steady at an average of about £1,700 a year. During
the four years dealt with in the audit of 1522 they had totalled
only £6,978 11s. 6½d., leaving a balance on hand of
£21,953 6s. 8d. besides produce. There were unfortunately
other expenditures which were beyond the comptroller's
authority. Pensions, gifts, and allowances as usual took their
toll, but besides these he also had to make payment for various
unusual and large items. For one thing, the expedition of
exiled Scots to help the Danes cost over £1,900, and for
another, the governor gave Archibald Douglas of Kilspindie
some £95 from the customs returns. But even more important
there was the deficiency in Queen Margaret's revenues requiring a payment of £6,408 1s. 4d. which took a large
slice out of the surplus; and on top of that, the expenses of the
governor's household from December 21, 1521, to May
31, 1522, came to £4,033 2s. These amounts totaling
£12,502 1s. 3d. would leave only some £9,450 along with

produce to be divided among all the smaller demands upon the revenues over a period of four years. Thus it was not surprising that when the Lords Auditors of the Exchequer completed their work, Robert had to record a final deficit of £3,176 10s. 4½d. The surprising thing is that under the circumstances his shortage was not greater.[28]

One interesting sidelight on Robert's relation to the deficit is that Gavin Douglas, Bishop of Dunkeld, when in London early in 1522 wrote to Wolsey in a letter of bitter complaint against Albany that the comptroller and treasurer kept the king in rags despite the fact that he was reportedly in their debt to the amount of £12,000. It may have been, of course, that the rumor of the amount of the debt was wrong. On the other hand that may have been the sum which they had jointly advanced to the government until the accounts were closed in June. As for his keeping the king without proper clothing, one must always remember that Robert was by no means the only one responsible for the king, and that Gavin Douglas was hardly an unbiased witness. His violent attack on Robert does show, however, that the latter was regarded as one of the principal supports of Albany's regime.[29]

IX

Growing Power and Influence

The primary purpose of Albany's return to Scotland in 1521 had
been to persuade the Scots to attack England. Once back,
however, he did little in this direction since for the moment the
better policy seemed to be the pursuit of peace. Henry VIII,
on the other hand, had decided that it would serve him best if
Scotland were to experience the ravages of his armies. Therefore, raids and attacks were mounted along the borders to
persuade the Scots not to support the French. The only result
of these actions was that the Scottish parliament convened on
July 18, 1522, and declared war on England. Yet, despite their
apparent determination to fight, the Scots merely made a token
demonstration. Having learned their lesson at Flodden, they
were content to limit themselves to defensive action. The
principal sufferers in the clash seem to have been Scottish
merchants trading to the Netherlands, who now fell under the
emperor's ban since their country was at war with his English
ally.[1] Happily, this state of affairs did not continue for long. As
Henry was now contemplating a further attack upon France, he
suddenly changed his plan and agreed to a truce. This led to
long-drawn negotiations, continually opposed by the French
king who wanted the Scots to invade England.[2]

Albany meanwhile had found that if he were to achieve

anything as ruler of Scotland, he would first have to concentrate on achieving peace and stability within the country. To do this was no easy task. The greatest of the Scots' problems was the success of the English king and his Warden of the Marches, Lord Dacre, in winning by means of bribes the support of a considerable number of Scottish nobles. The queen mother, in her usual fickle fashion, having now deserted the governor once again gave her support to the English interests. This all meant that Albany had to perform an almost impossible task. Since he could depend upon few people, at least few who held positions of power, his work of governing the country was effectively nullified at every turn. It was probably because of this, and also because he was receiving little support from Francis I, that he now decided to return home. The Scottish nobles at first objected, but finally, having persuaded them to give consent, he set sail for France in the latter part of October.

Lindsay of Pitscottie declares that at this time the young king was recognized as ruling the realm and all the officers of the government, including the treasurer and the comptroller were replaced.[3] This does not seem to be the case, however, for the records show that Albany set up a council of regency consisting of the Archbishop of Glasgow, the earls of Huntly, Arran, and Argyle, and a French knight Gonzolles, and it was only after they had sworn that they would do nothing against his authority that he left.[4]

Furthermore, Lindsay is not correct in his statement about the change of officers, for Robert, as comptroller, was summoned to court on December 15 by a certain John Shaw, baker, probably on the charge that he had not paid some bill. He protested that no sentence should be passed against him until he was given another chance to appear; and for the time being the case seems to have been dropped.[5] It is quite clear from this that he was still in office.

Much more important to Robert than Shaw's suit was the

growth during the autumn of 1522 of the quarrel between Edinburgh and Leith. It is probable that, encouraged by the upset state of the country, law enforcement being practically nonexistent, the Leith men were taking advantage of the opportunity to ignore Edinburgh's rights. The seizure of lumber by Robert and his friends in 1517 had established such a dangerous precedent in this regard that in 1519 the city fathers re-enacted the earlier regulation that no one could buy goods coming into Leith until the importer had entered them in the town books and the town treasurer had fixed the prices. Only then could even the comptroller and treasurer have first choice for the king's use. Furthermore, they decreed that nobody in Leith might salt, pack, or export fish except the comptroller acting for the king. To enforce these regulations the authorities insisted that the water-baillies hold their court on the foreshore of Leith and that they should take action against any who contravened the burgh's privileges. Likewise the monopolists of Edinburgh insisted that the selling of malt, beer, and wine in Leith taverns was illegal.[6] The Edinburgh burgesses were determined to maintain their control of the port town.

It must have caused much heart burning, therefore, when the Edinburgh authorities realized that the indwellers of Leith, led by the comptroller, were openly ignoring their statutes. During the short conflict with England in the summer of 1522 Robert "and his nychtbouris of Leith had coft [purchased] XX schippis prisis." Moreover, they had gone so far as to buy goods imported into the country, without first having them priced by the city authorities. Then, to cap the whole thing, Robert in direct contravention of the rights of Edinburgh had been buying up large quantities of fish which he salted, packed in his own cellar in Leith, and shipped abroad.[7] In fine, the inhabitants of Leith had been playing fast and loose with Edinburgh's sovereign rights.

The outcome of these misdemeanors was that the Edinburgh

authorities decided they must bestir themselves to keep Leith from declaring its independence. Therefore Patrick Barron, a baillie of Edinburgh, was instructed to sue Robert Barton and his neighbors before the Lords of the Council. The exact date of the case's commencement is not recorded but on January 17, 1523, James Logan, one of Robert's Leith henchmen, appeared protesting that the Lords should not proceed against Robert nor should they compel him to answer for he had not been able to obtain an advocate as the Lords required. One cannot but feel that this excuse was simply a means of delaying judgement, since on January 19, Robert appeared in person with the same plea for postponement. Even the Lords apparently became suspicious, however, for two days later they themselves appointed Robert Lesley to act on the defendant's behalf. At the same time that this maneuvering was going on, John Logan, son of the Laird of Restalrig, appeared and insisted that the Lords should do nothing which would be to the prejudice of his heritage or to the privileges of the Town of Leith.[8] It looks as though the Laird of Restalrig was perhaps a little sorry that his ancestors had been so free with their grants to Edinburgh. His reference to the privileges of Leith also seems to be rather strange, for Edinburgh had done its utmost to destroy any privileges which the port might possess. That Robert and his friends, however, felt that they had some rights worth defending soon became clear.

On January 24 the trial really began. Robert appeared before the Lords of the Council with a "respite" dated October 22, 1522, exempting him from all lawsuits for nineteen years. Albany had granted this just a day or so before sailing, probably to keep him from being continually troubled with minor suits. Magnanimously, however, Robert said that he would not invoke the grant as a means of escaping trial, but he did wish it to be recorded that on this occasion he had waived his rights with the proviso that his action would not become a precedent.

Adam Otterburn, procurator for Edinburgh, then asked instruments that Robert had admitted buying fish from the Bishop of
Aberdeen, preparing them for export, and purchasing goods
from foreign ships. When these were added to an earlier
admission that he and his friends had bought twenty prizes, the
case seemed settled. At this point in the argument Patrick
Barron intervened with a charter under the Great Seal granting
power to the Edinburgh authorities to sue the breakers of their
freedoms, to obtain escheat of their goods, and if necessary to
summon the king's forces to insure the enforcement of the law.
One-half of the offenders' goods were to go to the king and
one-half to the building of the church and to the "common
wele" of the town. He stated that he had explained this to
Robert and twenty-three others from Leith who were present
in the court.[9]

To this series of accusations James Logan presented the
reply of Robert and his confreres, craving the court to record
that he was ready to prove that the people of Leith were in the
habit of buying prizes coming into their harbor. The Laird of
Restalrig also protested that nothing should be done to limit the
freedom of the Leith inhabitants.

In the face of these conflicting claims, the Lords no doubt
found it difficult to make a clear decision. On one side were the
wealthy burgesses of Edinburgh, while on the other were the
men of Leith led by one as wealthy as any Edinburgh merchant,
and who besides was a royal official upon whose continuance in
office depended to a large extent the government's financial
operations. The final sentence, therefore, was carefully and
cautiously worded. The Lords forbade the inhabitants of Leith
to deal with foreign merchants until their wares had been
recorded and priced in the town's books. As for buying prizes,
that they said, was a matter for the Admiral's Court. Although
this judgement did not free Robert, David Falconer, Edward
Cockburn, John Kerr, and the other Leith inhabitants from the

Edinburgh monopoly, it seems to have tacitly admitted that they could deal directly with foreign merchants once the town treasurer had made a record of the imported goods. At the same time it must be noted that, in spite of Partick Barron's rather threatening exposition of the penalties that Edinburgh could exact from the breakers of her privileges, he made no attempt to enforce them, nor did the Lords order the inhabitants of Leith to reimburse Edinburgh for their illegal acts. They seemed to feel that such a drastic sentence would be unwise.

In the matter of prizes, if the Lords were unwilling to make a decision, the men of Leith had no such scruples. No sooner had the Lords given judgement than Sir Robert Logan of Restalrig appeared to protest that the inhabitants of Leith had always been in the habit of buying prizes. Since the king, however, was still only a child, he would not press his claims, but when the time was ripe he would reopen the whole matter before the court. Three days later, Robert himself appeared and declared that notwithstanding the decree given against him and the others of Leith he was prepared to prove that they were "in continuale use of bying prisis."

As a result of these declarations the Lords seem to have decided that they had better settle the matter once and for all. Consequently, they continued the case to the first Friday of February. A day or so before this date Patrick Barron, apparently suspicious that the Lords would again avoid the issue, declared that even if the Lords did not deal with the question of prizes as promised, Edinburgh should have letters of execution against the right of the inhabitants of Leith to purchase these ships.[10] For the time being nothing more was heard of the matter, for since hostilities had ceased no prizes were available for purchase.

The Edinburgh authorities, however, do not seem to have felt that this settled the controversy, for they were continually on the lookout for possible contraventions of the law by the comptroller. This is evidenced by the charge they made against him on February 4 declaring that he was dealing illegally with strangers. Robert replied by denying the accusation and pointing out that the goods in which he dealt, he had brought into the kingdom "on his own adventure." It was, therefore, none of Edinburgh's business what he did with them. This reply seems to have settled the case.[11]

About this time Robert's interest in trade took a new turn, for once again the question of the establishment of a compulsory staple came to the fore. The years since 1512 had been so taken up with war and conflict that Scottish merchants who had ventured abroad had been allowed by the government to go wherever they pleased, which seems to have been to Veere rather than Middelburg. That Henry Van Borselen, Lord of Veere, held the position of Conservator of Scottish privileges was no doubt of considerable help in attracting the Scots to the latter town.[12]

Once peace had settled on the North Sea, however, Middelburg again bethought herself of the possibility of attracting Scottish trade, to which end an envoy was dispatched in 1515 with letters to various officials, and to the Duke of Albany to whom they promised a yearly gift of £50 (Flemish). Although they received no immediate response to their advances, they soon enlisted the help of David Falconer who had lost his ship the *Bona Fortuna* to the Duke of Gueldres through the perfidy of the authorities at Veere.[13] It may have been on his advice, therefore, that they wrote sometime between June 21, 1516, and June 18, 1517, to an unnamed merchant in Edinburgh. They told him that Falconer had reported that both he and all the merchants of Scotland favored Middelburg as the site for the staple and asked him to do everything he could to favor their cause.[14] From later developments one may deduce that the recipient of this letter was Robert Barton.

Added to these moves, even while Albany was in France, the city kept sending envoys to discuss the matter with him and eventually made an offer of 11,000 guilders for the privilege. In return for this sum the Scots were to frequent the Middelburg market exclusively, where they were to receive special consideration and privileges. On these terms the agreement eventually was signed with the proviso that Middelburg would pay the money promised two weeks after the arrival of the first Scottish ship.[15]

Although a good many Scottish merchants no doubt did not favor any such move, by February 27 the Scottish Estates had ratified the agreement with Middelburg, had proclaimed it, and prepared to send over two or three ships as a token that it was now in operation. At the same time they wrote to Middelburg asking that protection be given to the Scots' ships since Veere and the other ports which they had passed over in Middelburg's favor might try to cause trouble.[16] It was not Middelburg's discontented rivals, however, who were to cause trouble, but the authorities of the city itself.

Once the government had given its approval, the Scottish authorities informed Robert Barton, as one of the chief merchants, that the staple was now in existence and asked him to dispatch a ship to make the contract effective. Robert, in partnership with Edward Cockburn of Leith and William Anderson a burgess of Edinburgh, agreed and in February, 1523, sent the *Thomas*. But when the ship arrived in Middelburg, an Englishman by the name of John Kadde instituted proceedings against its owners on the grounds that it was his vessel. Anderson who had sailed in the *Thomas*, was arrested, the cargo was appropriated by the Duke of Gueldres, and the sailors were imprisoned for some twenty-one weeks. Naturally this highhanded procedure roused the ire of the Scots, who flatly refused to send over any more ships. Another reason for Scottish discontent was that Middelburg did not pay the 11,000 guilders within the specified time of two weeks after the arrival of the first ship.[17] The consequence was that the whole arrangement fell to the ground. It is possible that the Middel-burg authorities' knowledge of Robert's earlier dubious activities persuaded them that perhaps the Englishman's claim against the *Thomas* was correct. But why they failed to pay the agreed sum to the Scottish government is incomprehensible.

Robert and his partners appealed to the council for help, but apart from its sympathy and an order to arrest all Zeeland ships in Scottish ports nothing came of their action. Seven years later the aggrieved shipowners had still received no compensa-tion. Middelburg's action had nullified the treaty as soon as it had come into effect.[18]

It was at this point that Robert had to turn his attention from the Dutch to dangers closer to home. Henry VIII and Charles V of Spain were planning another attack on France and her Scottish ally. In March, 1523, the Venetian ambassador reported that Henry had sent twenty ships against the Scots while at the same time he had dispatched land forces to harry the borders.[19] Without adequate leadership the Scots found they could do little either to keep peace within their own boundaries or to defend themselves against attack from without.

It was for this reason that the council finally had to make up its mind to send to France for Albany. On Thursday, June 18, the harassed regents gathered in Edinburgh to plot their course; and as speed was of the essence, they ordered six ships under the command of Robert Barton and David Falconer to stand by that they might carry a report to the duke. There then ensued a lengthy discussion which eventually achieved agreement. Since the English were threatening another invasion, the Scots' only hope was to bring Albany back to lead the kingdom's forces. Therefore, on June 23, the regents issued the following instructions:

> The lordis ordanis that lettres be written chargeing Robert Bertoun of Ovirberntoun, comptroller to our soverane lord, that he within xxiii houris nixt eftir he be chargit tharto, prepar

and mak his litill gallioun redy to pas in France with writings
concerning the common weil of this realm undir the pane of
tinsale of all his movable gudis, and that the marinaris that
war ordanit of befor to pas in the said schip mak them redy to
pas in the samyn to the effect forsaid undir the pane of deid.[20]

They wanted rapid and effective action. Robert was noted not
only for his celerity of movement, but also for his friendship
with the duke. Therefore, he was the ideal emissary.

At this point a difficulty arises. Despite the fact that Robert
received orders to leave for France, the only reference we have
to the voyage refers to a John Barton. For this we may choose
between two explanations. It is possible that those reporting
the presence of John, who were Italians, heard the name
"Hob à Barton," Robert's nickname, and mistook it for "Jok à
Barton." On the other hand, it may have been that in the face of
English threats of invasion Robert sent his son John, who might
have been about twenty-three years of age, as his deputy. There
are one or two references in the records to a John Barton about
this time, and this may be the man. In the light of the Lords'
strict orders, and the fact that John Barton would be rather
young for such a venture, it would seem, however, that Robert
was probably the Barton in question.

All that we know about the ensuing voyage comes from a
report of August 13, sent by Lord Fitzwilliam, commander of
the blockading English fleet, to Cardinal Wolsey, and although
it leaves out much desirable detail, it is possible to gain from
it some idea of what happened. It looks as though Robert or
John, very soon after he received his orders, set out for Dieppe.
With him went a number of other Scottish vessels to convoy the
returning governor. The French king and Albany himself,
however, do not seem to have agreed with the Scottish plan,
as it would have resulted in an overt act of hostility against
England. The Scottish commander, perhaps because of his inability to persuade Albany to sail with him, may thereupon have

decided to return home, or he may have felt that he should move his squadron to Boulogne. But whatever the reason he sailed out of Dieppe, losing two of his ships on the way. He then put into Boulogne where he lost another two vessels at the entrance to the harbour, leaving him with a total of seven.

Fitzwilliam does not explain how the Scots lost the four ships, nor why they sailed into Boulogne. He simply reports that he arrested off Boulogne a Piedmonstese hoy whose crew told him that John [sic] Barton had taken them prisoner and had maltreated and robbed them in order to make them explain the presence of the English fleet. When they had pleaded ignorance he had marched them blindfolded to prison where he had kept them for some time. His comment on the English fleet had been: "A foul evil take them. I have lost two ships coming into this haven whereof my part was 2,000 crowns; but it forceth not, for the King of Scots will be King of England shortly."[21]

From this report it would look as though the Scots had not come to blows with the English, but perhaps because of extremely rough weather had felt that it would be better to seek shelter in Boulogne, rather than risk a battle. This conclusion is borne out by Fitzwilliams' explanation that he was prevented from going in to destroy the Scottish squadron by the strong wind which forced him to leave lest his ships be wrecked. He declared, however, that he would place a guard off the port in order to prevent the Scots from escaping, so the governor would have to obtain other vessels if he were to sail safely to Scotland.[22]

Although it was important that the fleet could not bring Albany home, the commander's comment to the Piedmontese is of even greater significance, for if he were Robert Barton it gives an insight into his economic position at the time. That he had 2,000 crowns invested in two ships indicates that, despite the lack of reference to his activities in official records, he may still have been heavily involved in Scottish shipping and commerce. Occupied with affairs of state, apparently he was increasingly becoming an investor rather than a participant in Scottish trade. He was depending upon the employment of his funds rather than the sale of goods to increase his fortune.

By what date he was back home is not known, but whenever he arrived he must have become involved immediately in preparations to repel the English incursions. On August 3, the Lords of the Council appointed a committee consisting of the Abbot of Culross, the Dean of Glasgow, the Archdeacon of Caithness, the comptroller, Mr. Adam Otterburn, and Mr. Francis Bothwell to "convene incontinent," to devise means for transporting munitions for the army of defense. Despite all efforts of the committee and the Lords to raise an army with which to repel English attacks, however, the Scots accomplished little, for their enemies raided and burnt the border towns and villages at will.

Robert did not have much time to help in the collection of supplies, for on September 23 the Duke of Albany with ample French forces and money arrived in Scotland. This change of the wind caused many of those who had been veering over to the side of the English faction to tack hastily back to the pro-French party. The trend thus begun was further strengthened by the continued English raids which brought no advantage to their perpetrators and only grief to their victims. The regent's first move after his arrival was to mobilize an army to repel the English attacks, the comptroller being given the responsibility of organizing the transport of the troops. On October 5 the stewards and baillies of various crown lands were ordered to provide Robert with the necessary carriage horses along with harness and fodder for thirty days. The officials themselves were also to come to perform their feudal services at the head of the king's tenants. The order, however, was generally disregarded, so on October 22 another was issued, to be carried to the various officials involved by heralds, macers, and pursuivants who were to proclaim that they must come on pain of life, land, and goods.

After this the army gradually gathered, but it was late in the season. English gold had corrupted the venal nobility, and the common people were jealous of the regent's French auxiliaries. All this, coupled with the fact that the Earl of Surrey had an army somewhat larger than that of the Scots, prevented any decisive action. His army having refused to cross into England, Albany in disgust returned to Edinburgh, disbanded his forces, and on the insistence of parliament which had now turned against him, sent the French troops back home. Altogether, the whole affair had been a dismal fiasco.[23]

Although the expedition had very largely occupied his attention during the latter part of 1523, Robert had also continued his work as comptroller, traveling up and down the country inspecting royal lands, keeping an eye on fairs, and checking the accounts of various officials, with the result that in the comparative peace of the early months of 1524 and in preparation for the Audit of the Exchequer, he was able to take action against a number of defaulters.[24] For instance he sued the Earl of Athol for failing, in flagrant disobedience to the council's orders to pay the crown the rents and dues of the wardship of the Earl of Buchan. A little later he took action against Patrick Tyvy who had obtained the office of Custumar of Perth by Privy Seal in contravention of the comptroller's rights of appointment. Then on March 18 he returned to the attack against the inhabitants of Dysart for exporting salt without permission and without paying customs. Finally he brought suit against John Creighton of Ivernyte for having misappropriated the rents of the royal lands of Kinclevin.[25]

Although he won in nearly all these actions, Robert was not able to meet the Government's financial needs, for the results of the audit held during March and April, 1524, were very disappointing. He did not succeed in making the officials pay what they owed to the crown, for only eight sheriffs appeared for audit and they were all from the Lowlands. Their total contribution was a paltry £87 7s. 3d. Although the baillies of burghs did better, fifteen of them paying a total of £208 18s. 8d., many communities made no return. He was more successful, however, in forcing custumars and baillies *ad extra* to give in their accounts which amounted to £1,682 7s. 4d. and £6,138 6s. 8d. respectively, along with victuals. Altogether, including certain extras, the total income for the preceding 25 months amounted to £9,745 and produce, a considerable drop from the yearly average of around £7,250 in the 1522 audit. The disappearance from the 1524 lists of a number of the burghs, shires, and custumars which had appeared in 1522 shows that political disorganization had taken its toll.

Despite the decline in revenues, expenditures had surpassed them by only £1,986, which was considerably less than the adverse balance of £3,176 in 1522. But when the latter figure was added to that of the current audit, Robert was left with a total deficit of almost £5,000, a very serious gap in the country's finances. As usual, Albany was the expensive item on the budget, for his expedition against England had required almost £1,300, while his household expenses since the preceding September had amounted to over £2,300 as against £3,000 for the king's household during the whole twenty-five months.[26] The duke's presence, therefore, largely explains Robert's difficulties.

In the light of this state of affairs and of the treasurer's deficit of £3,692 for the past six years, it is not surprising that parliament now issued a proclamation ordering all baillies to make proper returns under pain of the loss of their offices.[27] One of these delinquents was the custumar of the burgh of Cupar, David Grundeston, who was short £50. Robert therefore laid charges against him, the case coming up for hearing on June 1, and as Grundeston did not appear, the Lords gave judgement against him by default. They ordered that his goods be distrained and that he give up his cocket seal, which meant his removal from office.[28] Yet because of the general chaotic condition of the country it was simply impossible to enforce the law against all the defaulters.

The fact of the matter was that the intrigues and bribery of Henry VIII and Dacre were bringing results. By the beginning of May, with the country nearly bankrupt, the Scottish nobles more and more opposed to him, and the French completely indifferent to his fate, Albany decided to leave. After many discussions with the royal council, it was agreed that he could be absent for three months, at the end of which time he either had to return or relinquish the regency. Albany tried to persuade the Scots to appoint Gonzolles treasurer, and to promise that nothing would be done without the latters's advice. This, however, they refused to do, rejecting also his request for a loan of 40,000 crowns. In high dudgeon, therefore, having committed the king to a group of nobles and clergy, he set sail for France on May 20, 1524, never to return.[29]

That Robert was at court and may have been a party to the negotiations between Albany and the council would seem to be indicated by his witnessing of a charter under the Great Seal on May 6. If this surmise is correct, it may be that at this time he began to feel that perhaps the Duke of Albany was a somewhat expensive luxury for Scotland. One can well imagine his sense of relief, at least as comptroller, when Albany left without having obtained the large loan he had requested.

Yet the last period of Albany's regency had not been disadvantageous to Robert personally, as during that time he had made decided advances both economically and socially. For one thing, he had obtained possession of the £3 8s. lands occupied by William Howison and the 3 mark 5s. 4d. lands occupied by Patrick Dickson, both lying in Crawmond Regis which was situated between his lands of Over Barnton and the Mowbray estate of Barnbougle. The owner, James Crawmond of that Ilk, had given these properties as a pledge for a loan to Alexander Strathauchin de Carmyly, who now resigned them to Robert presumably in return for the sum that was owing.[30] This was another addition to the family property.

The increase of his landed estate no doubt pleased him, but at the same time he was continually faced with the necessity of defending his investment in the wardship of Barnbougle. During the autumn of 1522 Alexander Hepburn of Richardtoune had been "uplifting" the rents of the lands of East Cragy, Linlithgow. Robert, annoyed at this interference with his rights, haled the offender before the council which ordered Hepburn to return part of the wheat in question. Even more aggravating was the attempt by one Robert Stewart to gain control of part of the Barony of Inverkeithing by means of a charter of the Duke of Albany granted shortly before his final departure for France. Robert naturally objected strongly to Stewart's action, but the Lords of the Council, refusing to take decisive steps, contented themselves with suspending the case by referring the whole matter to the next parliament, which they said, alone had power to deal with a grant by the governor.[31] Robert's indignation at the duke's action may have begun the process of turning him away from "the French interest," although he made no immediate move in this direction.

While wrestling with the difficulties of bringing to fruition his plans for Barnbougle, he took an important step in another direction by the betrothal of his daughter Margaret to the son of Sir James Sandilands of Calder. This was a typical example of the alliances that wealthy middle class families were beginning to make with members of the lower nobility not only in Scotland, but throughout western Europe. Such marriages often solved the nobility's financial problems while satisfying the middle class desire for social advancement.

Sir James Sandilands of Calder, who at this time was 42 years of age, had married Marion, only daughter of Archibald

12

Forrester of Corstorphine, sometime before 1508 and by her had two sons, John and James. As his income from his lands of Calder proved to be insufficient for his needs, he had borrowed 1,500 marks from Adam Hepburn, Provost of the Collegiate Church of Bothwell, putting up West Corswoods, Blackhall, Cammelt Chapel, East and West Handapwoods in the Barony of Calder, and the Halls of Airth in the Barony of Airth as collateral. Until the repayment of the money the provost could draw at least part of the revenues of these lands for his own use. How long the loan was in force is not stated, but Sandilands eventually came to the conclusion that it would be better business for him to make some arrangement with a wealthy merchant, whereby he could liquidate his debt to Hepburn and perhaps retain the lands in his own hands. It was at this point that Robert Barton entered the picture.

Who actually commenced the negotiations is not indicated, but by July 11, 1524, Robert and Sir James had come to a satisfactory agreement. John Sandilands, the elder son, and Margaret, both about fifteen years old were to marry when they came of age. If John should die in the meantime, James his brother, as the next in line was to become Margaret's husband. For his daughter, on the other hand, Robert was to provide a dowry of 2,000 marks, 1,500 immediately and 500 at the time of marriage, and with the first sum Sir James was to liquidate his debt to the Provost of Bothwell. The lands returned to Sandilands as a result were then to be granted to Margaret and her heirs, although until the marriage she was to receive no revenues from them. Upon her marriage she would resign the lands for a clear life-rent of £100 per annum, while at the same time Sir James would resign his barony in favor of her husband. To safeguard the rights of the young people thus involved, if either should refuse to go through with the marriage, Margaret was then to hold the lands and draw their revenues until Sir James paid back the 1,500 marks on the high altar of the Lady

Kirk of Leith. If after the marriage her husband desired to put her away he would have to pay her £100 per annum as long as the separation lasted. Should John and James both die or become wards of the crown prior to the marriage, Margaret was to remain in possession of the lands until they were redeemed at the price of 2,000 marks. Finally, if canonical impediments were found after the marriage, Sir James promised to obtain dispensations as often as needed, in order to assure the validity of the union.

As a guarantee that the agreement would be carried out fully, it was recorded in the book of the Official of Lothian to make it enforcible by ecclesiastical censures. Then on July 21 it was brought before the Lords of the Council that it might be placed in their minutes, giving it the authority of one of their acts.[32] These precautions were probably insisted upon by Robert as he was the one who was risking his 1,500 marks. He did not need to worry, however, for Sir James was apparently eager to carry out the contract. By October 20 the Provost of Bothwell had been paid off and Margaret granted the lands in question. Then, in June, 1526, John was given possession of the barony of Calder at the time of his father's departure on a pilgrimage to Rome, perhaps as penance for the murder of a certain James Somerville.[33] Robert's financial power had thus enabled him to ally himself with one of the country's noble families, another step on the road upwards.

Meanwhile important developments were taking place on the political scene. With Albany out of the country, Queen Margaret and the major nobles, led by Arran, Lennox, and Crawford, decided that the time had come to end the duke's regency and "erect" the young king as ruler. To this plan Henry of England gave his wholehearted support, feeling that if this action were taken he could probably dominate Scotland's government. At the same time, those opposed to Angus believed that by establishing the king as ruler of the country they would prevent the earl from again gaining control. As a result of all this reasoning, on July 31 the queen mother and the nobles assembled at Holyrood decreed that the king having now come of age (13 years!) should assume the governance of the realm. Henceforth, the Duke of Albany had no authority in the country, and the Scots would govern themselves.

That Robert was present at this ceremony would seem to be certain from the nature of the office which he held. As soon as the king was "erected," however, the council decided that since all the present holders of government offices had been appointed by the Duke of Albany, they should be removed and new incumbents appointed. Therefore, on August 1, all the chief officials having presented their resignations, the king declared their offices vacant. He then proceeded to appoint his own men, or rather those who enjoyed the confidence of Margaret and her supporters. Strangely enough, however, a number of those resigning were returned to office, and among them Robert Barton.[34] Apparently neither Margaret nor any of the others felt that they could do without him. Money was the government's great need, and Robert appeared to be the only one who could keep the king and his administrators supplied.

X

The End of the First Term of Office

The period from August, 1524, to August, 1525, was a difficult one for Scotland, and a particularly busy one for Robert, who was involved in the domestic politics of Denmark as well as in those of his native land.

Although Queen Margaret in alliance with the Earl of Arran had succeeded in establishing young James V as king directed by a council which she dominated, her troubles were by no means over. For one thing her much-hated husband, the Earl of Angus, presently in England, was hoping to come home to take over control of the country. Meanwhile, on the other side of the political fence, there had gathered a considerable group of the nobility and the middle class led by James Beaton, the Archbishop of St. Andrews, who continued to favor the Duke of Albany, desiring his return to Scotland. In the face of this threat, Margaret was of the opinion that her best means of staying in power was the support of her brother Henry. Consequently, she was prepared to talk peace with England, while at the same time refusing absolutely to reinstate Angus. As the English, on the other hand, did not show themselves enthusiastic about her attitude she then began to look again to France. With these various political crosscurrents flowing strongly, it is not surprising that for many, life in Scotland was not merely difficult but at times decidedly precarious.[1]

In the midst of this uncertainty Robert continued to fulfil his functions as comptroller. He was not able, however, to limit his interests solely to the financial side of the administration, for on September 15, 1524, parliament drew up a list of twenty-eight men of whom six, according to the queen's discreation, were always to be in attendance on the king. One of these was the comptroller.[2]

Margaret may have had some misgivings about Robert's appointment owing to his known support of Albany, but as his presence in the comptrollership seems to have been absolutely necessary she may have had little choice in the matter. Moreover she may have believed it wise to keep a line open to Paris. Thus despite any doubts she may have felt, if his report be correct, his influence with the queen-mother must have been considerable, for he claimed that he was largely responsible for the release of the pro-French Archbishop of St. Andrews whom the queen had imprisoned because of his activities on Albany's behalf. Serving Margaret and at the same time working with Albany's supporters, Robert may have been attempting to bring about a unification of the forces within the country for the purpose of countering the English efforts to divide and rule.

This interpretation is given some credibility by his actions at this time. Taking advantage of the presence of the Duke of Norfolk in Edinburgh as the bearer of Henry's congratulations to his recently "erected" nephew, Robert applied for a safe-conduct for two ships, presumably one of which at least was his own, to go to Lynn for "stuff" for King James.[3] That he received the desired document is not indicated, but probably he did not, for one of his ships while sailing shortly afterwards to France, and perhaps also to Lynn, was seized by a Flemish privateer aided by two English vessels.[4] This was distressing enough, but—what was worse—Robert's ship was bearing a letter to the Duke of Albany, in which he informed the duke of the state of affairs in Scotland, particularly of the need of food and fuel at Dunbar Castle held by the duke's representative Gonzolles, and also told of his efforts on behalf of the imprisoned Archbishop of St. Andrews. Revealing as it did Robert's continuing friendliness to Albany and the French cause, the letter should certainly have destroyed all credit he possessed with the queen. On the other hand, knowing Margaret's capacity for double-dealing, and also that she was again beginning to veer towards France, one cannot but suspect she was perhaps privy to the letter, having had Robert write it lest it should become known to Henry VIII. If such were the case, it was a wise move, for when the letter came into Wolsey's possession, he promptly forwarded it to Norfolk telling him to use it to discredit Barton with the queen mother and to persuade her that her only hope lay in English support.[5]

Before Norfolk could take any action, however, another English envoy, Dr. Magnus, had left London for the north. One thing which neither King Henry nor the Earl of Angus desired was the return of Albany to Scotland. Realizing this, George Douglas of Kilspindie had warned Norfolk on October 24 that unless something were done quickly Margaret and Arran, her principal supporter, would be back on Albany's side. He pointed out that she had released Albany's chief advocate, the Archbishop of St. Andrews; for, having received little help from England and none from most of the nobles, she felt that her only hope was France. In the face of this situation, Wolsey had hastily dispatched Dr. Magnus, one of his most tried and trusted negotiators, to Edinburgh in the hope of counteracting any pro-French moves. He instructed him carefully, telling him to obtain from Norfolk the letter which Robert had sent to France, in order that he might use it to persuade the queen to follow her brother's advice.

To deal with the Scots, and particularly with Robert Barton, was not quite as easy as Wolsey had anticipated. As soon as Robert knew that the English had captured the ship carrying the letter to Albany, he made a public acknowledgement of having written the duke, probably pointing out that he believed he was acting for the best interests of the country. With the pro-French element now in the ascendant, there was little fear that he would get into trouble. By this move he stole much of Magnus' thunder. The English ambasssador reported to Wolsey that he would say nothing about the letter, since by so doing he would only cause trouble to himself and the English cause. Any mention of the letter, he judged, would certainly alienate Robert who was "gretely in the quenes favour," and what was more, he did not take the letter too seriously, for since Robert was so friendly with the queen, he, Magnus, felt that Albany's return would only endanger Robert's position of influence. His interpretation of the letter was that it was one of pretended friendship which Albany would ignore since it came from the queen's party.[6] It is quite possible, however, that Magnus was wrong, and that the letter was part of an attempt by Robert to bring Margaret and Albany together to resist English encroachment.

This latter interpretation of Robert's letter receives support from the misfortunes which befell Magnus on his first interview with Margaret. A few days after his arrival in Edinburgh he was summoned to the queen mother's presence, probably at Holyrood, and to his embarrassment, when he arrived he found ten or twelve Edinburgh women, with the queen, complaining bitterly that the English had aided some Flemings in capturing their husbands and goods despite the pretended peace between the two countries. That they were referring to the capture of Robert's ship is clearly indicated by Magnus' comment that they were put up to this action by the comptroller. Robert was employing this strategy to defeat the English attempts to gain the queen's confidence while he was at the same time endeavoring to steer her and Arran towards France.[7]

His success in this direction manifested itself in Magnus' report to Wolsey on his attempts to have a secret meeting with Arran. He had made arrangements to meet the earl in the abbey chapel at Holyrood, but when the queen got wind of what was happening, she ordered the two of them to meet at court. When he arrived, he discovered Arran closeted with Robert and the queen, discussing the affairs of the country. Any conversation under such circumstances could accomplish little, for the queen kept a close watch on all his attempts to talk to the earl or the comptroller.[8]

The tide at this point, however, began once again to change. The time allowed for Albany's return was now long past but there was still no sign of his resuming his office in Scotland. Thus it was not surprising that even the pro-French element gradually came to feel that the Scots must make the best terms they could with England. In this they were encouraged by the return of Angus, with Henry VIII's approval, to take control of the government. His principal ally in this endeavour was Dr. Magnus who, concentrating on winning Arran and the Archbishop of St. Andrews over to the English faction, gained such success that Angus felt himself justified in attempting to seize the king. In this coup he did not succeed, but he did force the queen to come out openly against Albany and his royal French master. Matters finally came to a head on December 11 when James and the Scottish nobles issued a formal statement of deposition stating that Albany had forfeited all further claim to be regent. The government then dispatched the Marchmont Herald to France to inform the duke that his term of office was over, and that he should instruct Gonzolles who still held Dunbar Castle to turn it and its artillery over to the government. At the same time, the herald was ordered to tell Francis I of the Scottish decisions, to inform him that they were considering peace with England, and to demand that the Scottish artillery which Albany had taken to France be returned. He was also to remind the French king that because of their friendship with France, Scottish merchants had been prevented from trading in England, Flanders, Spain, and elsewhere, but that at the same time they had received very unfriendly treatment in France itself. This final section shows that the middle class, probably with Robert Barton, the one merchant on the council, acting as its spokesman, was becoming rather doubtful of the advantages of the French alliance. Indeed, it may have been that Robert and his friends were largely responsible for the inclusion of this statement in Marchmont's message.

The reason for believing this is that Robert, himself, seems at this point to have been turning more definitely towards the English side as is suggested by a letter of Magnus written to Cardinal Wolsey. Recognizing Robert as something of a key figure in the government, he seems to have gone out of his way to gain the comptroller's favor, an attempt in which he was apparently successful, and which may have helped to turn Margaret also away from the French. On December 27 he reported to Wolsey that he had warned the queen that she should stay in alliance with her brother. Then he continued:

Albeith I have diverse tymes written unto your grace of the suspicion that I have had in the countroller here called Robert Barton, moore commynly knowen and called in Englande Hob-à-Barton, I fynde gret kyndnes in hym soe that nowe he and I be right famylier, and myche better he is mynded towardes Englande than to Fraunce, and after that maner I am privea he counsailleth the quenes grace and especially aviseth her not to loose nor offende the Kingges highness her broder, and by hym I doe and shall knowe many thingges. He is a man of gret substance for these partes and wolde nowe seche for his eas and saving of his gooddes, and supposeth if Englande and Scotlande doe booth take oon waye it shalbe mooste specially for the common weall of all Scotland.

He added also that David Falconer and his other friends were of the same mind.[9]

These statements of the English ambassador are of no little interest and importance for one's understanding of both Robert and his changing view of Anglo-Scottish relations. Stedman dismisses Magnus' statement saying that Robert was merely fooling the ambassador, being still really a Francophile.[10] This does not seem to be borne out, however, by one's impressions either of Robert or of Magnus. Robert always appears to be a forthright individual, quite prepared to fight for his rights and his possessions, but not given to deceit. Dr. Magnus, on the other hand, was not the person who would easily be taken in by professions. Moreover, the later history of Robert's dealings do not bear out the idea that he was acting hypocritically. Holding a position of power and influence in the government by virtue of his "gret substance" he was seeking above everything else for peace, which could alone bring Scotland prosperity and himself freedom from many worries. Therefore, he may well have come to the conclusion that peace with England was far more important that the continuation of a costly alliance with a faithless France. In this he would by no means be alone.

If this were his position, events taking place while Magnus was writing his report would certainly act as a confirmation. At the end of November, the Earl of Cassillis had gone to England to discuss peace, but a peace which would include France. According to the imperial ambassador, Wolsey countered by saying England could not sign a treaty without the emperor's consent, and furthermore that the Scots must acknowledge Henry's "pre-eminence," or that he would ravage their country. Cassillis then replied that this demand would require further discussion with the home government, and so returned to Edinburgh. He did, however, succeed in one matter which lay very close to Robert's heart, for he brought back word that Robert's ship which had been captured by Flemish privateers would be restored on the payment of 150 crowns. The ambassador's success would further strengthen Robert's feeling of favor towards England.[11]

Events now began to move rapidly to a climax. Margaret was determined that she and Henry Stewart, her new paramour would rule the country. On the other hand most of the leading nobles including the earls of Angus, Cassillis, Lennox, and Argyle and the Archbishop of St. Andrews, the Bishop of Aberdeen, and the Prior of St. Andrews desired that they too should participate in the government, a position strongly supported by the English. To this Margaret did not agree, for she would not admit Angus, her much-hated husband, to any position of authority. Neither was she prepared to welcome back the Duke of Albany, for his return also would bring about a diminution of her control. In the early days of January, 1525, therefore, a tug of war took place between French and English interests, each trying to win Margaret over in order to gain possession of the king. She, in turn, hoped to use both parties to enable her to remain in power.

Robert had by now apparently moved completely out of the French camp. On Sunday, January 15, 1525, Magnus gave a luncheon or dinner at which the comptroller along with the lords Maxwell, Johnston, Drumlanrig, Emmysfield, and others were present. When the meal was over they all betook themselves to the Castle where Margaret, suffering a sort of mild seige by the opposition, was keeping the king out of the hands of Angus and the Archbishop of St. Andrews. On their arrival, they found Gonzolles presenting his credentials as a full-fledged ambassador of France to James and his council, and trying to persuade them that Albany, who was then in Italy, would be able to influence the pope in whatever they desired. Magnus thereupon produced a letter received from the pope, and requested that Gonzolles leave the room while the king read the letter to his advisers. After some argument with the council,

which seems to have been pro-French, Gonzolles retired and
the king read the letter, which advised him to follow his Uncle
Henry's advice. Magnus followed the perusal of the papal
communication by asking why the French had appointed as
ambassador the man who refused to surrender Dunbar Castle
to its rightful owners. This seems to have brought the meeting
to a close in favor of the English. Robert's intimate relations
with Magnus and the pro-English element at this time give
strong support to the idea that he had become more favorable
to them.[12]

Yet, although he had seemingly forsaken the French interests
it looks as though many had come to regard Robert more as a
balance wheel than as an English partisan. One is brought to
this conclusion by events which followed almost immediately.

About this time the Lords of the Council, among whom
would be Robert, prepared certain articles to which they
desired the queen to agree in order that they might all confer
together in the matter of peace with England. This she haughtily
refused, summoning to Edinburgh those magnates and prelates
whom she felt loyal to her, to give her their support. Few,
however, were prepared to aid such an unpopular and obviously
selfish leader. Most of the aristocracy seem to have been of the
opinion that Margaret's greatest need was common sense and
that one of the few people able to persuade her to act sanely
was the comptroller, who was then with her. On January 24
Gavin Dunbar, Bishop of Aberdeen, wrote Robert that a week
earlier he had received from him a letter, which may have
explained the situation, or which may have contained the
queen's summons. Having heard that she had rejected the
Lord's proposals for a conference, the bishop expressed his
satisfaction that it was impossible for him to come to Edinburgh
as he had promised, for obviously Margaret would not listen to
good council. He hoped that Robert would succeed in making
her see some reason, and declared that he was prepared to work

only for the king and the common weal. On the same day the
Earl of Rothes also wrote to Robert stating that some of the
lords were planning a meeting the following week in Stirling.
However, even though the Archbishop of St. Andrews had
advised him to attend he would not, which had annoyed many
of the nobles. He also expressed his fervent hope that Robert
would succeed in giving the queen sound advice for she needed
it badly.[13]

On January 25 the Earl of Angus and Archbishop Beaton, the
chancellor, having met at St. Andrews, whence the Bishop of
Aberdeen had written the day before to Robert, drew up a
statement calling for the king to be placed in the hands of a
council to be chosen by a parliament to meet at Stirling on
February 6. In the meantime, they held that since Margaret and
Arran were unlawfully in control of the king's person, his
orders should not be obeyed. At this point the whole political
framework of the country seemed to be dissolving, for Magnus
reported in his letter of February 2 to Wolsey:

> I see no person in surety but such as are able to defend them-
> selves, for that for want of order of justice I do not conceive that
> reason, law nor honour is considered. The gates be so sure
> barred up, that Justice came not nor may have power to issue
> forth and pass abroad.[14]

To prove his case he enclosed with his letter copies of the
letters sent by the Bishop of Aberdeen and the Earl of Rothes to
Robert the preceding week, indicating not only the state of the
country, but also that he and the comptroller were at that
moment working hand in hand. He further added that he had
advised the queen not to go to Stirling, but to let the nobles
come to her as to do the king a service, hoping that in this
way she might be able at least to save face.[15]

By this time Margaret, persuaded probably by Magnus and
Robert, saw that she must come to terms with the lords gathered

at Stirling. To this end, therefore, on condition that Angus would assert no matrimonial authority over her or her property, she agreed to the establishment of a governing council of which she was to be permanent president. This apparent concession brought only a truce, for almost immediately afterwards she dispatched letters to the Duke of Albany who was in Italy, urging him to return and assume power as governor. Unfortunately for her, her message was intercepted in Milan, the whole plot becoming known and the Angus party thereby receiving additional strength.[16] Further prestige now accrued to this faction by the Earl of Cassillis' successful negotiation of a three-year Anglo-Scottish truce. In the face of such growing English influence there was not very much that Margaret could do. She kept appealing to Albany to push her divorce in Rome, but that was about all that was possible. In the parliament of February the Earl of Angus had gained almost complete control of the Council of Regents, and when she refused to attend the next parliament held on July 6, he set up a rotating system of two regents to remain with the king for three months at a time, he and Gavin Dunbar, Archbishop of Glasgow, being the first two occupants of this office. By this means he at last gained control of the government.[17]

That Robert was in favor of the rise of Angus, even if he did not taken an active part in it, would seem to be manifested in his relationships at this time with the earl. It was probably to help Robert meet the financial needs of the crown that Angus had had parliament pass an act on February 15 revoking all recent grants from the king's property, on the ground that the royal household could not be adequately supported unless the comptroller received all the revenues from the royal estates. In return for this Robert was no doubt prepared to do what he could for Angus.

This would explain why, on May 3, the Lords of the Council registered in their *Acts* a promissory note of the Earl of Angus

to Robert Barton for a loan of £100 which he was to repay by
June 24 "but fraud or gile."[18] It is possible that Robert was
more or less forced to lend this money to Angus, but it is more
probable that he did it as a matter of business, particularly as
there seems to have been more to the transaction than meets
the eye. There is in the agreement no mention of security for
the loan, and no statement concerning the giving and taking of
interest. Robert's requirement of these two things may have
been responsible for another agreement signed the same day
and registered in the *Acts* five days later. In the latter document
he promised Queen Margaret, who had placed in his care her
ward, the Earl of Huntly, to produce the earl on her demand
under pain of 20,000 marks damages. It is possible that as long
as Huntly was "feft to remane wit" Robert, that the latter would
draw the revenues owing to the queen as Huntly's tutor.[19]

On the surface it looks as though this transaction had nothing
to do with the loan to Angus, for it was the queen who turned
over the earl to Robert, an act which may have been the result
of her rather than Angus' obtaining from him a much-needed
loan; she was always in need of money, as shown by her attempt
in February to borrow from Dr. Magnus. However, after
Robert had registered his agreement with the queen mother,
the earls of Angus and Arran along with Lord Fleming appeared
as guarantors to Robert for the 20,000-mark penalty. Under
these circumstances it looks very much as though they had
"persuaded" the queen to hand over Huntly and his revenues to
Robert while they guaranteed that he would not have to return
the earl until Angus repaid his debt.[20] If this be the explanation,
it is probable that Angus was borrowing the money for Margaret
or the young king. Robert may well have refused to loan the
needed money directly to the queen mother, insisting that
Angus and Arran as those who were really the rulers of the
country should be parties to the whole transaction.

In this connection it is interesting to note that there is very little reference during this year to Robert's business activities. In March, 1525, he exported some 40 chalders of "small" or refined salt for which he was obliged in return by the council to import the same quantity of "great" salt used for packing fish. Apart from references to his sending ships, which may or may not have been his, to France and England for goods for the king, this is the only evidence indicating that he was still interested in commerce. There is little doubt, however, that his trading activities continued, although perhaps handled by his wife or the sons of his first marriage. The latter hypothesis is borne out by the fact that it was one of his sons who was sent to London for a safe-conduct for the ship sailing to Lynn.[21]

Similarly not much information is available concerning his interests in real estate. On September 12, 1524, he received a grant of the wardship of all the lands of the late Thomas Forestar of Stralharny along with the right to marry the late Thomas' son George as he saw fit.[22] Whether or not he paid for this grant is not clear, but even if he did, he no doubt considered himself fortunate since any money expended for it was a very sound investment. A little later he found himself obliged to fight for part of the Lordship of Drummond, of which he had been the guardian since 1520. A certain James Sutherland had obtained, by a charter of the Great Seal, the stewartry and coronership of Balquihidder and the forestership of Glenorchy and Drummond which he had turned over to John Drummond of Innerpeffrey. Robert carried the case to the council which suspended Sutherland's charter until he should prove his rights and reinstated Robert in full control, responsibility, and income.[23]

The lack of information concerning Robert's business activities may be a consequence of his preoccupation not only with Scottish politics, but also with the misfortunes of Christian II of Denmark. By the beginning of 1524 this monarch had successfully alienated not only the Swedes and the Hansa, but also every class in his kingdom, except the merchants. Although the latter would have fought for him, the assumption by his cousin, Frederick Duke of Schleswig-Holstein, of the leadership of the rebels in 1522 and the subsequent refusal of both French and Scots to give him any aid so discouraged him that in April, 1524, he fled to Holland. This move actually led to further complications, for France now recognized Frederick as king in the hope of persuading him to participate in an invasion of England, while at the same time the Emperor Charles V, who was Christian's brother-in-law, and Henry VIII of England supported the exile. All this made life very difficult to those Scots who favored Christian while definitely disliking Henry, and also for those pro-English elements who at the same time wished to do business with Denmark. Meanwhile, since most of Christian's naval forces had remained loyal to him, they endeavored continually both to stir up rebellions in Denmark and to attack all those carrying on legitimate trade with the new King Frederick's subjects. To these forces the Scots sometimes gave their aid, while at other times they became their victims.[24]

To gain the active support of the Scots, Christian again dispatched to Scotland Dr. Alexander Kinghorn who early in November, 1524, reported confidently that French interest was on the wane, which meant that Frederick would receive no Scottish assistance. Robert Barton and David Falconer, on the other hand, had both offered him the use of their ships, while others had volunteered to serve as soldiers. He hoped that with these forces he would be able to prepare the way for Christian's return.[25]

At this point confusion was injected into the situation by an act of piracy against a Dutch ship by one Robert Fogo, captain and part owner of the *Litill Martin* of Leith, whose two partners were Alexander and Robert Barton. Fogo, while transporting a group of Edinburgh merchants to Danzig in May, 1524, had captured a Dutch vessel worth 13,000 gulden with which he returned to Leith, sending on the *Martin* to Copenhagen. On his arrival in Scotland the Edinburgh authorities, complaining to the Council that his action was illegal and dangerous, immediately demanded that the vessel and cargo be turned over to their care until the matter was settled by the courts. That these fears were not unfounded became clear very soon after the *Litill Martin* had anchored in Copenhagen; word leaked out as to what they had done, and the crew found it expedient to slip quietly on board and set sail for home without bothering to inform their passengers, whom they left to face charges of piracy. When the *Litill Martin* arrived back in Edinburgh the wives and families of the deserted men immediately raised a great outcry. This forced the council, despite Fogo's attempt to explain away everything, to take cognizance of the matter. They wrote Frederick of Denmark to assure him that what the Scots had done was perfectly legal, but that if anyone had any complaints for him to appear before them and he would promptly receive justice.[26]

Up to this point Robert had been involved in the matter only insofar as he was required to go bail for Fogo. The Dutch, however, were not inclined to bother with action in law courts when they could take what they wanted with relatively little trouble. Therefore, when Edward Crawford of Leith sailed into Copenhagen sometime early in June, 1524, he was immediately arrested on the demand of Alberycht Wangork, one-third owner of the ship taken by Fogo. Although Crawford fought the case in the Danish courts he could not obtain the release of his vessel. He was not the only one to suffer, for in quick succession the Dutch seized, apparently with Danish help, the *Cristofre*, the *Nicholas*, and the *Hoy*, the last-named being Robert Barton's own property.[27] This led to a further outcry in Scotland. Robert, who had apparently sold out his interest in the *Litill Martin* to David Falconer and Robert Cardine, insisted before the council (December 7, 1524) that

Fogo should return to Denmark to stand trial, and that the present owners should keep scatheless the Scottish merchants who had lost their ships. To this latter demand the Lords agreed but did nothing more.[28]

There the matter might have rested for some time had it not been for the appearance during the spring of 1525 in the port of Leith of Hans Sanderson, the Danish captain of the *Fleand Gaist* sailing out of Amsterdam, who was quickly faced with a suit by the five owners of the *Cristofre*. Accusing him of having seized their vessel the previous year, they demanded that he should restore both vessel and cargo. To this Sanderson agreed, providing as his securities Gilbert Menzies provost of Aberdeen, Robert's erstwhile foe over the matter of the Aberdeen customs; William Anderson, Edward Crawford of Edinburgh, and Robert Barton, the latter three all having suffered from Dutch reprisals.[29]

How it came about that at least three of Sanderson's four guarantors were victims of Dutch attacks is difficult to say, but the explanation may lie in the fact that Sanderson had joined Christian II's forces and had come over to recruit both ships and men for an invasion of Denmark. This surmise seems to receive support in the injunction, issued by the council on May 8 to those captains in Leith who might be preparing for war, forbidding them to attack the king's friends and informing them that they were hereafter to do no raiding except with the council's permission.[30] It may be that the Leith men were readying their ships to go to the aid of Christian. To give his men much-needed support, Christian had called upon both Robert and his friend David Falconer to fulfill their promises, which they did sometime before June. Sverin Norby was at this time holding Landskrona against Frederick's troops while another officer, Claude Kniphoff, was busy attacking the enemy on the high seas. On June 1 the commanders of Frederick's Danish forces investing Norby, complaining that they were having difficulties maintaining sea communications owing to the activities of Kniphoff, Barton, and Falconer, admitted that there was no hope of achieving very much against Christian's forces unless the Lübecker's came soon with their fleet.[31]

That Robert was not on this expedition is indicated by a letter which he wrote to Christian from Edinburgh on June 2. Acknowledging the exiled king's commission apparently appointing him his agent and delivered by the Denmark King-of-Arms, he promised that he would do everything he could to provide aid by preparing a small fleet to co-operate with the former's forces. He then went on to point out that Christian still owed him 2,500 gold florins for the *Lion*, but as the exiled monarch had once again promised to reimburse him, he would commit all his resources to his aid.[32] While this letter may give the impression that Robert was being foolishly and sentimentally loyal to Christian who was already a lost cause, the fact is that with the letters of marque against Frederick's forces, it was possible that he could recoup himself for all the losses already suffered in Christian's service. It was a case where romantic loyalty could be made to pay tidy dividends. That profit was involved very quickly became evident. Sometime around the beginning of July, Claude Kniphoff sailed into the Firth of Forth with a number of prizes. Magnus Bilde who was representing Frederick of Denmark in Scotland immediately complained that Kniphoff's presence was to him a source of danger, but the accused produced Robert, with whom he may have been staying since they were old friends, as his guarantee that he would do Bilde no harm. The chancellor then raised the question as to whether Kniphoff's captures were legally prizes. This the council discussed at great length, eventually coming to the conclusion that they were, since Christian was at war with the states whose ships Kniphoff had taken. Robert, who was probably a member of the council at this time, no doubt had much to say in favor of this decision.[33]

Although Kniphoff had thus far succeeded in persuading the
Scots to accept him as a genuine privateer, according to the
late R. K. Hannay, perhaps on Robert's advice, he now made a
mistake. On July 13 when the council had agreed that Kniphoff's captures were true prizes, it had also instructed him to
enter them in the Edinburgh books so that the ships and their
contents might be properly priced. After the king had been
first served, followed by the Lords of the council and the town
of Edinburgh, others could then buy what was left. Kniphoff,
however, instead of fulfilling the regulations, remained at
anchor in the Firth of Forth selling the contents of the prizes,
and perhaps the prizes themselves, to anyone who was willing
to come out and buy. This meant not only that the privileged lost
their privileges, but what is more even the city authorities were
not receiving what was their due. Therefore, on August 3, as a
result of complaints by the Edinburgh council, the Lords ordered
Kniphoff to leave, under threat of arrest, which he did.[34]

Hannay believes that it was his involvement in Kniphoff's
illegal operations in the Firth of Forth which now led to Robert's
removal from the office of Comptroller of the Royal Household. No doubt he had a reputation for consorting with dubious
characters such as Robert Fogo or John Watson of Dundee for
whom he provided security when they were accused of piracy,
but there is no evidence that he was linked with Kniphoff's
disobedience to the Lords' orders. It seems rather that the real
reason for his disappearance from the comptrollership was his
lack of success in balancing the royal budget.

While participating in the politics of his own country and in
the attempts of Christian II to regain the Danish throne, Robert
had continued to fulfill his duties as comptroller. The only
difficulty was that owing to the chaotic political state of the
country it was impossible to collect the money due the crown,
and as previously mentioned, he was obliged to continue to
lend funds out of his own pocket to Angus and the queen

mother since he could not obtain the royal revenues from those responsible for their collection. All he could do was take action against the delinquents before the council and eventually make the best bargains possible in the hope of obtaining at least part of what was owing.

A good example of his technique is to be found in the case of John Beaton of Creich, nephew of the chancellor, and chamberlain of Fife. At the audit in April, 1524, Robert had obtained judgement against him because of his failure to pay the overdue rents of the lordship. Yet despite the Lords' decision Robert had apparently held his hand in the hope of coming to a peaceful solution with the defaulter, a policy which now promised to be successful. On September 8, Robert and Beaton met, probably in the former's house, and drew up an agreement in which Beaton promised to pay within ten days £400 of the £500 which was his total debt, and if he failed to do so, to pay double the promised amount. For the balance, Robert was to take action against the tenants and occupiers of the lands, the chamberlain promising to help him as much as he could, to obtain the dues still outstanding. The Lords registered the agreement in their minute books, but they seem to have decided that Beaton should no longer hold the office of chamberlain, for they appointed the Earl of Crawford and the Bishop of Galloway to answer in the next account for all returns from the Lordship.[35] By such means Robert was able to salvage at least something for the government, an achievement which no doubt gave him favor in the eyes of those in the places of authority.

It may have been sometime near this date that Robert wrote two letters which are interesting examples of his writing, although they have no other significance. They were written to George Good, probably a burgess of Edinburgh who was a writer of the rolls in the Exchequer and who acted frequently for the baillies of Lauder, Banff, and Ayr.[36] As one of Robert's clerks, Good would have to issue orders or writs for the granting of saisin, or possession, to new tenants. These letters show the rather informal way of dealing with such business matters in those days:

> George Gawd, tak the rentall of Fyf fra the Arsdan and powt in thes berar and hes wyf and tak fra him iiij mark and other xiiij mark for the entra siclyk. Robert Bartan, Controller.

> George Gawd, I haf send to you yowr awn wedow of Stewart-toun. Schew brengis yerly proffet. Ther es na yer be scho well haf an new gawdsawn. Herfor rentall thes man has schow dessyres and tak an merk fra her. Robert Bartan, Controller.[37]

There is perhaps a touch of humor in the reference to "yowr awn wedow of Stewarttoun," which may give a little more light on the man's character.

The winter 1524-25 proved to be disastrous for the royal finances, as the near anarchy of Angus' rule cast the shadow of bankruptcy over the country. On May 19 Mr. John Campbell, the treasurer, appeared before the Lords to complain of the great sums of money which he owed to various merchants, one of whom would probably be Robert, and to the chancellor James Beaton, Archbishop of Glasgow. He, himself, had also provided some £3,000 to help balance the budget. He explained that not only was the cost of governing the country increasing, but revenues were falling rapidly since those responsible for administering the royal casualties were appropriating the money for themselves. It was a serious situation, and one which always accompanied the breakdown of a feudal government. Campbell demanded that the Lords of the Council take some kind of action to meet the shortage.[38]

Apparently the reason for Campbell's appearance with his complaint at this time was that Beaton was pressing him for the repayment of a loan of £860. Campbell agreed to meet his demands towards the end of the year, in two installments, and this in turn enabled him to force the Lords to acquiesce in two very important requests. One was that they would not postpone days for dealing with criminal cases, which were usually profitable to the crown because of the fines and penalties received. The other was that they would not give away crown lands and other royal feudal rights, for by so doing they were depriving the king of his proper revenues. Anyone guilty of contravening these regulations was to pay to Beaton the £860 promised by the treasurer.[39] The Lords' agreement to these proposals indicates that the situation was becoming desperate.

That Robert was sitting on the council about this time, and that he was not receiving enough money to meet his expenses, would seem to indicate that he was not only heartily in favor of this decision, but also that he had a part in putting it into effect.[40] Indeed it was probably as a result of this action of the Lords that he spent the month of July bringing suits against defaulting officials. On the 7th of the month he instituted proceedings against the tenants of East Farny in Fife for withholding from the king an annual rent of £5 6s. The next day he brought suit against the authorities of Cupar for their occupation of the mill of Russillis for which they owed £25. As the defendants made no attempt to justify themselves, the Lords ordered that letters be issued to force payment. Immediately following this decision Andrew Matheson appeared on summons of the comptroller and admitted that he had taken all the rents and dues of the lands of Luthre, Fife, as long as he held the office of chamberlain. Sir Lawrence Alexanderson also admitted that ever since he had received the grant of the land from Matheson he had done the same. Robert demanded, therefore, that they be obliged to make good their defalcations. Three days later John Beaton of Creich, chamberlain of Fife who had apparently regained his office, came to an agreement with the comptroller on the advice of the council whereby he made composition of £589 14s. 11d. for the rents in food and kind which he had appropriated. The same day the Lords gave

judgement at the instance of Robert against Malcolm Drummond
and David Murray for failing to pay £148, rents and dues
accumulated since 1521 from the lands of the port and isle of
Tulibanquhare in the lordship of Strathearn. Then on August
2 John Creighton of Innernyte, former chamberlain of Kinclevin, made composition by paying 200 marks (£133 6s. 8d.)
for his shortages.[41] As the figures mentioned in these suits
alone amount to £753 1s. 7d. it is rather easy to see why the
comptroller had been finding it difficult to make ends meet.

Another aspect of the attempt to "crack down" on defaulters
is seen in the case before the Lords (July 27) involving the ward
and marriage of the heir and lands of Sir William Keith of
Inverugy. Albany had made the grant in January, 1521, to the
Earl of Errol who had in turn regranted it to John Hay, Provost
of Guthrie. It looks as though Robert in his capacity as comptroller had demanded some sort of accounting, perhaps even
the payment of certain sums promised by the holder of the
wardship. The heir of the Earl of Errol, the original grantee,
stated that he had no connection with the property at all since
his father had given it to Hay, while Hay tried to point out that
he had never really held the land. Both sides were thus trying to
escape the responsibility of answering to the crown for the
grant. Robert, however, insisted that since the heirs of Inverugy had remained in the earl's hands, the latter was responsible,
and that the council should give no judgement concerning the
crown's claims until he as comptroller, had been formally
summoned to present his case.[42] As one can see, not only
violence, but the frustrations of lawyers made it no easy matter
to collect the money owing to the king.

It seems it was about this time that Robert made an innovation
in the method of keeping the royal accounts, by separating the
records of the expenditures of the royal household from the
general accounts of the government.[43] This had already been
done in the case of the accounts for food, but now *all* household

receipts and expenditures were to be recorded separately. This would facilitate control of the personal expenditures of the king, and enable the comptroller to make sure that the queen mother and the regents did not misuse funds ostensibly provided for James V's needs. Such a procedure undoubtedly did not increase his popularity with Angus and his satellites in the government.

Yet a mere change in accounting methods could do little for the country's finances. Therefore on July 30 he appeared before the council with the demand that, since the charges of the household were increasing more rapidly than income, the Lords take action to meet the threatening deficit. Only if those in control stopped wasting or misappropriating royal funds and endeavored to see that the money owing to the crown was paid, would the Exchequer Audit, at that moment in progress, produce anything like balanced accounts. As it was, the hope of coming even near a balanced budget was extremely dim.[44]

To his pleas, however, the council seems to have paid no attention. Consequently when the audit was completed late in July his premonition of a deficit proved to have been well founded, although the shortage for the year's operations was not as bad as he may have expected. For one thing, ten, instead of eight sheriffs, as in 1524, remitted a total of £410 10s. 3d. in place of the previous £87 7s. 3d. But what may have been of even greater significance was that over half of them came from north of the Forth and two from the shores of Moray Firth: Elgin and Forres. Similarly twenty, instead of fifteen, baillies of burghs paid in some £481 8s. 8d., an increase of almost £275 over the previous remittances. The royal custumars likewise showed an increase of over £270 when they paid some £1,910, of which Edinburgh alone was responsible for £1,440. Moreover the baillies *ad extra* also reported that their receipts had gone up more than one third over the previous year. In this connection

we might just add that Beaton of Creich paid in £1,676 3s. 10d.
for part of Fife, while the Archbishop of St. Andrews' deputy
Lawrence Alexanderson, remitted £252 10s. 10d. as well as
victuals, for the rest of the shire. The total income amounted to
over £13,300 in cash along with victuals which when sold came
to some £610 bringing the total to around £14,000, an increase
over previous years.

Despite this apparently favorable development, since the
successive governments of Margaret and Angus had not stressed
economy, the expenditures on the royal household for the
preceding sixteen months amounted to £6,800. This was a big
increase over the annual average of £1,500 for the two years
dealt with in the audit of April, 1524. When all the other disbursements were added in, Robert found himself with a
deficit for the year of £1,035 15s. 10½d., a sum which, by
various allowances, he reduced to £774 5s. 3d. Although this
appears to be a relatively modest shortage compared with some
of former years, one must remember that Robert began the
year with a debt of £4,705 6s. 8d. so that in August, 1525, he
was almost £5,500 "in the red", without any sign of his being
able to get out.[45] What is more, there is every likelihood that
he himself had loaned the government a good part of this sum
and continuance in office might only mean that he would have
to provide more from his own pocket in order to keep the
government solvent.

Just what Robert thought about this state of affairs we do not
know, but on August 7, 1525, it suddenly appears that he was
no longer comptroller, Sir James Colvile of Ochiltree, a loyal
Angus partisan, having taken his place. At the same time
Robert and his colleague Nicholas Cairncross were replaced as
the custumars of Edinburgh.[46] Was he removed or did he
resign from the offices he held? That question is of some interest both in itself and for understanding of what happened
later on.

R. K. Hannay believes that the Earl of Angus and his advisers discharged him because of his illicit dealings with Kniphoff. This would mean that they had removed a trusted financial official in order to protect the Edinburgh monopoly. In the light of the council's earlier actions this seems hardly likely, for the Lords usually contented themselves with saying that the people of Leith should obey the law, leaving the matter there. On the other hand, there is a complaint by Cairncross, Robert's fellow custumar, that he had been removed from office although he had fulfilled his duties honestly and soberly. This may indicate that the Edinburgh authorities annoyed at his collusion with Robert in some of his practices, did have a hand in the removal of both at the same time. The only difficulty is that the exact date of Cairncross' protest is nowhere indicated. It may be that he was not removed at the same time as Robert, but rather by Colvile after his assumption of the comptroller-ship.[47] Consequently, the theory that Robert was discharged does not seem to have very much in its favor.

It is much more likely that Robert simply resigned, as he had a good many reasons for so doing. Since he had become comp-troller some seven years earlier he had held a most thankless and frustrating post. Only in one year had he been able to close the audit with a surplus. On every hand he had been prevented from straightening out his accounts; and what is more, to help meet expenses, he had lent the government considerable money of his own of which they still owed him £774. When one adds to this the undoubted disfavor with which he was regarded by those whom he tried to make pay their bills, he could certainly not have been happy in his work. It had cost him much in time and money, and had brought only unpopularity and frustration. One could hardly blame him for quitting such a position when the opportunity offered.

Whether this is the proper interpretation or not is impossible to say for we lack evidence. All one may assert positively is

that as of August 7, Robert was once again a private citizen, free
to run his own business and to carry on his own affairs. It must
have been with a very great sense of relief that he returned to
Leith that afternoon, knowing that he was no longer responsible
for the financial welfare of the kingdom.

XI

Freedom Once More

Although Robert was now out of office, by virtue of his position in the community he could not entirely divorce himself from his political environment. Consequently, throughout the period 1525-1528 while he busied himself with trade, banking, and other private matters, he was repeatedly involved in affairs of state. Moreover, since he seems to have been one of the few people able to remain on at least speaking terms with all parties, probably because they all looked to him for financial help, he may have wielded a greater influence then is usually recognized.

During the months following his departure from the royal household, Scotland experienced a number of political changes. The Earl of Angus, being named tutor to the king until November, immediately assumed complete control of the country, albeit against the wishes of the queen mother and some of the leading nobles. But while the objectors did not possess the power to resist the earl's authority they could still cause him considerable trouble, particularly in the Highland districts where the queen mother had taken refuge under the protection of the Earl of Moray. Thus when November 1 rolled around, Angus, although supposed to hand over the king to the care of another group of nobles headed by the Earl of Arran and the Bishop of Aberdeen, refused to do so because he felt his authority would thereby evaporate. His only recourse was to establish a virtual dictatorship in order to maintain his power and position, which he did. For this he was henceforth even more deeply hated by Queen Margaret and her followers, who were just as anxious as was he, to rule the country. The anti-Angus party made up of great landowners such as the earls of Cassillis, Eglinton, Arran, and others even attempted to overthrow him by force, but meeting with defeat, they submitted and awaited a more favorable opportunity.[1]

Meanwhile Angus, who represented the English as well as his own interest in the country, had been working hard to obtain peace with England. The Lords of the Council supported by an ambassador from France had attempted to lay down a number of restrictive conditions, but with the defeat of Francis I at Pavia (1525) France had so lost her attraction for the Scots that Angus eventually succeeded in reaching an agreement with Henry VIII. Peace once more reigned between the two countries, a condition which would meet with the approval of all those who, like Robert, were attempting to make a living by trade and commerce, as well as those who suffered from the depredations of the apparently uncontrollable borderers. Although for this and other reasons many were ready to support Angus, a considerable number, and above all the queen mother, held for him an undying hatred. Margaret, who had already decided to break with him completely, had in June made representations to the Duke of Albany to obtain the papal decree anulling her marriage, and now appealed to him to push her petition. As Angus was asserting his right to control her property, to take up her revenues, and generally to exercise *jus mariti*, she was most anxious for a complete separation. For the next three years, while the case was pending at Rome, this conflict between the queen mother and the earl lay behind much of the turmoil in Scotland, and it was a clever man who could avoid becoming involved. The country was a constant battleground with the parties changing like the patterns of a kaleidoscope according to what they considered to be their interests.[2]

The continuing conflict did not improve the royal finances as the new comptroller only too quickly discovered. On August 14, about a week after his appointment, Sir James Colvile of Ochiltree appeared before the Auditors of the Exchequer with his resignation. He stated that he had been charged to make payments for the royal household from the king's lands, but since the Lords of the Council had authorized the custumars of Edinburgh to pay out of their returns sums of between £200 and £300 to various individuals as well as monthly pensions, they did not have enough for him and without their remittances he simply could not meet the king's bills. He therefore wished to demit his post. The Auditors, feeling that this was out of their jurisdiction referred the matter to the Secret Council who persuaded Colvile to continue.[3] There is little doubt that he was in a very difficult situation, which is highlighted by the number of suits which he instituted against various defaulting receivers of royal revenues. In the following December he pursued George Inglis, custumar of Ayr, for £146 11s. 9d., the Earl of Cassillis, chamberlain of Galloway, for £129 7s. and 100 cattle, and the Earl of Eglinton, chamberlain of Stewarton, for 18 chalders of meal.[4] There were, no doubt, many other similar cases, but these are sufficient to demonstrate that the new administration of the Earl of Angus had not brought peace or stability to the country.

In March, 1526, at Angus' instigation the king, being at that time 14 years of age, officially assumed supreme control with power to appoint and dismiss officials. But while James was ostensibly the ruler, the one who actually wielded the royal authority was the Earl of Angus supported by the Earl of Arran, but opposed by the queen mother, Archbishop Beaton of St.

14

Andrews, and the earls of Lennox and Glencairn. The outcome was a battle between the two parties near Linlithgow early in September, 1526, resulting in the death of Lennox, the capture of Glencairn, and the flight of Beaton. Although the king did not approve of this turn of events, he could do little about it, so was obliged to cooperate with the inevitable. Angus dominated the country, apparently using the royal revenues as he pleased and governing with a strong hand.[5] In the light of these developments Robert, no doubt, felt only relief that he was now free to devote himself to his own affairs.

One aspect of these affairs to which he could turn his attention was trade, and although the evidence concerning his commercial interests is scanty, what there is gives us some inkling of their nature and size. For instance on August 21, 1525, he sold to the new comptroller 2 chalders, 1 boll of meal, valued at 20s. the boll, and probably acquired by local trade.[6] Some two months later William Murray of Tullibardine, between Gleneagles and Castle Drummond, held up and robbed John Hildow, one of Robert's servants of 48 long pikes, worth 6s. 8d. each, two stones of gunpowder worth 48s. each, and 6 ells of white woolen cloth, worth 5s. an ell. The goods thus lost were being taken to Castle Drummond of which Robert still held the ward and were all, no doubt, imported from abroad.[7] Moreover, in 1528 he and George Wallace of Edinburgh were jointly involved in sending a ship to Bordeaux for wine, indicating his interest in this profitable aspect of trade.[8] Added to this he continued to deal largely in hides and fish, which he and his son John brought from Stirling, Anstruther, Crail, Dundee, and other more northerly ports, exporting them, sometimes without paying the customs, primarily to France. Despite the fact that his consignments were not very large—60 skins, 7 lasts of herring, 6 lasts of salmon, and the like—they formed a considerable proportion of Edinburgh's total exports. What he brought home is not known, although there is a reference in 1528 to a remission of £20 customs due by him on a cargo from England.[9]

The mention of goods imported from England may reveal that besides trading on his own Robert was acting as an agent for a group of London merchants. The reason for drawing this conclusion is to be found in his representing Robert Palmer and his associates of London in their endeavours to retrieve goods of which they had been despoiled in the spring of 1526. Henry Bardnare of Leith, commanding *The Ship of Henry Bardnare* of which he, Hugh Douglas, and Robert Bruce, Robert's friend, were owners, had seized a Spanish ship laden with Palmer's goods. When the matter came to court, the Lords of the Council convicted Bardnare of piracy and ordered the stolen goods to be delivered to Robert for safekeeping. What eventually happened does not appear in the records, but it seems likely that the Englishmen received satisfaction. The importance of this episode is that it indicates further Robert's attitude to the English and possibly his commercial relationships with them.[10]

His continued preoccupation with trade, evidently made him acutely conscious of the necessity of freeing it from its medieval restrictions. Thus he seems to have led the opposition even to the comptroller's right of first purchase of ships' cargoes for the crown. Although he understood this matter only too well, in September, 1527, he broke into a ship "arrested" by the comptroller and "at his awin hand" took out two lasts of salmon which he sold. Naturally enough the government sued Robert, but as he obtained a royal order forbidding the Lords to continue this case he succeeded in slowing up the wheels of justice until July, 1529. At that time, after Angus had been expelled from the country, and the king had finally assumed complete control of the government, Robert gained his freedom from the charge on the grounds of "insufficient evidence."[11] This does not mean that he was acquitted, but only that the pursuers could not prove his guilt. In these circumstances and in the light of his

previous record one cannot but suspect that his antipathy to
trade controls had led him to this action.

This interpretation of his attitude would seem to be confirmed by his stand on the ever-present question of the establishment of a compulsory staple in the Low Countries. As will be
remembered the plans to set up a staple in Middelburg in
1523 had been somewhat disturbed by that city's seizure of
Robert's ship the *Thomas*. In some way not entirely clear, this
difference had been either patched up or ignored in return for
the payment of 11,000 guilders to the Scottish government, and
the staple had been proclaimed. This would have settled the
matter had it not been for the refusal of the Scottish merchants,
perhaps because of the treatment meted out to Robert, to carry
their goods to Middelburg. In high dudgeon, therefore, the
Dutch burghers had written the governor, the council, the
chancellor, the secretary, and Robert Barton the then comptroller, demanding that the agreement become immediately
effective. What Robert's reaction was is not known, but one
may well imagine that unless he had received compensation for
the *Thomas* it would hardly be favorable.[12]

Before anyone could take action on the matter, however,
war had broken out between France and the Empire, in January,
1525. Commerce on the North Sea came to a standstill. More,
the Conservator of Scottish Privileges, partially remedied the
situation by obtaining from the king and council the promise that
when peace returned they would restore the staple to Middelburg.[13] But peace did not bring the staple to its promised resting
place, with the result that negotiations continued, spurred on
by the newly " erected" king's financial needs.[14] At this point the
authorities of Middelburg, claiming that the treaty of 1522 was
still in force, commenced arresting all Scots not sailing to their
port. The result of this action was an immediate outcry from
the merchants of Edinburgh, Aberdeen, Stirling, St. Andrews,
Perth and Dundee who presented a protest before the council

on June 21, 1526, through their provosts and other representatives, including Robert Barton of Over Barnton. The nature of the complaint is not indicated, but it did have the effect of postponing all action on the staple until July 14, in order that the merchants might have time to consider the plans for the staple and to make a report.[15]

On June 27 the comptroller, who meanwhile had been providing for the household out of his own pocket, refused to supply any more funds. The council instructed him to continue until July 14, at which time the merchants would report on the staple, promising to pay him from the money expected from Middelburg or "be ane gratitude of the merchandis of the realm." When the crucial date actually came around it was obvious that the opposition to any staple had gained strength. The council therefore, bowing to public opinion, put off the representatives of Middelburg until October 1, while at the same time levying a tax upon all the burghs for the privilege of their merchants being able to sail wherever they pleased.[16] To the sum raised in this way the Lord of Veere added 1,000 marks which he donated to the Scottish government in the hope of gaining the staple for his town. It was therefore something of a shock when William, Master of Glencairn, obtained a letter under the Great Seal, perhaps from Angus, establishing the staple at Middelburg.[17] Immediately the opposition was in full cry. The government itself seems to have been so startled by this action that it seized the Dutch representatives in Edinburgh, literally holding them as hostages for the return of the letter which had been smuggled out of the country. By November 30, 1527, the document was back in Scotland and for the time being the idea of a staple seems to have fallen into abeyance.[18]

In all of the controversy over the erection of a staple at Middelburg there is little doubt that Robert had borne a considerable part. He had been present at the meeting of the royal council when the opposition had first shown itself earlier in the year, and he probably had continued to lend his weight to the movement. For so doing, he had two reasons. One was, of course, that he had been badly treated by the authorities of Middelburg when he had sent his ship over to inaugurate the staple. Probably of equal importance, however, was his apparent opposition to trade restrictions or controls of any kind. They would only tend to limit his freedom to go where the prices were highest. In this he was evidently like many other merchants throughout history. Consequently, when the Lords temporarily set aside the staple, levying instead a special tax on the burghs, although he may not have liked to pay the impost he undoubtedly felt that this was better than Middelburg's plan.

Besides the question of the staple, another aspect of Robert's commercial interest was his seeking compensation for his losses at the hands of privateers. He had as yet received nothing from either the Spaniards for the loss of the *Black Barque* in 1520, or from the English for the seizure of the *Mary Katerine* in 1524. Consequently he persuaded Margaret, when she was in power, to write both her brother and Margaret of Austria requesting reimbursement. Neither, however, seems to have felt obligated to fulfill the Scottish demands. Nor was Henry any more acquiescent to similar demands forwarded by Angus over James V's signature. The English king merely replied that if Robert felt himself aggrieved he could take the matter to the Admiralty Court in London. To this James countered that the custom was to settle these matters at the border, but nothing more came of the protests. Robert had to write the losses off as one of the risks of business.[19]

In attempting to recoup himself for at least one other alleged loss Robert may have been somewhat more successful. Sometime in June, 1526, a ship loaded with timber and under the command of a John Fraser, factor of Sir Vincent Lunge, lieutenant of Norway, arrived in Leith, but as soon as it cast anchor, Robert Barton, John Cant, and Robert Bruce had it seized in reprisal for four lasts of salmon and some other goods which they claimed some Norwegians had taken from them. On the Lords' considering the case, with the understanding that David Falconer was prepared to act as guarantor for the payment of the money owing to the Scots, they allowed Fraser to sell his cargo. What happened then is not told, but it looks as though Fraser may have left the country without meeting the demands of Robert and his friends. At any rate, on December 1 he was once more before the council, for Robert Barton and Robert Bruce had obtained his arrest on the same charge, this time when he was in port with a shipload of victuals. It may be thought that this was merely a continuation of the original case, but from the fact that the two charges give different descriptions of Fraser's cargoes, and also because John Cant's name is now omitted, it looks as though this was a second charge owing to the fact that Fraser had left the country earlier, without satisfying the pursuers. Moreover, the lapse of some five months between the two cases would seem to support this interpretation. As Falconer, this second time, also appeared as surety that Robert and his colleagues would be reimbursed, Fraser was again released from arrest.[20] There for the moment the matter rested.

Yet for all his apparent interest in trade Robert seems to have devoted his attention even more consistently to "banking" and to investment in real estate. On August 16, while still bearing his old official title, he was faced with the demands of a Charles Campbell to pay 100 marks for the returns of the process of apprising against the lands of the Laird of Drummelyar. These had been loaned to Malcolm, Lord Fleming, on condition that they would be repaid at the end of the preceding November, Robert giving security for repayment to the extent of the 100 marks. As Robert paid the sum demanded without demur, one cannot but suspect that this was the old medieval method of circumventing the ecclesiastical prohibition of the taking of usury. Fleming no doubt reimbursed him in return.[21]

An even clearer example of Robert's banking activities appears about the same time, when a writ was issued for a charter to be drawn up confirming Patrick Houston's grant of all the lands of Lany, sheriffdom of Edinburgh, to Robert, his wife Elizabeth, and Robert, junior, their heir. Simultaneously a letter of regress was granted to Houston promising that on the redemption of the property he would be received back as the king's vassal. Turned over to Robert as security for a loan, Lany would provide by its revenues interest payments until final reimbursement. The confirmation of this interpretation is that Patrick's son John and his wife appear as owners of half the lands of Lany in 1531, showing that by that date Patrick had repaid at least part of the debt.[22]

That this aspect of his business was growing was indicated by another agreement to which he was a party. Patrick Hepburn, supported by various guarantors, made a contract with Robert to transfer money to Rome for his promotion to the Priory of St. Andrews. Robert was to send £400 (sterling) to a "sicker" bank in London which would then transfer the money through a bank of Bruges or Antwerp to a Mr. John Douglas, representing various Scots in Rome. If Hepburn's promotion did not take place Robert was to obtain sufficient letters of exchange so that the money could be used either in Rome or Flanders. The English bank was to expedite the sending of the money to Rome and was to see to the bringing back of the papal bulls. Hepburn paid £500 (Scots) down and promised £2,250 (Scots) forty days after the arrival of the banker's receipt. He also gave Robert the right to increase the amount to be paid in Rome by 500 or 600 ducats if necessary and agreed to pay all expenses at the rate of £3 15s. (Scots) for £1 (Flemish). The agreement as befitted one involving such a large sum of money, was registered in the books of the Lords of the Council, with various cautioners promising to reimburse Robert if Hepburn failed to do so.[23] This transaction not only demonstrates something of Robert's wealth, since he may have had to provide the cash for the London bank out of his own assets, but it also shows that his "credit rating" was indeed of the highest, even on the English market.

It was no doubt in connection with this piece of business that Dr. Magnus, who had come back to Scotland some time earlier, on the day of the Lords' registration of the agreement wrote to Cardinal Wolsey supporting James V's request for a safe-conduct for Robert and his servant John Chisholm. He asked that the permit remain in force for one year so that they could pass and repass with merchandise at will. Magnus adds that both Chisholm who was coming to obtain the safe-conduct, and Patrick Sinclair, a clerk of the King's Kitchen who was accompanying Chisholm, had been of the greatest help to the English cause by providing him with much information.[24] They were prepared to tell the king all that they knew. From these comments on Robert's servant, it would seem that he was still pro-English in his outlook and friendly with Dr. Magnus. Unfortunately there is no information as to whether Robert received the safe-conduct or whether he went to England. All that is known is that Hepburn obtained the priory and that by May 29, 1527, his guarantors had reimbursed Robert fully for his expenses.[25]

Clergymen and fellow merchants were not, however, Robert's only clients, for it would seem that he was acting as the agent for a number of the nobles. On December 18, 1527, John Grant of Fruthy, William Leslie of Buchan, and Patrick Grant in Ballindalloch appeared before the Lords and asked that their obligation to Robert for 300 marks be recorded in the *Acts*. This represented a sum owed by them to the Earl of Rothes, which Robert had promised to pay on their behalf in return for their guarantee that they would reimburse him before the next Feast of Epiphany (January 6).[26] He would, no doubt, receive adequate consideration for discounting their note.

Most important of all his activities were his dealings with the Angus-controlled government—dealings which at times must have caused him no little concern. It will be remembered that Queen Margaret had handed over the young Earl of Huntly to Robert for safekeeping on the guarantee of Angus and other leading Scots. Angus, however, now decided that this arrangement was no longer desirable, and during the meeting of parliament in Edinburgh in November (1526) he obtained the queen mother's consent, whether by force or not we do not know, for Huntly's transfer to his own tender care. Parliament then ratified the move, declaring that Robert was no longer responsible to produce the young earl on Margaret's demand.[27] From this it would look as though Robert may have lost both the security and the interest which were his due for the loan he had made to Angus, since there is no evidence that the earl made any attempt to reimburse him at this time.

This was not the end of the question of Huntly as far as Robert was concerned, however, for on August 19, 1527, an agreement between him and Angus was ratified by the Lords of the Council. Unfortunately the text of the document is missing, but it probably was a contract whereby Angus handed back to Robert the custody of the earl while he was absent on an expedition to the north of Scotland. Robert accepted the responsibility of taking care of the young nobleman, giving as surety for his safekeeping and redelivery by December 15, a guarantee to pay 10,000 marks. Angus was back in Edinburgh by December 4 and Huntly being turned over to him, the agreement was cancelled.[28]

This arrangement indicates that although out of the government, Robert was still on friendly terms with Angus, a friendship no doubt stimulated by the fact that as one of the wealthiest men in the country he could be very useful in times of financial stringency. It was probably because of this that he received a considerable number of special favors. For example, when in

1517 the Earl of Arran had led an army against the castles of Hume and Wedderburn held by Angus' followers, Robert had failed to appear with his retainers. Then more recently when Angus had attacked Cockburnspath, Robert had shown the same unwillingness to give his support. Since both of these expeditions were in the name of the king, for these omissions he would normally have suffered deprivation of his feudal holdings; but nothing of the sort took place. Instead, on June 19, 1526, he was freely pardoned for his *proditoria absentia* from the two expeditions.[29] Similarly in December of the same year he obtained, over the king's signature, exemption from all personal appearance in any sheriff's court, and "of all passing apoun assisis." This meant that he was freed from attendance under pain of fine, at any sheriff's court which was supposed to meet every forty days, and also from being summoned to take part in courts which the crown appointed for a specific purpose.[30]

It may have been that the favor of Angus also made possible at this time another step forward in Robert's social ascent as well as his provision for his family. Robert, his son by Elizabeth Crawford, and Barbara Mowbray of Barnbougle, his ward, were now both probably about fifteen or sixteen years of age. Since he and Elizabeth would undoubtedly be anxious, owing to the upset condition of the country, to see the earlier agreement made with John Mowbray put into effect as soon as possible, he brought the matter to parliament, in order that Robert junior's name might be changed to Mowbray. There might have been objections from various quarters but when Robert presented his request supported by John Logan, Laird of Restalrig and Robert's feudal overlord in Leith, Gilbert Wauchop of Nudry, and others, parliament which was dominated by Angus concurred, clearing the way for Robert junior to become the Laird of Barnbougle and the Baron of Inverkeithing.[31] Thus Robert provided for another member of his family, this time his youngest son.

The marriage of Robert junior gives abundant evidence of his father's importance, an importance which, strangely enough for Scotland of those days, rested upon his business and his wealth. Few Scottish merchants had risen to such a position by the end of the third decade of the century, although there is little doubt that the middle class was on the march. This second alliance, therefore, which Robert had made with one of the houses of the lesser nobility was a sign and a forerunner of what was to come. Some Scottish merchants, although far behind the leaders in trade in lands such as England and France, were pressing forward by means of their financial power to positions of greater social prestige and higher rank.

While carrying on a "banking" business and acting as an agent for other people including the Earl of Angus, Robert had also been able to devote considerable attention to his own holdings in real estate, which led him into a number of court battles. As pointed out earlier, he had obtained from the crown the ward and marriage of David, Lord Drummond, but by some means or other, Sir James Shaw of Sauchy had gained possession of the young man's person which he refused to surrender. Consequently, in final desperation, early in the year 1527 Robert took action against Sir James, had him declared a rebel and "put to the horn," which meant that all his property was forfeited. Robert then bought from the king for the nominal sum of £20, Sir James' lands. This was probably a move to force the disobedient noble to obey the king's orders, for once deprived of his property he quickly submitted, relinquishing David Drummond to Robert. Had someone else purchased the escheated property meanwhile, Sir James would have been able to regain possession only with considerable difficulty, but as Robert, who was interested primarily in obtaining possession of his ward, held the land, he turned it back to the original owner once his demands were satisfied. Robert's action in this case shows not only his ability to use the courts to accomplish his purposes, but also, by his returning of the land to Sir James, his apparent unwillingness to make enemies unnecessarily. He probably could have held the land even though he had gained possession of Drummond, but he did not, no doubt winning Sir James' friendship for the future.[32]

An even greater victory was his forcing of the newly installed ninth Earl of Crawford to relinquish his hold on the lands and villages of Balhungy and Ardesty, and two parts of the lands and village of Downycan, Forfar. Although Robert had purchased these from the earl's grandfather in 1511 he seems never to have enjoyed undisputed possession since 1512. Up to 1527 he had probably been too busy with government affairs to assert effectively anything more than his title to the property. Once he was free of the encumbrance of the office of comptroller he began to take action, and on November 8 he sued the Earl of Crawford before the Lords of the Council. He charged the earl, his father Alexander, and his grandfather John with having unlawfully taken up the rents of his land, practically ever since its purchase. The loss resulting from this amounted to 7 chalders of bere worth 16s. the boll and 3 chalders of wheat worth 18s. the boll as well as £30 for the yearly rents and dues of Kirkbuddo. The earl failed to answer Robert's summons both at this time and on the 22nd, so the Lords proceeded with the suit, ordering the swearing in of witnesses. When the case came up finally for trial on December 16 the Earl of Crawford was present and protested that since he had been unable to answer the previous summonses, nothing should be done to his prejudice. But when the Lords were prepared to give sentence the following day he was again absent, and as he made no defense Robert obtained a verdict against him, with authority to collect the sums involved.[33] This was no small victory as Crawford was a powerful noble whose support was actively sought by both political parties in the country.

That Robert was always prepared to wage a fierce battle to

protect his possessions appears also in a rather curious case in which a certain James Johnson of Edinburgh sued him for an unnamed sum of money before the official of the Archbishop of St. Andrews. The dispute must have been over a contract, a marriage, or a will, cases subject to the church courts. Robert, finding himself ordered to pay, appealed to Rome, but his action did not prevent Johnson from seizing his property until he carried the matter to the council. This body postponed the case until May 19, 1528,[34] after which it disappears from sight, although Robert no doubt regained possession of his lands. That he appealed to Rome is rather curious for it is one of the very few references to his having any dealings with the church. In fact, one is struck by their scarcity. Only when he was faced with the loss of property by an ecclesiastical judgement did he think of carrying the matter to the highest ecclesiastical courts.

Although primarily occupied during this period with his various business projects, Robert had by no means lost interest in what was going on in the world at large. Thus even during his respite from official responsibilities in Scotland he continued to concern himself with the affairs of Denmark. Despite Christian II's inability to regain his throne the Scots were very sympathetic to his cause. For one thing, Frederick, the new Danish king, did not treat Scottish merchants too well; and for another, Christian's envoy, Dr. Alexander Kinghorn, spent considerable time in both England and Scotland endeavoring to persuade the two kingdoms to provide aid for the exiled monarch. Most important of all, however, it seems that Christian himself paid a visit to Scotland as well as to England, during which he may have stayed with Robert Barton. His success was such that Henry VIII tried to persuade the emperor to do something, and both the earls of Moray and Angus lamented over the exile's misfortunes, wishing that they could help him; but none of them took any action. The Archbishop of St. Andrews, one of the most practical, or at least the most truthful of his sympathizers, told Christian that about all he could do was invoke the help of God.[35]

The only person who seems to have been ready to do more than talk was Robert. For one thing he provided money to purchase the release of certain of Christian's sailors and skippers who had been arrested by the Scottish authorities, probably for piratical activities. In return he received, on September 23, 1527, from Gottschalk Ericsson, Christian's chancellor, one tun of the best gunpowder, ten and a half tuns of bombard powder, 98 pikes, 58 halberds, 300 hand bombards with their necessary equipment as security for the £27 5s. which he had expended. But his support of Christian went even further than this. Some years later it was proven by Robert's heirs that he had actually expended around this time, on Christian's behalf, some 10,000 gulden for munitions and the like, for which he had received no repayment.[36] These facts speak for themselves. Moreover a letter from Frederick I to Francis I in January, 1528, indicates that he regarded Robert as one of Christian's chief allies. He reported that since Christian had been in Scotland seeking aid from Robert Barton and David Falconer, he hoped that the French king would use his influence with James and the nobles to prevent these two supporters of the exile from putting any schemes against him into effect.[37] For the time being, however, Frederick needed to have no fear, since Robert would soon be busy with more important matters closer to home, as new developments were about to take place on the Scottish political scene.

XII

Recalled to Duty

James V, by 1528 in his seventeenth year, at a time in history when maturity came early, was beginning to resent the influence and domination of the Earl of Angus. At the same time his mother and various nobles, jealous of the earl's position of predominance, fanned the embers of the king's antagonism, with such effect that in the last days of May it burst forth into full flame. Immediately finding widespread support, on June 19 James issued a proclamation prohibiting Angus or any of his party from coming within seven miles of his royal person. There matters rested for a little more than two weeks, during which time James gathered sufficient forces for the next move. On July 6, surrounded by a strong group of anti-Angus nobles, he came to Edinburgh where he proceeded to change his principal officials, appointing Gavin Dunbar, Archbishop of Glasgow, chancellor in Angus' stead, and Lord Maxwell provost of Edinburgh in place of Douglas of Kilspindie, the earl's uncle. Angus, himself, he commanded to retire north of the River Spey, while George, Angus' brother, and Douglas of Kilspindie he ordered to be imprisoned in alternate months as security for the earl's good behaviour.[1] It was the beginning of the end for Angus.

The finances of the country were now found to be in a very precarious state since Angus had appropriated for himself or his supporters most of the royal revenues, leaving the comptroller's coffers practically empty. Therefore, at a meeting of the council held in Stirling on August 10, the treasurer, who still had some money on hand, agreed to pay to the comptroller the sum of £2,000 with the understanding that the latter would return it when he had received the revenues due him from the royal property. As guarantors of the comptroller's promise, the Earl of Argyle, Erskine of Haltoun, and the comptroller himself bound themselves to see that, when parliament was held in September, Adam Otterburn of Auldhame, the comptroller, and Robert Barton of Over Barnton, or "uthir thre burges" would become security for the treasurer's loan.[2] The government was apparently planning to call in the "moneyed interests" to help maintain it in power.

Although there is no evidence that the financiers named gave the desired guarantees, it is certain that parliament, when it met, dealt drastically with the Douglases. Angus, George Douglas his brother, and Douglas of Kilspindie were all found guilty of treason and their possessions declared forfeited to the crown.[3] Angus, however, did not submit quietly to these decisions. He immediately dispatched his daughter and the young Earl of Huntly, who was still in his hands, south into England, and took steps to strengthen the defenses of Tantallon Castle and his other strongholds against any possible attack. At the same time, he issued a statement declaring that he was a loyal subject of the king but that he was being maligned and attacked by certain royal advisers who were his enemies.[4]

In reply to Angus' preparations James made two halfhearted raids on Tantallon Castle and Coldingham Priory, another of Angus' holdings, but by these actions he accomplished little or nothing. He was apparently awaiting the organization of an effective army. One of his difficulties was lack of arms. It was probably at this point that Robert again entered the picture for he still had in his possession the munitions deposited with him by Gottschalk Ericsson, the agent of Christian II of Denmark. These he now turned over to the Scottish king for employment in the attack on Angus. James, strengthened by this acquisition as well as by the rallying to his colors of many of the nobles and common people, and by the seizure of some of the cannon in Dunbar Castle, Albany's stronghold, thereupon made his way southward to Tantallon. The fortress, however, was too strong to be captured and after some futile fighting the disappointed king returned to Edinburgh.

Then came the most depressing of all news. As the guns were being withdrawn from before the castle, Angus had sallied forth, capturing the whole artillery park and killing David Falconer of Leith who was acting as captain of the infantry. Although Angus immediately afterwards returned the cannon to the king, the latter never forgave him for the insult.[5]

Shortly after this unfortunate victory, Angus won another which lowered him further in the estimation of the middle class. On November 25 the *Litill Martin*, now owned by David Falconer's widow and her son Peter, went ashore just to the north of Berwick. The local inhabitants, aided by Angus' forces, thereupon despoiled it of both cargo and tackle, an act which did not add to the earl's popularity in the commercial circles of Edinburgh.[6]

During all this time the king's greatest need had been money. The income from the forfeited lands of Angus and his accomplices falling to the crown might have solved the problem but for the fact that even before parliament had pronounced judgement the anti-Douglas nobles like so many vultures had appropriated most of it. In these circumstances, James' only recourse was to refuse to grant the charters of assedation for these lands until the nobles had rid the country of the convicted traitors. Legally he had the right to collect the revenues from these lands which remained in his power until the nobles met his conditions. In the light of the scarcity of royal funds, one cannot but suspect that this may have been a maneuver demanded by the comptroller's guarantors, among whom was probably Robert Barton, in order that they might have some protection against a royal default.[7]

Meanwhile, the Earl of Angus had been moving towards his final downfall. On December 12, 1528, the representatives of England and Scotland signed a treaty providing compensation for the raids of the men of Liddisdale on England and guaranteeing mercy to the Douglases if they would humbly seek the Scottish king's mercy and surrender Tantallon Castle. As Angus, however, was not willing to accept this arrangement, a stalemate resulted which was not overcome until Robert Barton assumed his old position in the government.[8]

According to Lindsay of Pitscottie, the king, while at Stirling in March, 1529, replaced quite a number of his officers whom he mistrusted because of their Angus connections. Among these were Sir James Colvile of Ochiltree, the comptroller, and Sir Robert Cairncross, the treasurer, in whose places he appointed Robert Barton to whom he also gave the offices of "maister of his cunze," and Great Custumar of the Realm, the latter appointment being for life. On the day of this revolution (March 6), Colvile appeared before the Lords protesting that although he was always ready to fulfil the duties of comptroller, he would now, in the light of their action, no longer consider himself responsible to provide for the king's household. The only reply which he received from the Lords was their order to Robert to pay him one-third of his over-expenditures at the close of the next Audit of the Exchequer and the balance as he received revenues from the king's lands.[9]

Robert was not in office very long before he went into action. On March 8, two days after his reappointment, he obtained a letter under the Secret Seal guaranteeing that the king would

make no gifts of the royal casualties or property under the
Signet, Privy, or Secret Seals without his approval. This was
a very important move since it would enable him to block the
granting not only of royal lands, but also of any Angus lands
which might escheat to the crown on the earl's surrender. That
this was his intention became clear on the 12th when the king
issued a letter under the Secret Seal annulling all gifts of
escheated lands whether they were those of the Angus party,
of others guilty of major crimes, of any guilty of "wilful error
in assize" (i.e., giving false verdicts), or of criminals not
"convictit or declarit" guilty at the time of the gift or before
Robert had become treasurer and comptroller. The latter then
appeared before the Lords of the Council, demanding the
revocation of the grants of these escheats since they had been
obtained through inopportune solicitation without the advice
of the treasurer, contrary to a royal writ of 1526 and an act of
parliament. In response to this request, the Lords thereupon
annulled all gifts of escheated lands which were not counter-
signed by the treasurer. At the same time, Robert also insisted
that the council hear any royal case whenever he might present
it, lest the crown suffer loss through delay. To this likewise the
Lords agreed, and the same day had to stand by their decision
when the Laird of Colinton's representative appeared with a
protest against a summons of error which had been issued
against him on the complaint of Lord Livingstone. He complained that since it was not the day for royal cases, the writ
should be quashed. Robert, however, insisted that the Lords
should hear a royal suit whenever presented, and apparently won
his point.[10] By these means he hoped to straighten out the
country's financial tangle.

Having progressed thus far, Robert next turned his attention
to bringing about Angus' submission and departure from the
country. Since he had known the earl and had enjoyed his
confidence, his personal influence with him would be of no

little importance. Therefore, he assumed the responsibility of negotiating with the rebels for their surrender. From information contained in a letter issued under the Signet on March 23, it is clear that Robert went to Tantallon on the king's behalf where he carried on discussions with such success that he obtained the agreement of both sides in the dispute. Angus, his brother, and his uncle agreed to surrender Tantallon along with all their other strongholds on the Marches, to cast themselves upon the king's mercy, and to leave the country. The king on his part promised that he would then consider pardoning them. At the same time—and in this Robert's hand is very evident—James also consented that all Angus' lands should be handed over to the treasurer or other royal officials, while those escheated lands already granted to nobles would be recovered as soon as possible in order that they might be placed under the same supervision and care. The king also granted that anyone of whom Robert approved could bring him the key of Tantallon which he had promised on Robert's pleas not to demolish, and that even if Robert made requests on the rebels' behalf it would not be counted as a crime. In connection with this last provision he permitted Alexander Drummond, at Robert's intercession, to return home. The others, however, found themselves obliged to remove across the Tweed.[11]

The evidence concerning the negotiations and their results does not seem to bear out Calderwood's statement that when James chased out the Angus faction, seizing their lands, he was not acting honestly or fairly. It seems rather that he fulfilled his agreement, an agreement which was probably less drastic than it would have been had not Robert conducted the negotiations. Indeed, throughout this final act of the war between James and Angus, Robert appears as the dominant figure, striving to bring peace and some measure of security to the country. Neither the higher clergy nor the leading nobles

possessed influence with both sides in the quarrel, comparable
to that of the businessman of Leith.

This is borne out by one who was able to be more objective
than most observers. Alexander Kinghorn had arrived from
Denmark at the end of March, 1529, to take possession of the
arms and munitions which Christian had left in Robert's care
and with which James had equipped his expedition against
Tantallon. Robert explained the situation, claiming that the
king had compelled him to hand over the arms, and asking that
he should be given a month's notice before Christian wished to
use the supplies. If this were done he promised faithfully that
he would do Christian good service. Kinghorn in his report to
Christian explained that Robert was holding the reins of almost
all the government in his hands, being the king's chief adviser
on all financial matters, the chief accountant, treasurer,
customs officer, and master of the mint. He seems to have felt
that Christian need not worry about the return of the munitions
since Robert, who was his chief Scottish supporter, virtually
controlled the country.[12]

The comments of Kinghorn are very illuminating, as they
indicate the power Robert possessed. It looks a little as though
he had, in a way, succeeded to Angus' position by virtue of
his importance as a financier. The old order was beginning to
change when the businessman was replacing the feudal baron as
the real power behind the throne. Probably most Scots of
Robert's own day would not have seen this. That a Scot from a
foreign background, however, grasped the significance of his
position points to the fact that power was indeed beginning to
pass to a new element in society.

Robert's acquisition of power, on the other hand, never
made him forget his duties to the crown. Not long after the
temporary settlement of the Angus problem he went back to
another which had caused trouble during his previous term of
office. It will be remembered that in July, 1525, there had been

a dispute over the question of who should make composition or pay the price of the wardship of Inverugy. Robert had claimed that the Earl of Errol, the Royal Marshal, should do so as he had received the ward from the crown. Eventually the earl acknowledged this responsibility, but failed to make it good by paying the 2,250 marks due. It would look as though he had met the situation by remitting 200 marks and persuading Robert to act as his surety for the balance. On June 3, 1529, Robert finally succeeded in forcing the earl to come to an arrangement for liquidating the debt. The latter promised to pay 800 marks more by the end of the Exchequer, and 625 at each of the succeeding quarter days of Martinmas and Whitsun. The document containing this agreement Robert had recorded in the *Acts of the Lords* on June 4.[13] The same day he also had it enacted that the composition made with Lord Ogilvy for a slaughter which he had committed should be paid directly to him for meeting the overexpenditures of an earlier treasurer, Sir John Campbell of Lundy, who had been patiently awaiting repayment of the monies owing to his accounts.[14]

At the same time he was occupied with another difficult situation. During the first three weeks of June the king had been traversing the border lands trying to establish peace by forcing the local lords to submit or by hanging them without compunction. Finally at Jedburgh he had established a band or agreement for the good rule of the area, and the council had taken hostages whom they had incarcerated in Edinburgh Castle to make sure that the agreement was maintained. For some reason, not quite clear in the documents, the king felt this to be a wrong action. Therefore on July 14 William Scott of Balwerie, Robert Barton, and James Creighton appeared before the Lords of the Council and on behalf of the king, protested against their action in this matter on the ground that it would cause further trouble on the borders.[15]

Throughout the second and third quarters of the year Robert

must have spent much of his time with the king. He was at Jedburgh with the court in the middle of June, while on the 21st of the following month he witnessed one charter in Edinburgh and another on August 6, in Stirling.[16] It would look as though he was attempting to work out some effectual means of supervising the royal expenditures. There were, of course, normal fixed revenues such as returns from royal estates and customs, and customary expenditures such as payment for justice ayres, the purchase of clothes, food, and accommodation for the royal court. But there were at the same time the uncertain expenditures of the king who had continually to give donations of largesse, to pay gambling debts, and the like. These Robert now seems to have consolidated into a "Privy Purse Account," which would facilitate the keeping of records, if nothing else.[17] He also insisted that the royal revenues should not be held responsible for the payment of various unwarranted demands such as the upkeep of five Italian minstrels who had formerly been supported from the revenues of the chamberlain of Garioch.[18] A cleaning of the financial Augean stables seems to have been his ambition as well as the country's most urgent need.

His great opportunity to deal with the whole problem came in August with the opening of the Audit of the Exchequer. Under his eagle eye the accounts of custumars, baillies, and sheriffs were closely examined and searched for defalcations of every type. On August 6 the custumars of Whithorn and Wigtown, despite their pleas that the continual state of war had kept ships from their ports, were obliged to make a part payment to the comptroller, rendering accounts for the first time since 1521. Six days later Ninian Stewart, sheriff of Bute, tried to avoid paying certain rents to the crown on the ground that he had never received the revenues of the king's victuals and cattle from the lordship of Bute which he had rented for five years when Ochiltree was comptroller. Robert, however, stepped in insisting that he should pay all dues for which he was responsible and obliging him to give guarantees for his compliance. At the same session, as he had done at earlier audits, Robert also sued the baillies and provost of Dysart for the "custom salt" of all their salt exports, amounting to some £100 annually, with the demand that they should meet their obligations each year and not wait until he took action against them in the courts. Furthermore, he instituted a suit to force Dysart to meet its other fiscal responsibilities, which previously it had done only in part. In the succeeding days of the audit Robert successfully sued others such as David Grandestoune of Kingask and Duncan Campbell of Glenorchy who had interfered with the crown's lands or had failed to pay for lands which they had leased, to the impoverishment of the king.[19] He was determined that every official and tenant of the crown should pay the money he owed.

Yet in spite of all his efforts Robert was not able to end the financial year with a balance. Colvile, as comptroller, had run continually into debt, closing his accounts with a deficit of £530 in 1526, £1,245 in 1527, and £2,094 in 1528, despite an increase of the revenues by more than £1,000 a year. During the period from August 20, 1528, to March 7, 1529, he received £6,624 14s. 7d., but ended with a deficit of £2,184. Burdened with this inheritance as well as troubled by the turmoil of the country, Robert since March 7 had done his utmost to collect the royal revenues, but his success had not been outstanding. The total income for his six months' tenure of office was £2,330 and his "clear" deficit, which included the £1,000 to Colvile and the repayment of £774 5s. 3d. owing to himself since 1525, amounted to £3,536 18s. 11½d. Since he as treasurer, however, still had £1,102 on hand, he obtained the consent of the Lords to apply this sum against his deficit, thus reducing it to some £2,434, which still amounted to about one-third of the total annual revenues of £8,954. Something drastic would have to be done if the country were to attain financial stability.[20]

The difficulty of the situation was emphasized if that were possible, by pleas from various royal officials who were seeking supplies or payment for their various expenditures. Colin Campbell, Earl of Argyle, pleaded for supplies to enable him to deal with rebels who were causing trouble in the Isles. In answer to this request the Lords, with the consent of the treasurer, dispatched to the west one cannon, two falcons, two gunners, two wrights, and three barrels of powder. The limited amount of supplies indicates how poverty-stricken was the government. A few days later Patrick Wemys of Pittincrieff petitioned for money to pay the garrison of the castle of Inchgarvie. Added to this, in September Robert faced the necessity of reimbursing his predecessor as treasurer, the Laird of Lundy, for his overexpenditures, but fortunately he could postpone this as Lundy was out of the country. On top of all these demands, there were cases of some royal officials being overpaid while others had received nothing at all.[21] Altogether the financial difficulties of the government appeared insoluble, with everything in confusion and at cross-purposes, despite all that Robert might attempt to do.

From what has been said so far, it is clear that Robert since March had been very much occupied with "the king's business." This did not preclude, however, his continuing to carry on his own affairs, although there is little doubt that he was not able to take as much interest in them as when free of political responsibilities. For instance, although in February and early April there are two references to the mercantile activities of Alexander Barton, not until April 24 is there any evidence that Robert was once again turning his attention to such matters. At that time the ship of John Dolbuy arrived from Veere, and in it Robert imported 16 tuns of wine, more than half the cargo. On May 20 he received 2 tuns of wine from the ship of John Litill arriving from Flanders, and the same day he sent off 4 dakers

of hides aboard *Le Bark de Hadington*, destination not recorded.[22]
In all of this there is no reference to his own ships, nor is there
any evidence that he had still the wide contacts and customers
which had been his a few years earlier. As he was growing
older, he probably found that trade made too many demands
upon his time and energy, with the result that he engaged in it
only spasmodically and on a smaller scale.

More active was his interest in his landed estates. In the
middle of June, while the king was at Jedburgh dealing with
the troubles caused by adherents of Angus, he issued a charter
to Robert. The estate of Over Barnton with its castle, the manor
and lands of East Bewlaws, and the lands of Foulfurd which
Robert Barton junior had earlier received from his father but
which he now returned, the king erected into the free barony of
Over Barnton. This was a reward for Robert's services to himself
and his predecessors, particularly against the English, as well as
for Robert's expenses in his various offices. At the same time he
quitclaimed the lands of all dues, except attendance at one
head court a year, and promised that if ever the land came into
ward, it would be freed of all dues on payment of 40s. for each
year of the ward.[23] Although Robert had held the lands of
Over Barnton as a free barony since the original grant in 1507,
by this act he had all his land lying in the neighborhood of
Edinburgh consolidated into one holding on the most favorable
terms.

While thus consolidating and expanding his holdings Robert
also found himself under the continual necessity of defending
them against encroachment. During 1528 he continued to
press his suit against the Earl of Crawford. As has already been
seen, Crawford, his father, and his grandfather before him had
all been taking the revenues of Ardesty, Balhungy, and other
lands which in 1511 the grandfather had sold to Robert. In
December, 1527, he had obtained judgement against the
movable goods of the living earl, but as the latter had sold them

and had feed his lands to his son Alexander before September 2, 1528, he actually possessed nothing which Robert could seize. This was apparently a typical Crawford trick, but Robert was not finished. On December 7 the case came once again before the Lords of the Council who on Robert's petition ordered their judgement enforced against the Crawford lands.[24]

How the sentence was to be executed did not become clear until March 16, ten days after Robert had reassumed his office of comptroller. On that date the king under the Great Seal granted him the lands and mills of Kirkbuddo and of Hobmill held by the Earl of Crawford. Robert had finally succeeded in forcing the earl to compensate him for the rents amounting to £646 illegally taken from his lands of Balhungy, Ardesty, and Downycan by three generations of Crawford earls. To meet this bill the earl turned over to Robert the abovementioned lands which brought in an annual revenue of £34 15s. 2d. with the understanding that he could redeem them on payment of the principal sum. Thus Robert was to receive over 5 per cent on the money still owing, despite any ecclesiastical disapproval of the taking of "usury." Less than a month later Robert sold " terras et villas de Balhungy, et binam partem suam terrarum et ville de Downycane, in Baronia de Downy, vic. Farfare," to George Haliburton of Gask.[25] The disposal of this property freed him from the responsibility of carrying on a continual battle with the Earl of Crawford, while at the same time, he now had the assurance that from the recently acquired property he would obtain the revenues which were his due.

While working towards the settlement of this dispute over the Crawford lands Robert succeeded also in concluding a suit over his wardship of the Mowbray estates. Early in the reign of James IV, James Dundas of that Ilk had received from the king the promise of the guardianship of the Barony of Dunmany if John Mowbray its laird should die leaving a minor heir. This promise, however, James nullified along with many others when in 1493 he revoked all grants made while he, himself, was a minor. Nevertheless, on Mowbray's death Dundas claimed possession of Dunmany, and without any of the necessary legal formalities had since that time been lifting the rents of the lands of Echlyn, one of its properties. Naturally Robert, who had received all of Mowbary's estate in ward, resented this action but he does not seem to have pursued the matter very vigorously until 1528 when he was contemplating the marriage of his son to the Mowbray heiress. He then hailed Dundas before the Lords, who appointed arbitrators. As Dundas, however, refused to accept their decision, on February 11, 1529, Robert demanded immediate judgement which he obtained, the Lords ordering Dundas to pay the 200 marks he had collected. Although the plaintiff had made a strong bid to hold the land, he now submitted and Robert agreed to accept the misappropriated rents and drop the case without requiring the imposition of a penalty.[26]

Perhaps of more importance than either trade or real estate were his financial operations. As seen earlier, at the close of the audit in August, 1525, Robert was the creditor of a number of officials who had failed to remit amounts they owed the government. He had provided for these defaulters the necessary sums out of his own pocket as loans, presumably receiving interest for his service. Neither Lord Lyndsay of the Byres nor Campbell of Glenorchy, however, had met his obligation by the time Robert returned to office, as they no doubt felt that the upset condition of the country made it hardly necessary. This was not Robert's attitude, and in July, 1528, shortly after the king had taken over the reins of government, he sued both men before the council. This court took no immediate action but continued the cases until October with the assurance that if no defense were offered, the defendants would be made to pay.[27]

Another example of his financial dealings appears the following year on August 27 after the close of the audit when he became surety for Hugh Campbell of Loudon, sheriff of Ayr, who owed £500 to George Good and George Nicholl of Edinburgh, promising to pay them £250 at the end of September and a like sum at Christmas. In return for his backing of this note he received from Campbell the tacks of the churches and lands of Crawmond, presumably adjacent to his own of Crawmond Regis, and Abirleddy, which would no doubt bring him a good return on his money.[28]

Perhaps in the same category of "financial interests" was the continuing case of the piracy of Robert Fogo. Although the latter had gone to Denmark to stand trial, no one had appeared to press charges. Therefore, he demanded that the Scots who claimed over 9,000 gulden because of his action should bring the matter before the Lords of the Council. This was a foolish move for the council promptly found him guilty.[29] Fogo thereupon declared that since Robert Barton, William Clapperton, and others were involved with him they also should have to pay, perhaps because they had been shareholders in the *Litill Martin* or perhaps because they had received some of the loot. To this the council did not agree, with the result that Fogo and his associates in crime were ordered to make good the damage.[30] There the matter rested for the moment.

What occupied Robert's attention during the autumn and winter of 1529 is a matter of conjecture, although it is probable that he spent most of his time working on the question of the royal finances, for he was frequently with the court as it moved around the country.[31]

On May 19, 1530, in order to deal "with certain great matters," the king chose a special secret council in which he included Robert along with the two archbishops, a number of bishops, the earls of Moray and Rothes, the lords Erskine, Gray, Sir James Hamilton, and others.[32] It may have been that one of the special problems was that of finance, which would explain the need of the comptroller's participation. This

suggestion is perhaps borne out by a statement in a royal confirmation of a grant of land by David Chalmer of Seggidene to
Alexander Chalmer of Petty. The charter records that confirmation has been given with the consent of the king's familiar,
Robert Barton of Over Barnton.[33] Robert was apparently
continually looking over the king's shoulder to make sure that
he did not waste the royal patrimony.

Such vigilance was very necessary since rebellions in the
Highlands and a state of quasi-war on the Borders indicated that
the 1530 audit of the Exchequer might reveal serious shortages
in the royal finances. It was to help expedite the collection of
money owing to the crown, therefore, that Robert appeared
before the Lords on July 21 with a letter under the king's
signet, demanding that during the time of the audit, the Lords
deal with no summonses or other matters but those pertaining
to the crown. To this request the Lords gave their hearty
consent, issuing a decree that on account of the plague, the
Exchequer should be removed to Linlithgow where the audit
should be carried out as expeditiously as possible by limiting
all cases to those directly related to the Exchequer.[34]

The month of August must have been a difficult and trying one
for the man holding the combined offices of treasurer and comptroller. There seem to have been a good many instances in
which sheriffs and chamberlains arrived with accounts that
were not properly kept, or did not balance and so failed to
produce the revenues expected. At times, dishonesty and
financial ineptitude went hand in hand. In one instance, for
failure to pay their legitimate dues to the crown, Robert had
to take action against the abbot and monks of the Abbey of
Dunfermline.[35] But much more important were the defalcations of various lay officials. The account of Peter Scott,
chamberlain of Strathearn, was short by £173 8s. 8d., that of
Ninian Stewart, sheriff of Bute, already in difficulties, lacked
some £70, and that of James Grant of Fruchy, tenant of

Glencharny and Ballnadalloch, some 1,800 marks. In each case
Robert assumed the debt for them, paying the money owing to
the Exchequer out of his own pocket and taking their promises
to pay. By the end of the month Grant had met his obligations,
but apparently the others had not.[36] Only by Robert's personal
action in this way could anything be made out of the accounts,
but it was rather hard on the official who had to carry a considerable part of the royal debts on his own shoulders.

With regard to the defalcations of others Robert seems to
have been determined to force the matter through to a decisive
verdict. It may be that whenever he felt that the official involved
could pay, even out of his own assets, he attempted to make him
meet his obligations. One good example is the case of the custumar of Perth, Alexander McBroke, whose name seems to be
symbolic. His accounts were some £23 short of what they
should have been according to the cocket books. Therefore, the
clerks of the cocket were ordered to appear with their records
whose accuracy they had to guarantee by oath, and if McBroke
were still short of his proper return he would be obliged to
pay the balance out of his own pocket.[37]

While pressing hard upon inefficient and dishonest collectors
of revenues, Robert was also apparently employed in other
matters. On August 17, while in Linlithgow, he acted as a royal
justice, coming down with a heavy hand on John Lord Hay of
Yester, principal sheriff of Peebles. He had received from the
king the custody of two thieves whom he had handed over to
another John Hay for safekeeping. As the latter, however, had
allowed them to escape, Robert ordered the sheriff to be
imprisoned for his deputy's negligence.[38] This episode is the
only evidence that Robert ever acted in this legal capacity,
but it indicates how busy he was at this time.

On September 4 Robert presented his own accounts as
treasurer. The Lords Auditors were no doubt, somewhat
surprised and pleased at the result. From August 2, 1529, to the

above date, his total income had been £12,914 14s. 7d. while expenditures, despite expeditions to the west and to the borders, had come to only £12,236 8s. 2½d. leaving a balance of £772 12s. 9d. for the use of which he promised to give account at the next audit.[39] When one remembers the methods employed to collect the feudal revenues and the state of the country, one cannot but be amazed that Robert as a treasurer should have come up with such a result on the operations of the year 1529-30.

Unfortunately, it is impossible to determine how well he did as comptroller. It has been taken for granted by various editors of documents such as the *Register of the Great Seal*, the *Treasurer's Accounts*, and the *Exchequer Rolls* that in August, 1530, he was no longer comptroller. This, however, is not the case, but the difficulty is that his comptroller's accounts do not seem to be extant, except in some references to them in his 1531 returns. Consequently, one cannot give any exact information concerning the results of his financing of the household. That a good many of the responsible officials reported is evident. Moreover, Colvile received £265 from them, and when Robert had paid him the £1,000 in accordance with the Lords' earlier instructions, there remained only £933 still owing to Colvile from his previous deficit. But the £1,000 payment undoubtedly left quite a hole in Robert's accounts, probably being the reason for his large deficit of £7,467 8s. 4d. mentioned in 1531 as reported in 1530.[40]

Why did the household records not survive? It is impossible to say, but it may be that Robert's accounts revealed large-scale peculation by officials. If this were the case, a good many men would have been interested in destroying the incriminating documents. But whatever the explanation, it seems that Robert was becoming weary of carrying the country's financial load. He was probably over sixty years of age, which was old for those days, and the strain of providing a considerable part of the

16

capital for the government's operations was doubtless becoming too much for him. Consequently he seems to have felt that perhaps others might now shoulder the burden.

On September 10 he resigned his office as Lord High Treasurer, and sometime between October 30 and December 6 that of Comptroller of the Royal Household.[41] According to the charter granted to him in 1528 he was to be custumar of the kingdom for life, an office which, since it was apparently a sinecure, he may have continued to hold for the allotted time. The exact date of his resignation as head of the royal mint is not recorded, but it would seem certain that by the beginning of 1531, he had demitted all his public responsibilities, retiring finally to private life.

XIII

The Last Voyage

The decade of the thirties differed somewhat from the two which had preceded it. Whereas during the years 1513-1530 the ruler of Scotland had been a boy over whom various factions of Scottish nobles were continually squabbling and fighting, by 1530 that same boy had come to manhood with the determination that he would rule the country himself. The chief political party of the twenties, the Douglases, had suffered a mortal blow, resulting in the exile of its leader, the Earl of Angus, while the other disturbing force, Queen Margaret, had been successfully put in her place, so that James in his own name was now able to govern effectively. The only drawback was that his lack of funds kept him from attempting anything grandiose. Nevertheless, with peace and stability in the country, he could have a reasonable expectation of a modicum of prosperity which would in turn improve the government's financial condition. Thus, from the domestic point of view, the opening years of the fourth decade of the century held a promise of considerable improvement in Scotland's fortunes.

Somewhat the same optimism was also possible with regard to Scotland's foreign relations. Henry VIII of England was at this

time deeply involved in the matter of ridding himself of
Catherine of Aragon, a proceeding which might have serious
international repercussions. He was, therefore, very anxious
to remain on good terms with everyone, particularly the Scots,
since there was talk on the Continent of a crusade against
England. Such an expedition led by Catherine's nephew
Charles V of Spain and supported by the French and the Scots
would force him to fight on two fronts, a prospect he did not
relish, so for a time he was prepared to be almost polite, even
to his northern nephew. The latter, meanwhile, was also
seriously involved in the quest for a wife, a project which for
the next five or six years was to be a dominating factor in
Scotland's foreign policy. James found himself obliged to seek
a partner in many different courts of Europe, before he finally
succeeded in persuading the French king to give him his
daughter, Madeleine. Bapst in his work *Les Mariages de Jacques V*
gives a detailed account of James' search for a mate in which he
considered various princesses including the Duchess of Urbino;
Mary Tudor; Dorothea, the daughter of exiled Christian II; and
the Queen of Hungary. The negotiations concerning this matter,
however, although involving some excitement and interest,
threatened no war. Thus, as long as Henry of England was
occupied with his own marital problem, James was able to
carry on this relatively harmless foreign adventure without
either very great expense or serious danger.

Ultimately of much greater importance to Scotland than the
king's marriage was the influx from across the North Sea of
heretical religious beliefs. Although Martin Luther had nailed
his 95 Theses to the door of the church in Wittenberg on
October 31, 1517, his revolutionary views had obtained little
support in Scotland for a number of years. Patrick Hamilton,
it is true, was burned at St. Andrews in 1528 for preaching the
doctrine of justification by faith alone, but the new ideas did not
really begin to disturb the ecclesiastical or secular authorities

until the thirties. When they did come, they infiltrated into the country primarily from Denmark, where during the last years of Christian II's rule, Lutheranism had spread rapidly. By 1533 Christiern Pedersen's book, *Den rette vey till Hiemmerigis Rige* had been translated into broad Scots by John Gau, under the title of *The Richt Vay to the Kingdom of Hevine*.[1] This work, probably along with others, was imported into Scotland by both foreign and native merchants who were becoming the great carriers of Lutheran doctrine. Because of this commercial mode of transmitting evangelical views, the eastern seaboard ports were the principal points at which they gained entry to the country, and once in, they were hard to suppress. Moreover, the old Lollard tradition, which had never died, prepared at least some people to accept these doctrines. Despite all that church and state could do, Protestantism was influencing and even winning over individuals from among both laity and clergy. James, encouraged by the church, tried to restore orthodoxy, but he was able to achieve little against the tide which was now beginning to rise.[2]

In the midst of all this movement and development in the kingdom, Robert seems to have continued on his way, much as he had done before. Although he would be counted quite elderly in those days, his interest in what was going on around him, his decisiveness, his habit of asserting his rights, and his diligence in business, seem to have been much the same as ever.

Having officially brought his activities as Comptroller of the Royal Household to a close shortly after the end of the Audit of the Exchequer in August, 1530, he nevertheless continued to be responsible for all the accounts covering the period from the audit until his resignation. According to the record of September 7, 1531, he had received during these few months the sum of £2,019 4s. 2½d. and certain victuals, and had paid out £238 10s. 7d. which left a total balance, apparently including the victuals, of £1,981 19s. ½d. This sum the Lords applied to his deficit remaining in August, 1530, leaving an outstanding debt still owing to him of £5,485 9s. 3¼d. Colvile of Ochiltree who had once again become comptroller had received £9,000 18s. 7¼d. and victuals during his term of office, giving him a deficit of only £25 5s. 3½d., but when he added this to sums still due as a result of his earlier tour of duty, the government was in his debt for nearly £1,000.[3] Thus, the king and his councilors were able to administer the country only because Ochiltree and, more particularly, Robert were able to carry the country's debts.

It is at this point, however, that one of the complications in this situation makes its appearance. According to the practice of the time it was apparently permissible for the treasurer and the comptroller to make allowance in their Exchequer accounts for fees and charges which they owed to royal officials even though the latter had not been paid, presumably on the understanding that when the money came in, they would receive the sums owing. Robert had followed this practice, but once he was out of office, the various officials who were still unpaid began to demand that he should reimburse them for their services. He refused, claiming that this was not his personal debt, but that of the king, and when they took action against him personally before the courts, he appealed to the Lords of the Council for protection. He pointed out that the government still owed him a large sum of money, and that until it liquidated that debt, he could not meet all the royal servants' demands. The Lords thereupon (December 6) suspended the letters of suit, ordering that cases against him should be discontinued until the crown had reimbursed him for his expenditures.[4] The action of the council proved to be nothing more than a temporary respite, for during the Audit of the Exchequer in August, 1531, the Lords ordered Robert to pay the various scribes of the Exchequer the sum which had been allowed in his accounts for 1530 "conforme to the outdrawchtis of the samin."[5] This was a clear indication of the direction in which the wind was turning. He was soon to be faced with demands from various other individuals whom he would have to reimburse out of his own pocket.

No action was taken, however, during the 1532 audit, perhaps because Robert was one of the Lords Auditors which meant that he would be able to oppose any efforts to make him pay the crowns' creditors. But within some six months a certain Sir John Thomson, a priest, was suing him for wages which he declared Robert had not paid his brother who was one of the king's brewers. As he took the matter to the episcopal official of Lothian, Robert appealed to the council on the grounds that all such matters should come before it, and that the brewer had confessed on his deathbed that he had misappropriated some of the commodities under his care. The Lords thereupon forbade further action before the episcopal official which seems to have settled the matter.[6]

Not so successful was he in a number of similar cases. For instance, despite his protests that the council had guaranteed him protection he was ordered on May 27, 1533, to pay out of his own pocket some £23 owing to the family of the late Henry Borthwick, one of the king's gunners.[7] In December of 1537 David Lowry, a royal macer, sued him for about £16, his wages left unpaid for the years 1517, 1518, and 1522, while two weeks later the Falkland Pursuivant took action to obtain £10 which he had not received for his services during the year 1529-30. The Lords of the Council found Robert guilty on all points, ordering the issuance of letters to "poind" his goods.[8] These judgements were followed in the autumn and winter of 1538-39 by others equally unfavorable. Sir James Kincragy, Dean of Aberdeen, obtained judgement against him for £76, and Robert Fogo on January 16 was similarly successful in obtaining £20. The same day Robert Wood, "master brewster" to the king, claimed that the former comptroller owed him £56 4s., to which the latter replied that he had already given him 80 sheep in part payment. Wood tried to prove that the payment of sheep was for a debt owing to his "godmodir," but as his evidence was insufficient, the Lords ordered Robert to pay only 17 marks instead of the full amount.[9]

The case of this kind which had the most dramatic history was that of Duncan Dawson a collier who took action in March, 1534, to obtain £82, the balance owing to him of his "pur fee." The Lords of the Council after due consideration passed judgement against Robert, giving the pursuer the right to seize the ex-comptroller's goods for the debt. Dawson thereupon instructed the Ross Herald to take the action necessary to obtain the sum in question.

When the herald took action the records do not state, but according to his usual custom he went to a tavern which Robert had recently acquired in Edinburgh, and there he seized four tuns and a puncheon of claret, along with two small pieces of silver plate and a silver goblet. Having valued these as a part payment of the debt, he then demanded that Robert buy them back. Old though he may have been, Robert was by no means lacking in courage. Moreover, he probably felt considerable security in the knowledge of the king's favor. Therefore, he snatched the silver from the herald "and said planly that nane sic as he nor nane uthiris suld have ony thing pertening to him," and ejected the Ross Herald from the tavern. The old privateering spirit was by no means dead.

The herald thereupon broke his wand and took witness that Robert had refused to submit to the Lords' decrees. How long the council waited before taking action is not stated, but Robert, apparently to protect himself against further suit, in July, 1536, appealed to the king who issued an injunction to the Lords forbidding them to proceed with the matter. It was to no avail, however, for when the Lords summoned Robert to appear before them some time later, although he pleaded the king's discharge they declared it to be invalid since it had not been signed by the treasurer. In this decision they took refuge behind a law of parliament to keep the forfeited lands of the Angus faction from being squandered in gifts to importunate courtiers. The judgement which they then rendered was that Robert's goods should be escheated to the crown and he should be imprisoned for a year and a day.[10] The king, however, probably again intervened on behalf of his loyal old servant, for the sentence does not seem to have been enforced.

Yet whether enforced or not, the frustration and sense of ill-usage arising from these cases cannot but have been increased by his almost total lack of success in attempting to make those who owed him money pay their debts. As in his earlier term of office, he had met the shortages of many officials from his own pocket only to find that when he sought repayment the money was not forthcoming. Nor were the Lords of the Council too favorable to his efforts to force payment of these debts. Of some of the cases which he instituted during the four months December through March, 1530-31, against such men as Campbell of Glenorchy, Stewart of Garlies, and Crawford of Ayr, the outcomes are not revealed in the records.[11] But when the Lords of the Council quashed a judgement of a lower court against Ker of Dolphinston on the grounds that it was "unorderlie and without cognition in the cause," Robert's patience disappeared. He entered a vigorous protest that the council's action should not prevent him from suing for the payment of Ker's debt to the crown since he personally had assumed responsibility for it. Moreover, he claimed that the Lords had no right either to make him pay money except as recorded in his accounts or to compel him to change his accounts which were audited and closed.[12] Obviously he was afraid that the royal advisers might well attempt to make him pay debts which never had been his responsibility.

Such protests achieved very little. When during the summer of 1537 he instituted a suit against a priest, Sir William Rutherford, whom he accused of failing to see that certain penalties for which he had become surety at the justice ayre of Jedburgh were paid, he seems to have had no success. And just as little did he achieve in his other attempts which continued until December, 1538, to have the council enforce his demands.[13]

Why the Lords of the Council adopted this attitude is hard to say. One may surmise, of course, that all of Robert's lawsuits had no solid foundation. That the lower courts, on the other hand, accepted some of his claims would seem to indicate that in a number of instances at least, he had justice on his side. The correct answer may be found in the obligation which he received from the Lords on February 12, 1531, under the Secret Seal guaranteeing the gradual repayment of the money owed him by the king. The full text of the note makes the matter clear:

> We, be the tennour of this writ, with avis and of the lordis of our counsale and of our thesaure, oblissis us and oure successouris to content and pay to oure lovit familiar servitour, Robert Bertoun of Ovirbertoun, umquhile oure comptroller, his airis or assignais, the some of sex thousand, sevin hundreth lxxix lib. xv s. viii d., usuale money of this realme, in this maner eftir followand, that is to say, ane thousand pundis of the said money at our next chekker that is to be haldin this instant zeire, and the nixt zeire thareftir ane thousand pundis, and sa furth zeirlie, ilk zeire ane thousand pundis, unto the compleite payment of the said soume of sex thousand sevin hundreth lxxix lib. xv s. viii d., becaus the said Robert is fundin sa mekle superexpendit to us and to the auditouris of the saidis comptis.

The Lords registered this writ on February 23, just to make it the more certain; and in accordance with the agreement the treasurer paid the first £1,000 before the time of the Audit of the Exchequer.[14] It is possible that in promising to pay a sum larger than that which was actually owing they were not only taking care of interest, but also of the various claims which might be made against Robert or which he might make against others. If this were the case their attitude to the suits he instituted is somewhat more understandable, for they had made adequate provision for the liquidating of the royal debt.

Unfortunately for Robert, although the council's spirit was willing its accounting was weak, the result being that it was not able to pay the promised £1,000 out of ordinary revenue in 1533. Only after a tax had been levied on the ecclesiastical estate was the money forthcoming and even then with some difficulty.[15] The year 1534 saw a further payment of £1,000, which meant that the debt had been reduced in all by some £3,000.[16] But this was apparently the last instalment, for the king and his councilors had on hand other matters which demanded any available surplus.

It was not, however, that Robert had fallen from favor, for James V seems to have been deeply grateful for all that he had done while in office. This he indicated in a number of ways. For one thing, in May, 1531, he wrote a long and strongly worded letter to the Emperor Charles V demanding compensation on Robert's behalf for the *Black Barque* seized by Spaniards at Yarmouth in 1520. As Charles may not have been willing to listen to reason on this matter, a month later James again wrote, at the same time instructing the Snowdon Herald, who was conducting political negotiations with Charles at the moment, to speak to him about the matter. Yet for all this royal assistance Robert failed to obtain reimbursement for his losses. That the king was in earnest in making his demands, however, is shown by his going so far as to send the Falkland Herald to Spain in search of redress, and when he also reported no success, by his granting in 1539 of letters of reprisal to John Barton, Robert's son, and to Alexander his nephew. As Robert was too old to seek restitution in person the king bestowed upon the new generation the right to collect up to 20,000 ducats by force of arms.[17]

Another way in which the king indicated his regard for the former comptroller was manifested in the royal treatment of Archibald Douglas of Kilspindie, Angus' uncle, who in 1534 had returned to Scotland in the hope of being allowed to stay. To his pleas James would not agree, ordering him to leave forthwith. But until he could obtain passage on a ship he was permitted to live with Robert Barton. Although the latter had been on friendly terms with the Douglases in earlier days James was quite sure that he could depend on his primary loyalty to the crown.[18]

Two years later, in July of 1536, there is further evidence of the royal favor towards the former servant. On July 22 James granted to Robert protection from all lawsuits while he was out of the country on the king's business and for forty days after his return. In the same document he also forbade the Lords to do anything about Robert's deforcement of the Ross Herald referred to above. The reason for this grant was that Robert "be of gret age, febill and vaik in persoun."

Although not stated explicitly it would seem that James was planning to take Robert with him on his romantic voyage to France whither he was planning to go incognito to win a bride. Owing to bad weather, however, the voyage was abandoned after a few days, but it would seem obvious that Robert was not with the king, for on July 28 when James was still at sea Robert appeared before the Lords with the request that they register the royal letter of protection. Whether he sailed with the king when the latter went officially to France in September does not appear in the records although it is quite clear that his son John was present, returning in March, 1537.[19] James, himself, came home in May bringing with him as his bride Madeleine, the beautiful but consumptive daughter of Francis I, only to have her die within two months of their arrival.

The final act of royal grace to Robert took place the following year when James, after revoking all grants of land made since the beginning of his reign, restored to Robert and his son, Robert Mowbray of Barnbougle, because of the former's valor in the defense of the country against the English and his great expenditures in the office of comptroller, the lands of Over Barnton, East and West Bewlaws, and Foulfurd along with the property of Robert of Barnbougle which he had resigned for the purpose, as the Free Barony of Over Barnton. This grant James made with the approval of the Three Estates of Parliament, no doubt in the hope that it might help to relieve them of some of the financial obligation which they had to Robert.[20] On September 21, Robert and his son took formal possession of the recreated free barony. Thus to the end of his life Robert seems to have enjoyed the confidence and affection of his king.

With the ex-king of Denmark, Christian II, he was not nearly so popular. The Danish royal exile was still hopeful of regaining his throne with the aid of his sea captains, the division of his enemies, and the backing of the Scots. Of the last-mentioned Christian had pinned his hopes on Robert Barton and David Falconer, but now that Falconer was dead and Robert was old they were of little help.[21] The only thing which Robert might do was return the munitions which Christian had deposited with him some years earlier, but as they were no longer in Robert's hands owing to James' having used them against Angus, this would be difficult. To obtain his munitions Christian in 1531 wrote the Scottish monarch, but the latter would promise only that he would see that justice was done as quickly as possible. After a further delay James sent Christian another letter explaining that no court action could be taken until he remitted authorization for the institution of a suit against Robert in the proper form.[22] Whether this communication ever reached the addressee is not known, for in the preceding November he had fallen into Frederick of Denmark's hands to remain a prisoner for the rest of his life.[23]

Although this, as far as Robert could see, would be the end of his relations with Denmark, he was not to find relief quite so easily. Early in May, 1535, Peter Sauvenius, ambassador of Frederick's successor Christian III, arrived in Scotland seeking help, for his master was having difficulties with the Hanseatic League which had embraced the cause of Christian II. He brought a request that "Albert Bartuen" and "Albert Fagow" be sent over with five or six ships.[24] Apparently the Danes, forgetting the passage of years and remembering only the two Roberts' exploits, thought that they were still able to provide assistance. Thus both sides were vainly seeking Robert's help in the struggle for the Danish throne.

In this controversy it was Dorothea, a daughter of Christian II, and Countess Palatine of the Rhine who made the last move. Early in 1540 she wrote James a very sharp letter demanding that Robert be required to surrender the money and arms he had received from her father. The Scottish monarch replied to her demand by explaining that although he was always ready to see that justice was executed, he was quite sure that Robert had in no way been dishonest. Nevertheless to ease her mind he promised a full and complete investigation into the matter. Here, as far as it concerned Robert, the matter dropped, for before the inquiry could be made he had departed this life.[25] Thus the political problems of Denmark pursued him even to the end.

In much the same manner also, Anglo-Scottish relations kept forcing themselves upon him in his latter years. Although the two countries were officially at peace throughout the 1530's owing to Henry VIII's preoccupation with marital and religious problems, along the borders there was constant raiding which soon spread to the high seas. There are a number of references during these years to prizes captured by both Scottish and

English privateers, although the former seem to have marked up a better score by taking eight in March and seven on May 19, 1533. William Clapperton, John Ker, and John Barton, presumably Robert's son, were apparently doing well. Robert also, may have been involved financially, for late in 1532 or early in 1533 he along with Clapperton and some of the other sailors of Leith had a dispute with the Earl of Bothwell, Admiral of Scotland, over some prizes captured "at the west see." Yet the privateering was not all one-sided for Robert may have lost to English raiders in June, 1533, a ship carrying Mr. John Lauder to Flanders, on his way to Rome to sue the Archbishop of St. Andrews for not paying his taxes.[26] Thus in spite of the earlier influence of Dr. Magnus the old conflict with England had again raised its head.

His loss of a ship to English marauders points to the fact that his interest in his own trade had by no means ceased. This conclusion is supported by various other pieces of evidence. For one thing, when in 1531 a revolt broke out in the west James sent a plea to France for gunpowder. Whether he obtained it is uncertain, but about the same time Robert received £60 from the Lord High Treasurer to buy the necessary commodity, presumably abroad.[27] He was once again acting as a purchasing agent for the crown. Added to this he was doubtless also trading in his own interest, or perhaps his son John was carrying on the business. Although there are no extant references to Robert's commercial activities from 1531 to 1537, it is recorded in the Edinburgh Tron book for the latter year that in August he weighed two sacks 16 stone (about 1,000 lb. Troy) of wool, probably for export. During the following two years he sent abroad some five or six sacks of wool, as well as hides (eight dakers) and beef (eight lasts).[28] These were not large amounts, yet when compared to Edinburgh's total trade they represent the average or a little better than the average export per merchant.

Trade involved finance, and throughout this period Robert's

interest in banking was still considerable, although at times it is not easily separated from his other business activities. A good example was the case of the *Paul*. He had leased the vessel to Patrick Barcar who, however, suddenly died leaving his wife Helen Douglas and "sex small barnys" to carry on. The widow, with Robert's consent, appointed the captain and crew, only to have Robert Douglas, John Brown, and John Barton, perhaps some of Barcar's creditors, seize the ship and appoint a new crew. About this time Helen also died leaving her children to fend for themselves, and Robert to recover the ship any way he might. To safeguard his property Robert in 1538 demanded that the leader of the other party, Robert Douglas, appoint only a supercargo leaving the former captain and crew to operate the ship. To this Douglas and his associates finally agreed, on condition that he would not demand restitution without prior notice.[29]

Perhaps another indication of his activities as a financier is to be found in his dealings with Marjorie Bassindene, widow of Evangelist Passer. Passer, probably an Italian merchant or banker who had settled in Edinburgh, had become surety for their salaries to the six Italian minstrels of the king whom Robert had later struck from the payroll. On their removal from the royal household they had instituted suit against Passer who had in turn made demands for reimbursement from the treasurer. The Lords of the Council, before whom the matter eventually came, agreed that some recompense should be made, ordering Campbell, the treasurer, to pay Passer 240 marks. Of this sum he paid, on Passer's instructions, 40 marks to Robert, the balance apparently going to the estate of Passer who at this point died quite suddenly.[30] Robert may have received the money in order to pay off the Italian musicians, although this sum could have met only part of the bill since the Italians were still suing Passer's estate in 1538.[31]

This, however, did not complete his dealings with the Passer family, for shortly after Evangelist's death Robert apparently owed his estate some £240. The sum may represent a loan made to Robert or it may have been placed in his hands for the purpose of investment or of settling up the deceased's financial affairs, for Robert reported to the Edinburgh Burgh Council and also to the Lords of the Council that out of it he had paid a good many of Evangelist's debts, including even his funeral expenses.[32] The widow was not satisfied, however, insisting that he would have to return a larger balance than that which he had admitted.[33] The result was a long-drawn lawsuit which continued until February, 1540, when Robert was so old and feeble that his wife was obliged to act as his tutor.[34] Although nothing seems to have come of widow Passer's pursuit, it indicates the headaches that went along with high finance, even in the sixteenth century.

Another aspect of Robert's financial transactions appears to have been that which underlay his acquiring in 1538 the lands of Cragy in Fife from Henry Stewart of Rosyth. As this man had been responsible for the bringing to Scotland of James V's second bride, Mary of Lorraine, it may be that he had borrowed money from Robert in order to meet some of his expenses. Whether such was the case or not it would seem that his selling of his land in feu-farm to Robert for the sum of £40 down and an annual rent of one silver penny indicates that it was not the usual type of real estate sale, but was a customary method of obtaining cash on the basis of land as collateral.[35]

One last reference to what may have been another of Robert's financial ventures brings a new factor into the picture. Early in 1538 he took action in the Barony Court of Restalrig against William Clapperton, who had become surety for Andrew Purves, macer, to force him to pay 18 ounces of silver, and won the case. As Clapperton, however, found that the price of silver was not "liquid," which apparently means "determined," he refused. He was perhaps feeling the effect of the influx of

precious metals from America which had resulted in the fall in
the value of silver all over western Europe. On Clapperton's
objection, Robert carried the matter to the Lords, demanding
that the defendant's goods be seized, but they appointed the
Laird of Restalrig and his baillie as arbiters to determine the
true price of the metal. When they had accomplished this task,
they were then to see that Clapperton paid his bill.[36] This
would seem to be one of the earliest references in Scotland to
the current fluctuation in the value of silver.

While both trade and finance continued to occupy his attention during the last decade of his life, probably Robert's most
absorbing interest was that of adding to and caring for his real
estate. Even this, however, was closely bound up with his other
business ventures. Much of the land he held, like that of Cragy
in Fifeshire, he had originally received as security and interest
for loans, or was in his hands as a result of the direct investment
of his money.

One example of the latter type of transaction was his purchase
in 1531 from the crown jointly with John Drummond of
Innerpeffrey and Alexander Robertson of Sauchy of the ward,
reliefs, non-entries, and marriages of the estate of the late
Patrick Buttir of Gormo for 500 marks, with a down payment
of £200. The only difficulty about this transaction was that the
widow, Janet Gordon, Lady Lyndsay, refused to hand over the
property to the three guardians.[37] While the council hesitated to
eject the widow, Robert sued Drummond for the debts of the
latter's late father. It may have been that the obtaining of the
guardianship over the lands of Gormo had had something to do
with the Drummond debts, so that when Lady Lyndsay resisted,
Robert took the more direct method of obtaining his money.[38]
This seems to have ended the partnership, for the king then
turned the lands over to Dame Janet and James Hering of
Glaslune.[39] This venture had not met with conspicuous success.

In August, 1531, a short time after the unsuccessful attempt to profit from the lands of Gormo, Robert took the important step of selling to Thomas Erskine of Haltoun, the king's secretary, the lands of Kirkbuddo, and the mill and lands of Hobmill, which he had received in 1529 from the Earl of Crawford as security for the repayment of £662 6s. It would look as though he was attempting to dispose of some of his Forfar properties, which owing to their situation far from his own area of activity had never been very profitable. As the proceeds of the sale had probably reimbursed him for the sum of money which the earl owed him, he would not suffer any loss by the transaction. That this sale did not liquidate all his holdings in Forfar, however, is quite clear for on December 13, appearing before the Lords in connection with a suit against the Earl of Crawford, he protested that any decision reached should not be to his prejudice with regard to the lands of Kirkbuddo and Elphinstone. As there is no record of his disposing of the latter property, it was apparently still in his hands.[40]

Much more vital to Robert at this time, or perhaps a little later, seems to have been a question concerning the wardship of the lands of the Lord of Drummond. From what one is able to piece together from the documents, it seems that by late in 1534 David, Lord Drummond, was married and had purchased from Robert the wardship of his lands, his entry being ratified by a royal charter on January 5, 1535. However, Robert had already given John Drummond of Innerpeffrey and William Drummond of Stobhall a tack of part of the land, including Innerpeffrey, Fairdow, and Auchterarder. Not only had the two men failed to pay Robert any rent for these properties, but they now refused to hand them back to Lord Drummond. Robert, therefore, took action before the Lords of the Council on February 15, 1536, claiming £135 from John and 500 marks from William, for the preceding two terms' rent. Having proved his claims, he forced the two men to meet his demands. David, on the other hand, had a somewhat more difficult time, but by 1538 he finally succeeded in ousting John Drummond from the lands which he was attempting to retain.[41]

The culmination of Robert's real estate operations came in 1537 when, as mentioned above, King James, after the general revocation of grants, in recognition of his service and expenses on behalf of the crown returned to him and his son, Robert Mowbray of Barnbougle, an augmented Barony of Over Barnton. While the other lands were no doubt important, this property formed the core of Robert's financial edifice which was now established in one solid and permanent holding.

Yet while considering his country estate, one must not lose sight of the fact that Robert was first and foremost a middle class town dweller. He may still have held property in Leith, and from his dispute with Duncan Dawson the collier it is obvious that he owned a tavern in Edinburgh. Probably with "retirement" in mind about 1538, or perhaps a little earlier, he had acquired this property which would no doubt always be a money-making investment in Scotland. Robertson and Wood in their *Castle and Town* point out that many people who would not do so today, owned and operated such establishments in the sixteenth century. "It seems to have been considered a cherished privilege rather than a career of doubtful respectability." Thus, by moving to the "big city" and setting himself up as an Edinburgh tavern-keeper, Robert, it would seem, indicated his intention of spending the remaining days of his life in quietness and in an odor of respectability.[42]

Although it might be an odor of respectability which would surround his last days, there is some doubt that it would be an air of sanctity. Anticlericalism and perhaps even Lutheranism were making headway in the seagoing circles of Leith, for in July, 1532, the Kirkmasters of St. Mary's Church, Leith, were pressing demands before the council that certain recalcitrant Leith skippers be obliged to pay the traditional fees for the repair of the fabric. One of the leaders of the defaulters was a certain Adam Dais, who had some business connections with John Barton. That Dais' opposition was not the result merely of an unwillingness to pay out money may be indicated by John Knox's report that in 1534, being delated as a heretic, Dais was required to burn his faggot. It might be felt, of course, that it was his refusal to pay rather than heretical beliefs that caused his difficulties, but even if this explanation is correct, his anti-ecclesiastical attitude probably reflected that of a considerable number of the indwellers of the port.[43]

That Robert perhaps held the same opinions as Dais may be revealed by his support in 1533 of the refusal of Sir Thomas Erskine of Haltoun to pay the Bishop of Dunkeld £10 from the lands and barony of Kirkbuddo for the support of a chaplain in the Parish Church of Dundee. The bishop stated that the former owner, the Earl of Crawford, had made the church this gift, but as neither Robert, who had recently sold the land to Erskine, nor Erskine himself, seems to have known of it they rejected his claim. In this there could be some incipient Protestantism for Erskine was the uncle and guardian of John Erskine of Dun who had by this time joined the Protestant cause and was doing everything he could to forward its fortunes. But Protestantism or no, the Lords ordered the bishop and his chaplain to produce proof, which they apparently found impossible.[44] There the case rested until 1539 when a new incumbent renewed the bishop's demand, only to have a countersuit instituted with the result that nothing more happened, Barton and Erskine having gained the victory.[45]

While this contest had been in abeyance between 1533 and 1539, Robert had also fought the Bishop of Dunkeld on the issue of the tithes of the kirks of Aberleddy and Crawmond. As mentioned above, he had purchased them from Hugh Campbell of Loudon who in turn had obtained them from the confiscated estates of Douglas of Kilspindie. After the latter's

death Isobel Hoppar, Douglas' widow, attempted in 1538 to regain possession of the tithes, at the same time that the Bishop
of Dunkeld claimed that they belonged to him, while Robert,
who was in possession, refused to turn them over to anyone.
Although the outcome of the contest is unrecorded, it is quite
clear that he was not prepared to surrender his property at
the command of even the church.[46]

It is in 1536 that the clearest evidence is given of Robert's
disregard of the church's legal rights. The Bishop of Moray
sought to obtain the tithes of the churches of the lordship of
Drummond, which belonged to the bishop as Abbot of Scon,
but which Robert had apparently put in his own pocket while
guardian of the property. Robert rejected the episcopal
demands and the council took only very feeble measures to
make him pay. Finally the matter came to a head in the spring
of 1539, for the young Lord Drummond, who was being
pressed by the bishop to give restitution, tried to force Robert
to make a settlement. The latter, however, instituted a
countersuit, and from that time on the matter disappears from
the records.[47]

Although it is impossible to draw too many conclusions
concerning Robert's attitude to the church from this evidence,
his actions would seem to indicate that he was unimpressed by,
if not actually hostile to, the ecclesiastical authority of his day.
That there are few references to the church throughout his life
would seem to indicate a certain indifference to it, while his
contacts with Dais and the Erskines in his later years indicate
that in all probability he had at least heard of the new Protestant
doctrines, even if there is no evidence that he ever became
one of their adherents.

Much more important in his eyes than religion were the
fortunes of his family. It must have given him considerable
satisfaction, therefore, when in May, 1531, he attended the
nuptials of his daughter Margaret and John Sandilands. Margaret

resigned the lands which she had held up to this time, and the king granted them in conjunct-feftment to the young couple.[48] Robert had thus forged another link with the nobility.

Although he had apparently settled his son Robert's future in much the same way by marrying him to Barbara Mowbray, he still had problems in connection with this latter transaction. In the autumn of 1531 it was necessary for him to take action to protect Robert and Barbara from an attempt by the latter's mother to gain possession of some of the Barnbougle properties. Arbitrators were appointed to settle the case, which they may have done, for there is no sign of any further action.[49] Even this did not bring his worries to an end with regard to the Mowbrays, however, for when the king revoked all the grants made during his minority Robert's plans were again put in jeopardy. But, as has been seen, the problem was solved by the re-grant of the property with further additions. Thus he had made good provision for Elizabeth Crawford's son.

This raises the question of his provision for John, James, and Henry, his children by his first marriage, for it seems a little strange that the youngest child should have been the successor to the larger part of his estate.[50] Robert may have felt that his eldest son John was making his own way in the world without much need for help. He had been actively employed in the king's business early in the thirties, had been in France at the time of the royal courtship, and on July 5, 1537, sailed for Denmark as James V's ambassador to Christian III bearing letters of credence which referred to him as "virum ex familia nostra." Moreover in January, 1540, he received a grant of East and West Dudingstone from the Commendator of the Abbey of Kelso, a natural son of the king.[51] Yet there still may have been some conflict within the family over Robert's decision to recognize Robert Mowbray as the heir to the Over Barnton estates, for on March 10, 1539, the Mowbrays resigned

all their lands, including the baronies of Dunmany, Inverkeithing, and Barnbougle, to the king, receiving them back for
themselves and their son John with the provision that if their
line should die out, the property would go to John Barton,
"seniori filio Roberti Bertoun de Ovir Barntoun."[52] This may
have been an attempt to assuage John's annoyance at his
exclusion, but one cannot help feeling that Robert Mowbray
garnered most of the benefits accruing from the estate, the
remaining sons having to take what was left over, which apparently consisted of the lands of Cragy, perhaps the tavern in
Edinburgh along with some property in Leith, and the money
still owed by the crown.

There was, however, one other possible source of wealth for
the adventurous: the losses sustained through the capture of the
Bartons' ships by Spanish and Portuguese privateers. By 1538
the possibility of enforcing claims against the perpetrators of
these misdeeds seems to have attracted John's attention, for in
that year he appealed to the king for a grant of letters of
reprisal against the Spaniards who had failed to reimburse his
father for the capture of the *Black Barque* in 1521. Although this
might seem a somewhat belated attempt to collect such a debt,
it was nothing to the request which he made in the spring of
1540 when seeking authority to attack the Portuguese for their
robbery of his grandfather off the port of Sluis. James V wrote
the Portuguese king concerning this request, explaining that
it would be difficult to refuse John—"an active youth" (probably
about 35 years of age!)—unless the Portuguese offered some
recompense.[53]

This royal letter dated April 13, 1540, contains the last
reference to Robert's being alive. Appropriately enough it
dealt with the Portuguese attack which had really marked the
beginning of his career, and which at the close of his life was
again offering chances of wealth to a new generation of Bartons.
By June 7 he had passed away.[54]

His death undoubtedly came as no surprise, for he was regarded in 1536 as being old and feeble, while from a statement made by his son John after his death he had apparently been too sickly since 1538 to take an active interest in his business affairs. Indeed when in 1540 he had been sued by the widow Passer, his wife had acted as his tutor. All of this points to the fact that with advancing years, the conduct of his affairs fell more and more into the hands of his wife and children. To a man such as Robert this must have been humiliating and frustrating so that death would come as a true release.

XIV

Epilogue

We do not know whether or not Robert left a will. In all probability he did, and records show that his wife, Elizabeth, and her son, Robert Mowbray of Barnbougle, were his two executors.[1] In this capacity they were immediately confronted by three important matters: the settlement of the inheritance, the payment of creditors, and reimbursement by debtors. Considering that the two latter responsibilities required their dealing with the rulers of two states, acting as Robert's executors would not be easy.

First and foremost there was the problem of the division of the estate. By royal grant Robert had already secured for Robert Mowbray the barony of Over Barnton. As it did not, however, include all his real property, the remainder of the estate became the portion of John Barton who repeatedly appears as Robert's heir during the few years following the regrant of Barnbougle in 1537. As far as can be ascertained, the larger part of these holdings were the lands of Cragy obtained from Henry Stewart of Rossyth. Elizabeth seems to have been unwilling to surrender them without a struggle, with the result that John had her summoned before the Lords of the Council.[2] Although we have no evidence as to the settlement of the dispute, it would seem that John obtained his due.

The whole inheritance, however, was soon brought into jeopardy by the demands of Dorothea, Christian II's daughter. King James, on the insistence of Dorothea's representative, now held an official inquiry into what had become of the funds and stores which Christian II had committed to Robert's keeping. To answer this question, John Barton and Robert's executors produced documents which proved that although Robert had received some money from Christian, he had made a full statement of expenses to that monarch when the latter had come to Scotland, and moreover, out of his own pocket, he had spent for Christian's cause some 2,000 pieces of gold more than he had received. James informed Dorothea that when the evidence was submitted for examination, her representative, despite the fact that he could have continued to prosecute, decided to drop the case.[3] This finished the connection of the Bartons with the forlorn hope of Christian II.

As far as the executors were concerned, however, much more important than the ex-King of Denmark's debts were the monies owed to Robert's estate by the King of Scots. Although a certain amount had been paid off by the royal exchequer, there was apparently a balance owing of some £3,000, a considerable sum for those days. Elizabeth seems to have concluded that the crown either would not or could not pay its debts. She therefore entered into an agreement with the king and his council whereby Robert's two remaining sons, probably by his first marriage, James and Harry, were to receive between them some £80 a year from the royal treasury until the king should provide one or both to benefices; and she, in return, promised to forego the royal debts. The reference to "benefices" may indicate that these two sons were both clergy, but since there is no other evidence that either of them was, the term may refer simply to some office or some source of revenue which would produce a minimum of £40 a year for each.[4] The pension was paid until James V's death, but after that it disappears from the accounts, although both men were still living in the 1560's.[5] They played neither a great part in the history of the country, nor even in that of their own family, dropping out of sight without leaving any lasting traces.

What happened to the tavern in Edinburgh and any property in Leith is unknown. They may have been sold or they may have gone to James or Harry, but of this there is no sure or certain knowledge.

After Elizabeth's remission of the crown's debt to Robert's estate, she also disappears from sight. There are relatively few references to her in the sources except in connection with her son Robert Mowbray, so that it would seem that she had concentrated her attention primarily upon her home, aiding her husband only in cases of necessity. How old she was when Robert died, whether she ever married again, and when she herself died, are all questions for which there are no answers.

Much clearer is the picture of what happened to Robert Mowbray. Apparently counted among the nobles of the day, he was one of those who in August, 1540, composed the court ordered to try Sir James Hamilton of Finnart for aiding the exiled Earl of Angus. As many earls and other lords, all of whom held places of power and authority in the country, sat in judgement on the case, it would seem that Robert, the son of the Leith sea captain, had indeed risen to a position of importance.[6] On his father's death he had received full possession of the Barony of Over Barnton, which he united to that of Barnbougle, thus establishing very large holdings to the south of the Forth, just west of Edinburgh. Within less than a year (March 14, 1541), however, he sold part of the lands of Foulfurd within Over Barnton to Robert Cairncross, Bishop of Ross, whom his father had succeeded as treasurer in 1529. If there is any connection between this sale and Cairncross' earlier removal from office, it is not indicated.[7] Robert Mowbray was alive in 1549, but was probably dead by 1555, in which year there are references to John Mowbray of Barnbougle who was then in possession of the estate. In 1558 he is referred to as "the late Robert Mowbray," having died before reaching the age of fifty.[8]

More interesting to the follower of Robert Barton's career is Robert Mowbray's second son James who inherited the lands of Over Barnton. Not much is known about him, except that in November, 1558, he sold Over Barnton to Mr. Alexander Mauchan, an Edinburgh advocate.[9] This was the end of one phase of the family's development, and the end of one of Robert's great projects to build for himself and for his descendants a landed estate which would give them a place among the gentry. One cannot but wonder whether John Barton, if he had received the estate, might not have shown more appreciation of his inheritance.

Another member of Robert Barton's family was his daughter Margaret, who had married John Sandilands, Laird of Calder. Margaret's husband, perhaps under the influence of his father-in-law, showed certain favors to Archibald Douglas of Kilspindie when he was in Scotland seeking pardon and staying with Robert, for on March 14, 1541, he received letters of protection from James V for supplying Douglas with food. During the 1550's Sandilands was active in the political affairs of the country. Also, having espoused the Reformed cause, he gave his support and friendship to John Knox. What Margaret's views may have been on the question of Protestantism is not known, and they probably were not very influential since she seems to have been dead before 1560. John, after her decease, married a second time, but himself was dead by 1567.[10]

To continue the story of Margaret one step further, it should be added that her brother-in-law, James, in the 1550's became the Preceptor of the Order of St. John of Jerusalem. Then, aligning himself with the Protestant cause, he obtained possession of the lands of the preceptory as Lord Torphichen, the name of the principal holding. He, however, died without issue and left the lands to his grandnephew, Margaret's grandson, who thereupon took possession and assumed the title of Lord Torphichen. Robert's financial aid to Sandilands of Calder had eventually yielded much greater profits than he had probably ever expected.[11]

The story of Robert Barton, however, really comes to a close with the history of his son John. Before his father's death, John had paid 400 francs towards the expenses of the Falkland Herald who had been sent to Spain to obtain redress for the seizure of the *Black Barque*, and after Robert's passing he paid another 400 "crowns of the sun" for the same purpose. How far he was successful in obtaining compensation is not stated. All the information available is his demand that the other merchants who had suffered losses through Spanish piracy should pay their share of the expenses.[12] From his desire to have others share the costs, one might deduce that his efforts had been unsuccessful, but this cannot be said with certainty.

It is sure, on the other hand, that at first he failed to obtain a regrant of the letters of marque against the Portuguese for their robbery of his grandfather. On June 12, 1540, King James wrote Charles V of Spain explaining the situation with the comment that since the Portuguese had refused compensation, he could hardly deny John's request to be permitted the opportunity of taking reprisals. Charles replied by asking that the matter be held in abeyance until he had an opportunity to communicate with the Portuguese concerning this matter. As nothing came of the emperor's efforts, James, sometime after February, 1541, granted the letters, and John and his friends proceeded to take full advantage of their opportunities.[13]

By this time John had become a seaman of considerable reputation, as is indicated by his holding in 1542 the office of

Vice-Admiral of Scotland. Misfortune, however, dogged his steps. After the death of James V the French arrested him in Dieppe on the charge that he was a supporter of the English against France and Scotland. The Scottish merchants, the Archbishop of St. Andrews, and the government raised an immediate outcry against this action. At the same time, Robert and Alexander Barton, his sons, petitioned the King of France for his release, pointing out that he had been simply obeying the orders of the Douglases, who were now back in Scotland, dominating the scene, but that in truth he had served the King of France loyally against the English.[14] With such advocates there is little doubt that John was released, but how long he lived afterward is not known. It is only certain that he was dead by September 7, 1561.

The reason for the certainty of John's death prior to September 7, 1561, is that on that date the final act of the Barton drama began to unfold. Piracy and privateering had been gradually falling into disrepute, and in this year the council issued a proclamation forbidding Leith merchants to purchase pirated goods. The Reformation's stress upon honesty and hard work in the sight of God did not favor this dishonest if easy method of earning a living. The Privy Council, therefore, on the above date, summoned before it Robert Logan and his brother, William Logan; Alexander and Robert Barton, sons of the late John Barton; and John Mowbray of Barnbougle, all of whom claimed to have letters of marque against the Portuguese. A lengthy discussion of their rights ensued, but it had a foregone conclusion. In 1563 Parliament formally revoked the Barton's letters of marque forever.[15]

In a very real sense, this is the end of the history of Robert Barton. In 1558 the lands of Over Barnton had been alienated and in 1563 the letters of marque, upon which the fortunes of the family had been to a large extent founded, were canceled. A new day had arrived when other ways and other means of

making money were to be employed. It was a new world which
Robert would not have fully understood and in which he
probably would not have felt entirely at home.

As one looks back over Robert's career from the beginning
of the reign of James IV down almost to the end of that of James
V, and compares it with that of others of his own day, one
receives the impression that in many ways he was typical of the
age in which he lived. A member of the new rising commercial
middle class, his primary interest was not merely in the exchange
of goods for relatively small profits, but in operations bringing
the largest possible monetary returns. These gains he then
employed to make more money, either by lending to the
crown and to private individuals, or by acquiring real estate,
the most secure investment of the time. In all of this he was
by no means unique, for others were at this time making their
fortunes in similar ways all over western Europe.

Furthermore, carrying on the business of a merchant and
financier in rather uncertain times, he had continually to be awake
to opportunities, to risks, and to obstacles. This would make
him intellectually active, perhaps at times ruthless, but above
everything else efficient, or at least much more efficient than
the average feudal or ecclesiastical administrator of his day. It
was therefore no accident that he was called upon to shoulder
heavy responsibilities in the financial administration of the
country when disbursements were normally outrunning receipts. In this also he was typical of the contemporary middle
class, for the kings of Europe more and more were finding
themselves depending upon this group to help in bridging the
gap between medieval feudal incomes and modern administrative expenditures. The result was that the merchant class
gathered into its own hands new political power which it was
not slow to use to its own political, economic, and religious
advantage. That such was Robert's position is quite clear, for

by 1530 he seems to have been in control of most of the country's financial administration.

What he would have done in the face of the Reformation will never be known. His rather obvious disregard of the church and the fact that his son-in-law eventually became a prominent figure in the Protestant Lords of the Congregation may indicate that like so many of his fellow merchants he would have given his adherence to the movement to establish a reformed church.

Although Robert was a good example of a sixteenth century middle class self-made "tycoon," he was more than that. He was clearly a leader, a man of determination, sagacity, and vigor. Throughout his career he manifested the capacity to take the initiative and the courage to carry his projects through to their conclusion. The very fact that after four hundred years so much material is still available for the study of his life is a proof of his importance in his own times. Although he was seldom in the forefront of events, he was one of those men who often wielded more power behind the scenes than did those who have come down in history as the dominant personalities in early sixteenth century Scotland.

Bibliography

Primary Sources:

1. MANUSCRIPTS

BELGIUM:

Archives Générales de la Royaume de Belgique, Brussels:
Mss. Divers
Papiers d'Etat et de l'Audience
Trésor de Flandres, Ser. I

DENMARK:

Danish Royal Archives, Copenhagen:
Royal Correspondence, Scotland, A II
Sundtolregnskab

FRANCE:

Archives du Département du Nord, Lille:
Chambres des Comptes de Lille
Chambres des Comptes, Trésor des Chartres Commerciales
Compte de la Recette Générale des Finances
Lettres Missives
Archives du Département de la Loire-Inférieure, Nantes:
Registre de la Chancellerie de Bretagne, 1506, 1509
Paris, Bibliothèque Nationale:
Mss. Dupuy
Mss. Français
Mélanges de Colbert
Rouen, Bibliothèque Publique:
Déliberations du Conseil Communale de Rouen, 1515–1520

ENGLAND:

London, British Museum:
  Cottonian Mss.

SCOTLAND:
Edinburgh:
  City Archives:
    Burgh Court Book, 1507
  H.M. General Register House:
    Acta Dominorum Concilii, Vols. X–XLIII
    Acta Dominorum Concilii et Sessionis, Vols. I–XII
    Calendar of Royal Letters, ed. R. K. Hannay
    Curia Itineratis Justiciae, Transcript III, 1508–13
    Customs Records, 1500–1510 (miscellaneous)
    Customs Books, Edinburgh, 1510, (ca.), 1528, 1538–39
    Drummond Writs
    Inventory of Crawford and Balcarres Scottish Muniments at Haigh, Vol. I
    Liber Domicilii S.D.N. Regis, 1528–30
    Liber Emptoris S.D.N. Regis, 1531–32
    Liber Introitus de Edinburgh, 1510–11, 1512, 1528
    Liber Tronatoris Burgi Edinburgi
    Liveries for James V
    Mayne Letter Book
    James Nicholson, *Protocol Book*, 1549–1579
    Rothes Cartulary
    Vincent Strathauchin, *Protocol Book*
    Tyningham Letter Book, ed. R. K. Hannay
    Tyningham Ms.
  National Library of Scotland:
    Justiciary Records, Vol. II, 1507–11
    Law Tracts Miscellany, Advocates' Ms.
Private documents:
  Lord Torphichen's Muniments, Edinburgh

Moray Muniments, Darnaway Castle, Morayshire
Rosebery Muniments, Dalmeny

2. PRINTED DOCUMENTS

BELGIUM:

Inventaire des Archives de la Ville de Bruges, ed. L. Gilliodts-Van Severen, Bruges, 1876, IV–VI

DENMARK:

Aarsberetninger fra det Kongelige Geheimarchiv, ed. C. F. Wegener, Copenhagen, 1852–65, I–III

FRANCE:

Papiers d'état Relatifs à l'Histoire de l'Écosse au Seizième Siècle, ed. A. Teulet, Paris, 1851, I

GERMANY:

Die Hanserecesse von 1477–1530, ed. D. Schafer, *et al.*, Leipzig, 1894–1913, Ser. 3, V, VI, IX

HOLLAND:

Bronnen tot de Geschiedenis van den Handel met Engeland, Schotland en Ierland, ed. H. J. Smit, The Hague, 1942, II; 1

Bronnen tot de Geschiedenis van de Leidsche Textielnijverheid, ed., W. W. Posthumus, The Hague, 1911, II

Bronnen tot de Geschiedenis van Middelburg in den Landsheerlijken Tijd, ed., W. S. Unger, The Hague, 1923–1931, I–III

Bronnen tot de Geschiedenis van den Oostzeehandel, ed., N. A. Poelman, The Hague, 1917, I

Inventaris van het Oud Archief der Stad Middelburg, ed., J. H. de Stoppelaar, Middelburg, 1883

UNITED KINGDOM:

Abstract of Inventory of Charters Belonging to the Corporation of Dundee, Dundee, 1881

Accounts of the Lord High Treasurer of Scotland, ed., T. Dickson et al., Edinburgh, 1877–1911, I–IX

Acts of the Parliament of Scotland, ed. T. Thomson, Edinburgh, 1814, II

Acts of the Lords of the Council in Civil Causes, 1478–1495, London, 1839, I

Acts of the Lords of the Council in Civil Causes, ed. G. Neilson and H. Paton, London, 1918, II

Acts of the Lords of the Council in Public Affairs, 1501–1554, ed. R. K. Hannay, Edinburgh, 1932

Acts of the Lords Auditors of Causes and Complaints, 1466–1494, London, 1839

Ancient Criminal Trials in Scotland, ed. R. Pitcairn, Maitland Club, Edinburgh, 1833, I: 1

Calendar of Patent Rolls, Henry VIII, London, 1914, 1916, I, II

Calendar of State Papers Relating to Ireland, 1509–1573, ed. H. C. Hamilton, London, 1860

Calendar of State Papers Relating to Milan, ed. A. B. Hinds, London, 1912, I

Calendar of State Papers Relating to Scotland, ed. M. J. Thorpe, London, 1858, I

Calendar of State Papers Relating to Spain, ed. G. A. Bergenroth et al., London, 1862–82, I–IV

Calendar of State Papers Relating to Venice, ed. R. Brown, London, 1864–69, I–III

Calendar of Writs Preserved at Yester House, 1166–1625, Edinburgh, 1917

Charters, etc., Relating to the City of Edinburgh, 1143–1540, Scottish Record Society, Edinburgh, 1871

Epistolae Jacobi IV, Jacobi V et Mariae Regum Scotorum, ed. Thomas Ruddiman, Edinburgh, 1722, I

Excerpta e Libris Domicilii Jacobi Quinti, 1525–1533, Bannatyne Club, Edinburgh, 1836

Exchequer Rolls of Scotland, ed. G. Burnett *et al.,* Edinburgh, 1887–1898, X–XVIII

Extracts from the Records of the Burgh of Edinburgh, 1403–1528, Scottish Burgh Record Society, Edinburgh, 1869

Extracts from the Records of the Royal Burgh of Stirling, 1519–1666, Glasgow, 1887

Flodden Papers, ed. M. Wood, Scottish History Society, Edinburgh, 1933

Foedera, Conventiones et Acta Publica, ed. T. Rymer, The Hague, 1741, V–VI

Forty-Fifth, and Forty-Sixth, Annual Report of the Deputy Keeper of the Public Records, London, 1885–86

Hamilton Papers, ed. J. Bain, Edinburgh, 1890, I

Illustrations of Scottish History from the Twelfth to the Sixteenth Centuries, ed. J. Stevenson, Maitland Club, 1834

Ledger of Andrew Haliburton, ed. C. Innes, Edinburgh, 1867

Letters and Papers illustrative of the reigns of Richard III and Henry VII, ed. James Gairdner, London, 1863, II

Letters and Papers of Henry VIII, ed. J. S. Brewer *et al.,* London, 1862–1896, I–XV

Letters and Papers Relating to the War with France, 1512–13, ed. A. Spont, Navy Record Society, London, 1897

Letters of James IV, calendared by R. K. Hannay, ed. R. L. Mackie and A. Spilman, Scottish History Society, Edinburgh, 1953

Letters of James V, calendared by R. K. Hannay, ed. D. Hay, Edinburgh, 1954

Original Letters Illustrative of English History, ed. H. Ellis, London, 1825, Ser. 1, Vol. I; 1827, Ser. 2, Vol. I

Parliamentary Records of Scotland, Edinburgh, 1804, I

Protocol Book of W. Corbet, 1529–58, Scottish Record Society, Edinburgh, 1911

Protocol Book of John Foular, ed. W. MacLeod and M. Wood, Edinburgh, 1930

Protocol Book of James Foulis, 1546–1554, Scottish Record Society, Edinburgh, 1927

Protocol Book of Gilbert Grote, 1552–1573, Scottish Record Society, Edinburgh, 1914

Protocol Book of Gavin Ros, 1512–1532, Scottish Record Society, Edinburgh, 1908

Protocol Book of James Young, 1485–1515, Scottish Record Society, Edinburgh, 1941

Records of the Convention of the Royal Burghs of Scotland, 1295–1597, ed. J. D. Marwick, Edinburgh, 1866

Regality of Dunfermline Court Book, 1531–1538, ed. J. M. Webster and A. A. M. Duncan, Dunfermline, 1953

Register of the Privy Council of Scotland, ed. J. H. Burton, Edinburgh, 1877, I

Register of the Great Seal of Scotland, ed. J. B. Paul *et al.*, Edinburgh, 1882, 1883, II, III

Register of the Secret Seal of Scotland, ed. M. Livingstone and D. H. Fleming, Edinburgh, 1908–1936, I–III

Register or Chronicle of Butley Priory, Suffolk, 1510–1535, ed. A. G. Dickens, Winchester, 1951

"Report on the Erskine of Dun Manuscripts," *Fifth Report of the Historical Manuscript Commission*, London, 1876

Secondary Sources:

1. CONTEMPORARY ACCOUNTS

R. Holinshed, *The Scottish Chronicle*, Arbroath, 1805, III

John Knox, *The History of the Reformation in Scotland*, ed. W. C. Dickinson, Edinburgh, 1949, 2 vols.

John Leslie, *Historie of Scotland*, ed. E. S. Cody and W. Murison, Scottish Text Society, Edinburgh, 1895, II

Robert Lindsay, of Pitscottie, *The Chroniclis of Scotland*, ed. A. J. G. Mackay, Edinburgh, 1899, I

A Diurnal of Remarkable occurrents which have Passed within the Country of Scotland, ed. T. Thomson, Maitland Club, Edinburgh, 1833

2. BOOKS, ARTICLES, ETC.

P. Abercromby, *The Martial Achievements of the Scots Nation*, Edinburgh, 1715, II

C. F. Allen, *Histoire de Danemark*, Copenhagen, 1878, I, II

C. Anderson, *The Annals of the English Bible*, London, 1862

R. N. Bain, *Scandinavia*, Cambridge, 1905

J. Balfour, *Historical Works*, Edinburgh, 1824, I

E. W. M. Balfour-Melville, "Burgh Representatives in Early Scottish Parliaments," *English Historical Review*, LIX (1944)

N. E. Bang, *Tabeller over Skibsfart og Varentransport Gennem Øresund, 1497–1660*, Copenhagen, 1906, I

L. A. Barbé, *Sidelights on the History, Industries, and Social Life of Scotland*, London, 1919

P. W. Becker, *De Rebus inter Ioannem, Christianum II, Daniae Reges, ac Ludovicum XII et Jacobum Galliae Scotiaeque Reges*, Hafniae, 1835

S. T. Bindoff, *The Scheldt Question to 1839*, London, 1945

A. E. Borely, *Histoire de la ville de Havre et de son ancien gouvernement*, Le Havre, 1880

A. Boudier, *A Travers les Siècles*, Dieppe, 1950, Ser. 3

A. de la Broderie, *Hervé Porzmoguer*, Quimper, 1885

D. Calderwood, *The History of the Kirk of Scotland*, ed. T. Thomson, Wodrow Society, Edinburgh, 1847, I

A. Campbell, *History of Leith*, Leith, 1827

J. Campbell, *Lives of the Admirals*, London, 1750

A. E. Christensen, *Dutch Trade to the Baltic about 1600*, Copenhagen, 1941

V. E. Clark, *The Port of Aberdeen*, Aberdeen, 1921

W. E. Collins, "The Scandinavian North," *Cambridge Modern History*, Cambridge, 1907, II

A. Conway, *Henry VII's Relations with Scotland and Ireland, 1485–1498*, Cambridge, 1932

J. Davidson and A. Gray, *The Scottish Staple at Veere*, London, 1909

W. C. Dickinson, "Burgh Life from Burgh Records," *Aberdeen University Review*, XXXI (1946)

J. Dowden, *The Bishops of Scotland*, ed. J. M. Thomson, Glasgow, 1912

E. H. Dunkley, *The Reformation in Denmark*, London, 1948

W. Fraser, *The Douglas Book*, Edinburgh, 1885, II, IV

E. de. Fréville, *Memoire sur le Commerce Maritime de Rouen*, Rouen, 1857, I

J. A. Gade, *Hanseatic Control of Norwegian Commerce in the Late Middle Ages*, Leiden, 1951

J. Gairdner, *History of the Life and Reign of Richard III*, new ed., Cambridge, 1898

G. D. Gibb, *Life and Times of Robert Gib*, London, 1874, 2 vols.

V. Gibbs, *The Complete Peerage*, London, 1910–1953, *passim*

N. P. Gilmore, *The World of Humanism*, New York, 1952

I. F. Grant, *Social and Economic Development of Scotland before 1603*, Edinburgh, 1930

J. Grant, ed., *The Old Scots Navy, 1689–1710*, The Navy Record Society, London, n.d.

J. Grant, *Old and New Edinburgh*, London, n.d., I

R. K. Hannay, "Incidents and Documents, A.D. 1513–1523," *The Book of the Old Edinburgh Club*, Edinburgh, 1916, IX; "Shipping and the Staple," *ibid.*

C. E. Hill, *Danish Sound Dues and the Command of the Baltic*, Durham, N.C., 1926

J. C. Irons, *Leith and its Antiquities*, Edinburgh, 1898, I

J. Jorgensen, *Geschichte der Danische Literatur*, Munich, 1908

T. Keith, "The Trading Privileges of the Royal Burghs of Scotland," *The English Historical Review*, XXVIII (1913)

H. Koht, "The Scandinavian Kingdoms in the 14th and 15th Centuries," *The Cambridge Medieval History*, Cambridge, 1936, VIII

E. Lipson, *Introduction to the Economic History of England*, London, 1926, I

P. Lorimer, *The Precursors of Knox*, Edinburgh, 1857

T. M'Crie, *The Life of John Knox*, Edinburgh, 1855

A. J. G. Mackay, "Introduction," *The Poems of William Dunbar*, Scottish Text Society, Edinburgh, 1893, III

J. D. Mackie and G. S. Pryde, *The Estate of Burgesses in the Scots Parliament*, St. Andrews, 1923

R. L. Mackie, *King James IV of Scotland*, Edinburgh, 1958

J. MacKinnon, *The Constitutional History of Scotland*, London, 1924

———, *Luther and the Reformation*, London, 1930, IV

———, *The Social and Industrial History of Scotland from Early Times to the Union*, Glasgow, 1920

H. Maxwell, *The History of the House of Douglas*, London, 1902, II

F. Michel, *Les Ecossais en France*, Paris, 1862, I

J. B. Paul, *The Scots Peerage*, Edinburgh, 1910, 10 vols.

Percy's Reliques of English Poetry, London, 1906 (Everyman), II

N. Periaux, *Dictionnaire Indicateur et Historique des Rues et Places de Rouen*, Rouen, 1870

E. Power and M. M. Postan, *Studies in English Trade in the Fifteenth Century*, London, 1933

R. S. Rait, *The Parliaments of Scotland*, Glasgow, 1924

D. Robertson and M. Wood, *Castle and Town*, Edinburgh, 1928

C. Roger, *Historical Notices of St. Anthony's Monastery, Leith*, Leith, 1877

M. P. Rooseboom, *The Scottish Staple in the Netherlands*. The Hague, 1919

J. Russell, "Bonnington, Its Lands and Mansions," *The Book of the Old Edinburgh Club*, Edinburgh, 1933, XIX

Z. W. Sneller, *Walcheren in de Vijftiende Eeuw*, Utrecht, 1917

E. Stair-Kerr, *Scotland Under James IV*, Paisley, 1911

J. Stedman, *Memorial of the Family of Barton*, Bath, 1857

P. F. Tytler, *The History of Scotland*, Edinburgh, 1864, II

R. Wodrow, *Collections upon the Lives of the Reformers*, Maitland Club, Edinburgh, 1834

T. S. Willan, *The Muscovy Merchants of 1555*, Manchester, 1953

J. Yair, *An Account of Scotch Trade in the Netherlands*, London, 1776

H. Zimmern, *The Hansa Towns*, London, 1898

Notes to Chapter I

1 P. F. Tytler, *History of Scotland*, Edinburgh, 1864, II, 239 ff.

2 E. Stair-Kerr, *Scotland Under James IV*, Paisley, 1911, p. 26; James Grant, *The Old Scots Navy, 1689–1710*, London, 1914, pp. vii ff.; cf. also W. S. Reid, "Sea-Power in the Anglo-Scottish War, 1296–1328," *The Mariner's Mirror*, XLVI (1960), 7 ff.

3 R. S. Rait, *The Parliaments of Scotland*, Glasgow, 1924, pp. 351 ff.

4 *Ibid.*, pp. 33 ff.; J. MacKinnon, *The Constitutional History of Scotland*, Glasgow, 1924, pp. 212 ff.

5 J. N. Charteris, "The Tudor Dealings with Scotland, 1488–1524," (unpublished thesis, McGill University), Chap. I; Tytler, *op. cit.*, II, 265 ff.

6 I. F. Grant, *Social and Economic Development of Scotland before 1603*, Edinburgh, 1938, pp. 92 ff., 199–218.

7 G. Grub, *An Eccesiastical History of Scotland*, Edinburgh, 1861, I, 348 ff.

8 P. Hume Brown, *George Buchanan*, Edinburgh, 1890, pp. 41 ff.; cf. also A. J. G. Mackay, "Life of the Author," in John Major, *A History of Greater Britain*, trans. A. Constable, Edinburgh, 1892.

9 W. S. Reid, "The Scottish Counter Reformation," *Church History*, XIV, 1945, 104 ff.

10 D. Patrick, ed., *Statutes of the Scottish Church*, Edinburgh, 1907, pp. lx ff.

11 W. S. Reid, "The Lollards in Pre-Reformation Scotland," *Church History*, Vol. XII (1942).

12 I. F. Grant, *op. cit.*, p. 321; W. S. Reid, "Trade, Traders and Scottish Independence," *Speculum*, XXIX (1954), 210 ff.

13 I. F. Grant, *op. cit.*, pp. 287 ff.; W. S. Reid, *Economic History of Great Britain*, New York, 1954, Chap. 5.

14 E. de Fréville, *Mémoire sur le Commerce Maritime de Rouen*, Rouen, 1857, I, 294; F. Michel, *Les Ecossais en France*, Paris, 1862, I, 358; C. Innes, ed.,

The Ledger of Andrew Haliburton, 1492–1503, Edinburgh, 1867, pp. xl, lxv; I. F. Grant, *op. cit.*, pp. 321 ff.; J. MacKinnon, *Social and Industrial History of Scotland from Earliest Times to the Union*, Glasgow, 1920, p. 85. For an account of Scottish measures at this time, see J. Skene, *De Verborum Significatione*, Edinburgh, 1681, art. "Serplath," which indicates the prevailing uncertainty and confusion. *Liber Tronatus Burgi Edinburgensis* (Ms.), H.M. General Register House.

15 Fréville, *op. cit.*, I, 301 ff.; Michel, *op. cit.*, I, 360; D. Robertson and M. Wood, *Castle and Town*, Edinburgh, 1928, p. 281; T. Dickson *et al.*, eds., *The Accounts of the Lord High Treasurer of Scotland*, Edinburgh, 1877, I, clxxx, ccxviii, 69.

16 J. Davidson and A. Gray, *The Scottish Staple at Veere*, London, 1909, p. 94; E. Power and M. Postan, *Studies in English Trade in the 15th Century*, London, 1953, p. 43.

17 Michel, *op. cit.*, p. 360; MacKinnon, *Social and Industrial History*, p. 109.

18 T. D. Cook, *The Story of Rouen*, London, 1928, p. 169; A. Boudier, *A Travers les Siècles*, Dieppe, 1950, Ser. 3, o. 8.

19 Michel, *op. cit.*, I, 360.

20 H. Zimmern, *The Hansa Towns*, London, 1889, p. 255 f.; G. Waitz, *Lübeck unter Jurgen Wullenwever*, Berlin, 1855, I, 8; J. A. Gade, *The Hanseatic Control of Norwegian Commerce during the Late Middle Ages*, Leiden, 1951, p. 104.

21 H. Koht, "The Scandinavian Kingdoms during the 14th and 15th Centuries," *Cambridge Mediaeval History*, Cambridge, 1936, VIII, 535 ff.

22 Waitz, *op. cit.*, I, 12 f.; Koht, *op. cit.*, VIII, 547 ff.; G. F. Allen, *Histoire de Danemark*, Trans. E. Beauvois, Copenhagen, 1878, I, 254 ff.

23 Davidson and Gray, *op. cit.*, p. 85; T. A. Fisher, *The Scot in Germany*, Edinburgh, 1912, pp. 3 ff.

24 Allen, *op. cit.*, I, 10; S. T. Bindoff, *The Scheldt Question to 1839*, London, 1945, pp. 30 ff.

25 *Ibid.*, p. 16; Davidson and Gray, *op. cit.*, pp. 128 ff.; Z. W. Sneller, *Walcheren in de Vijftiende Eeuw*, Utrecht, 1917, pp. 2 ff., 12 f., 90 ff. 113 ff., 135.

26 *Ibid.*, pp. 69 ff.

27 *Ibid.*, p. 70 f.; Rait, *op. cit.*, p. 34; J. Yair, *An Account of the Scottish Trade in the Netherlands*, London, 1776, p. 84.

28 T. Keith, "The Trading Privileges of the Royal Burghs of Scotland," *English Historical Review*, XXVIII (1913), 455 ff.; MacKinnon, *Social and Industrial History*, p. 90 f.; W. C. Dickinson, "Burgh Life from Burgh Records," *Aberdeen University Review* XXXI (1946), 217; Davidson and Gray, *op. cit.*, p. 23.

29 *Ibid.*, pp. 43 ff.; MacKinnon, *Social and Industrial History*, p. 91; I. F. Grant, *op. cit.*, pp. 366–68; Keith, *op. cit.*, p. 460; W. M. Mackenzie, *The Scottish Burghs*, Edinburgh, 1949, pp. 62 ff.

30 *Ibid.*, Chaps. V and VI; Keith, *op. cit.*, pp. 465 ff.

31 Dickinson, *op. cit.*, pp. 214 ff.; Robertson and Wood, *op. cit.*, pp. 204 ff.; Mackenzie, *op. cit.*, pp. 97 ff.

32 *Ibid.*, pp. 75 ff.; Keith, *op. cit.*, p. 454 ff.; E. W. M. Balfour-Melville, "Burgh Representation in Early Scottish Parliaments," *English Historical Review*, LIX (1944), 82; T. Pagan, *The Convention of the Royal Burghs of Scotland*, Glasgow, 1926, pp. 19 ff.

33 J. D. Mackie and G. S. Pryde, *The Estates of the Burgesses in the Scottish Parliament*, St. Andrews, 1923, p. 1; Mackenzie, *op. cit.*, p. 77.

34 Yair, *op. cit.*, p. 90; cf. *The Parliamentary Records of Scotland*, Edinburgh, 1804, I, 292 f., 323; Keith, *op. cit.*, p. 460.

35 Davidson and Gray, *op. cit.*, p. 93; cf. I. F. Grant's list of the burghs in their order of relative importance, *op. cit.*, p. 353.

36 James Grant, *Old and New Edinburgh*, London, n.d., I, 32 ff.

37 *Charters and Documents Relating to the City of Edinburgh, 1143–1540*, Edinburgh, 1871, Nos. XXX, XLVII; Dickinson, *op. cit.*, pp. 215 ff.; Robertson and Wood, *op. cit.*, p. 53.

38 *Charters*, Nos. XXIX, XXXI, LIV, LXII.

39 Keith, *op. cit.*, p. 457.

40 J. C. Irons, *Leith and its Antiquities*, Edinburgh, 1898, I, 527 f.; *Charters*, Nos. XX, XXXV.

41 *Charters*, Nos. XXV, XLVI, LV; Irons, *op. cit.*, I, 42; Davidson and Gray, *op. cit.*, p. 36; *Extracts from the Records of the Burgh of Edinburgh, 1403–1528*, Scottish Burgh Record Society, 1869, pp. 3, 4, 14, 19, 23; *Law Tracts Miscellany*, collection in the National Library of Scotland, Edinburgh, pp. 528 ff.

42 T. S. Willan, *The Muscovy Merchants of 1555*, Manchester, 1953, p. 1 f.

43 Power and Postan, *op. cit.*, p. 71.

44 N. A. Poelman, ed., *Bronnen tot de Geschiedenis van den Oostzeehandel*, The Hague, 1917, I: 2, No. 2523; L. Gilliodts-Van Severn, ed., *Inventaire des Archives de la Ville de Bruges*, Bruges, 1876, IV, 10, 42, 43, 197, 334; Grant, *op. cit.*, p. 342; Davidson and Gray, *op. cit.*, p. 50 f.

45 W. S. Reid, "The Middle Class and the Scottish Reformation," *Church History*, XIV (1947), 137 ff.

Notes to Chapter II

1 J. Stedman, *Memorial of the Family of Barton*, Bath, 1857, p. 10 f.

2 *Ibid.*, p. 11; P. Abercromby, *The Martial Achievements of the Scots Nation*, Edinburgh, 1715, II, 522. Apparently Stedman gained most of his information from Abercromby and added a few embellishments of his own.

3 Stedman, *loc. cit.*

4 G. Burnett and A. J. G. MacKay, *The Exchequer Rolls of Scotland*, Edinburgh, 1877, XIII, 295; T. Dickson, *et al.*, eds., *The Accounts of the Lord High Treasurer of Scotland*, Edinburgh, 1877, I, lxii, 54, 66, 68.

5 M. P. Rooseboom, *The Scottish Staple in the Netherlands*, The Hague, 1919, p. 26 f.

6 Stedman, *op. cit.*, p. 11; G. Buchanan, *The History of Scotland*, ed. J. Aikman, Glasgow, 1845, p. 186.

7 For instance on April 15, 1483, a certain John Barton was pursued before the Lords of the Council by a group made up of Scots and Flemings for taking from them as English goods £465 worth of madder, alum, wax, and herring. The defendant claimed that these had been given to him

by judgement of a court in Honfleur but was required to prove it. (G. Neilson and H. Paton, eds., *Acts of the Lords of the Council in Civil Causes*, London, 1918, II, cxxxf.) This case has the "Barton touch" apparently pointing to the man who had been robbed at Sluis. Another reference is to a John Barton "senior" who appears in the *Exchequer Rolls* in 1507, and who in May, 1510, resigned his 4-mark land in Leith to the House of St. Anthony, in return for the 14s. rent of the land of the late John Dudingstone. A number of reasons, besides the fact that he was a resident of Leith, suggest that this was Robert's father. For one thing, he is referred to as "senior" indicating that he had a son John, which was true of the man in question. In the second place, although the connection with Dudingstone is somewhat uncertain, it is significant that John, the son of John Barton and brother of Robert, married Helen Dudingstone who may have been the heiress of the abovementioned late John Dudingstone, and owner of land at Bridge-end to the south of the property owned by John, senior (*Exch. Rolls*, XIII, clxxx; J. C. Irons, *Leith and its Antiquities*, Edinburgh, 1898, I, 555–57; J. B. Paul and J. M. Thomson, *Register of the Great Seal of Scotland*, Edinburgh, 1883, III, No. 2092). It is, therefore, not merely possible but also highly probable that John Barton, senior, lived at least until 1510.

8 Irons, *op. cit.*, II, 40.

9 J. S. Brewer, *et al.*, eds., *The Letters and Papers of Henry VIII*, London, 1896, XV, No. 779.

10 Robert Lindsay of Pitscottie, *The Chroniclis of Scotland*, ed. A. J. G. Mackay, Edinburgh, 1899, I, 227 f.

11 *Ibid.*, II, 369.

12 *Treasurer's Accounts*, I, lxxv; *Exch. Rolls*, XIII, clxxix.

13 *Treasurer's Accounts*, I, 129; J. D. Mackie, *The Earlier Tudors*, Oxford, 1952, p. 96 f.

14 *Ibid.*, p. 136 n.; A. Conway, *Henry VII's Relations with Scotland and Ireland, 1485–1498*, Cambridge, 1932, p. 30.

15 Buchanan, *op. cit.*, p. 163; Lindsay, *op. cit.*, I, 226. For comments on Lindsay's reliability see R. L. Mackie, *James IV of Scotland*, Edinburgh, 1958, p. 63.

16 Lindsay, *op. cit.*, I, 228 f.; Buchanan, *op. cit.*, p. 166.

17 *Treasurer's Accounts*, I, 125.

18 *Ibid.*, I, lxxv, cvi, 181, 190. He was confirmed in his fief of Largo about this time (p. lxxv).

19 Cf. *infra*, chap IV, note 36.

20 Neilson and Paton, *Acts*, II, 469 f.

21 T. Thomson, ed., *The Acts of the Parliament of Scotland*, Edinburgh, 1814, II, 235.

22 James Balfour, *Historical Works*, Edinburgh, 1824, I, 218; I. F. Grant, *Social and Economic Development of Scotland before 1603*, Edinburgh, 1938, p. 363; J. Davidson and A. Gray, *The Scottish Staple at Veere*, London, 1909, p. 73.

23 *Treasurer's Accounts*, I, 200, 217 f., 246, 247, 253, 254, 247.

24 *Extracts from the Records of the Burgh of Edinburgh, 1403–1528*, Scottish Burgh Record Society, Edinburgh, 1869, p. 119 f.

25 *Acts of the Lords of the Council in Civil Causes, 1478–1495*, London, 1839, p. 18.

26 *Ibid.*, p. 372.

27 *Loc. cit.*

28 *Acts of the Lords Auditors of Causes and Complaints, 1466–1494*, London, 1839, p. 186.

29 J. B. Paul, *et al.*, eds., *Register of the Great Seal of Scotland*, Edinburgh, 1882, II, No. 2238.

30 Rooseboom, *op. cit.*, p. 30; C. Innis, ed., *Ledger of Alexander Haliburton*, 1867, *passim*; H. J. Smit, ed., *Bronnen tot de Geschiedenis van den Handel met Engeland, Schotland en Ierland*, The Hague, 1942, II: 1, Nos. 60 f., 107. The author has followed Smit's interpretation of Haliburton's position: that he was not made a government representative until 1500.

31 W. W. Posthumus, *Bronnen tot de Geschiedenis van de Leidsche Textielnijverhid*, The Hague, 1911, II, No. 713; W. S. Unger, ed., *Bronnen tot de Geschiedenis van Middelburgh in den Landsheerlijken Tijd*, The Hague,

1926, II, No. 279; J. Yair, *An Account of the Scottish Trade in the Netherlands*, London, 1776, p. 92; J. Davidson and A. Gray, *The Scottish Staple at Veere*, London, 1909, p. 135.

32 *Haliburton's Ledger*, p. 89; *Ancient Laws and Customs of the Burghs of Scotland*, Edinburgh, 1910, II, 82.

33 *Treasurer's Accounts*, I, 217, 318.

34 L. Barbé, *Sidelights on the History of Scotland*, London, 1919, pp. 101 ff.; J. Gairdner, *History of the Life and Reign of Richard III*, Cambridge, 1898, pp. 268 ff.; Mackie, *op. cit.*, pp. 116 f., 143 f.; H. R. Williamson, *Historical Whodunits*, New York, 1956, pp. 53 ff.

35 *Treasurer's Accounts*, I, 301 ff.

36 J. Gairdner, *Letters and Papers Illustrative of the Reigns of Richard III and Henry VII*, London, 1863, II, 185 f.; R. K. Hannay, ed., *Acts of the Lords of the Council in Public Affairs*, Edinburgh, 1932, p. lx.

37 *Exch. Rolls*, XI, lxii; XIV, xciii; *Treasurer's Accounts*, I, clii.

38 *Ibid.*, I, 343.

39 *Ibid.*, I, 344.

40 Gairdner, *Richard III*, pp. 321–23; *Exch. Rolls*, XI, lxif.; A. B. Hinds, ed., *Calendar of State Papers Relating to Milan*, London, 1912, I, No. 541; H. Ellis, *Original Letters Illustrative of English History*, London, 1825, Ser. 1: I, 32 f.

41 G. A. Bergenroth, ed., *Calendar of State Papers Relating to Spain*, London, 1862, I, No. 221; R. Brown, ed., *Calendar of State Papers Relating to Venice*, London, 1864, I, No. 755.

42 *Acta Dominorum Concilii*, XIV, 159; Gairdner, *Letters and Papers*, II, 185 f.

43 John had already retaliated against the English, for on January 10, 1497, James IV had issued letters of protection to him stating that he was seeking reprisals for damage which they had caused him, his friends, and his relatives. The English prize in Leith in April of that year may have been one of John's captures. (Smit, *Bronnen*, II: 1, No. 112; *Treasurer's Accounts*, I, 330.)

44 The reason for believing this is that on the shore at Roscoff there stood a chapel to St. Ninian, obviously the donation of Scottish merchants

who had dedicated chapels to the same saint in both Bruges and Copenhagen. It is believed also that this was the port at which Mary, Queen of Scots, landed in 1548 when fleeing from Henry VIII's "rough wooing."

45 *A.D.C.*, XIV, 159; *Registre de la Chancellerie de Bretagne* (ms.), Archives du Département de la Loire Inférieure, 1506, fo. 59; 1509, fo. 22; A. de la Borderie, *Hervé Porzmoguer*, Quimper, 1885, p. 10.

Notes to Chapter III

1 *Supra*, p. 8 f.

2 Gilliodts-Van Severen, ed., *Inventaire des Archives de la Ville de Bruges*, Bruges, 1876, Ser. I, Vol. VI, 450.

3 J. Davidson and A. Gray, *The Scottish Staple at Veere*, London, 1909, p. 143.

4 W. S. Unger, ed., *Bronnen tot de Geschiedenis van Middelburgh in den landsheerlijken Tijd*, The Hague, 1926, II, Nos. 283, 285.

5 H. J. Smit, ed., *Bronnen tot de Geschiedenis van den Handel met Engeland, Schotland en Ierland*, The Hague, 1942, II: 1, No. 144 and n.2.

6 Unger, *op. cit.*, II, Nos. 286 ff., 312. £1 gr. Fl. equalled 10s. Scots.

7 A. E. Christensen, *Dutch Trade to the Baltic about 1600*, Copenhagen, 1941, pp. 35 ff.

8 N. E. Bang, *Tabeller over Skibsfart og Varentransport Gennem Øresund, 1497–1660*, Copenhagen, 1906, I, 2, 3.

9 V. E. Clark, *The Port of Aberdeen*, Aberdeen, 1921, p. 17.

10 *Extracts from the Records of the Burgh of Edinburgh, 1403–1528*, Scottish Burgh Record Society, Edinburgh, 1869, p. 59.

11 *Ibid.*, pp. 76, 78, 89.

12 J. C. Irons, *Leith and its Antiquities*, Edinburgh, 1898, I, 130; *Acta Dominorum Concilii*, XIII, 85, 118 f.

13 T. Dickson, *et al.*, eds., *Accounts of the Lord High Treasurer of Scotland*, Edinburgh, 1900, I, 247, 248, 319, 321, 325.

14 *Ibid.*, II, 108, 117.

15 Unger, *op. cit.*, II, Nos. 286, 312.

16 *Treasurer's Accounts*, II, 143, 349, 356, 358, 370, 379.

17 *Ibid.*, II, 231, 241, 271, 273.

18 C. Innes, ed., *Ledger of Andrew Haliburton*, Edinburgh, 1867, pp. 73, 82, 167, 192.

19 *Ibid.*, pp. 71, 211; *Extrs. Edinb. Recs.*, p. 72.

20 *Haliburton's Ledger*, pp. 60, 264; *Customs Accounts* (ms.), 1500? (a fragment in H.M. General Register House, Edinburgh).

21 *Haliburton's Ledger*, p. 236; G. Burnett *et al.*, *The Exchequer Rolls of Scotland*, Edinburgh, 1888, XI, 233.

22 *Ibid.*, XI, 273, 378.

23 J. Skene, *De Verborum Significatione*, Edinburgh, 1681, p. 11, "ane certaine measure and quantitie of herring, quhilk perteins to the King as an pairt of his custumes, and annexed propertie."

24 J. Neilson and H. Paton, eds., *Acts of the Lords of the Council in Civil Causes*, London, 1918, II, 397.

25 W. MacLeod and M. Wood, *The Protocol Book of John Foular*, Edinburgh, 1930, No. 65.

26 J. Erskine, *An Institute of the Law of Scotland*, ed., A. MacAllan, Edinburgh, 1838, Bk. II, tit. iii, 28.

27 M. Livingstone and D. Fleming, eds., *Register of the Secret Seal of Scotland*, Edinburgh, 1921, I, No. 642.

28 *Exch. Rolls*, XI, 376.

29 *Treasurer's Accounts*, II, 23, 29, 32.

30 *Exch. Rolls*, XII, 89, 91.

31 *Reg. Sec. Seal*, I, No. 767; *Treasurer's Accounts*, II, 34, 37, 148.

32 *Exch. Rolls*, XII, 161, 164.

33 J. Russell, "Bonnington: Its Lands and Mansions," *The Book of the Old Edinburgh Club*, Edinburgh, 1933, XIX, 148; J. B. Paul *et al.*, eds., *Register of the Great Seal of Scotland*, Edinburgh, 1882, III, No. 2092; *Acta Dominorum Concilii et Sessionis*, XII, 194 f.; J. Stedman, *Memorial of the Family of Barton*, Bath, 1857, p. 32, is here very far from the truth concerning Barton's family.

34 *Treasurer's Accounts*, II, 353, 371.

35 *Ibid.*, II, 206, 216, 375, 380. James had obtained both horses and books from abroad two years earlier (p. 21).

36 *Ibid.*, 234 f.

37 *Exch. Rolls*, XII, 91, 164, 263, 273, 466 f; XIII, 98, 230, 365; *Customs Books, etc., 1500–1677* (ms.), H.M. General Register House, Edinburgh. *Liber Introitus de Edinburgh, 1500–1511* (ms.), H.M. General Register House, Edinburgh; this is probably the book of Thomas Dikson, rector of Toray (cf. *Exch. Rolls*, XIII, 366). The Bartons' exports were as follows:

September 10 , 1510 Andrew Barton (rex) to Berwick		3 pieces of wax (wt. 260 wax stones)
		3 lasts (of hides?)
Oct. 6,	John Barton to Dieppe	76 sides of bacon
	Robert Barton	3 lasts, 2 dakers, 6 hides
Oct. 27,	Andrew (destination omitted)	2 lasts, 10 pipes of tallow
Nov. 10,	Robert to Veere	10 bbl. tallow
Nov. 17,	Andrew (rex) to Dieppe	40 bbl. tallow, 1,000 calf skins
	Robert	13 bbl. tallow
Dec. 3,	Robert to Dieppe	17 dakers (hides); 10 bbl. tallow
	Andrew (rex)	2 lasts hides, 24 bbl. tallow
Dec. 17,	Andrew (rex) to London	7 pieces wax (wt. 623 wax stones)
Jan. 4, 1511,	Robert to Dieppe	$7\frac{1}{8}$ dakers hides, 5 bbl. tallow, 400 calf skins
March 4,	Robert to Dieppe	6 puncheons, wax

March 7, Robert to Dieppe	5 puncheons, wax
April 2, Robert to Dieppe	3 pieces, wax (wt. 226 lb.)
Andrew (rex)	3 pieces, wax (wt. 226 lb.)
April 24, Andrew (rex) to Dieppe	12 lasts, 7 dakers, hides
Robert	2 pieces, wax (wt. 52 wax stones)

38 *Exch. Rolls*, XII, 164; XIII, 393.

39 *Treasurer's Accounts*, III, 95, 240, 246; *Exch. Rolls*, XII, 260.

40 *Sundtoldregenskab* (ms., Royal Danish Archives), 1503; *Exch. Rolls*, XII, 262 f. John Barton paid the Sound Tolls twice in 1503, although no exact date is given.

41 *Treasurer's Accounts*, III, 182.

42 R. L. Mackie, *et al.*, eds., *The Letters of James IV*, Edinburgh, 1953, No. 277.

43 J. Herkless and R. K. Hannay, *The Archbishops of St. Andrews*, Edinburgh, 1907, I, 184, 192 ff.

44 *Exch. Rolls*, XII, 260; *Treasurer's Accounts*, II, 287; III, 95.

45 *Ibid.*, II, 240 ff., 478.

46 *A.D.C.*, XXIII, 64, 87, 117.

47 *Ibid.*, XXII, 67, 78, 98, 112; R. K. Hannay, ed., *Acts of the Lords of the Council in Public Affairs*, Edinburgh, 1932, p. lxv.

48 *Reg. Grt. Seal*, II, Nos. 3647, 3648; *Reg. Sec. Seal*, I, No. 2305, 2318.

49 *Foular Protocol Book*, I, No. 746.

50 *Reg. Grt. Seal*, II, No. 3198; *Treasurer's Accounts*, IV, 6; *Moray Muniments* (ms.), Darnaway Castle, Box 31, Div. I, bundle 1.

51 *Reg. Grt. Seal*, II, No. 3214.

52 *Letts. Jas. IV*, Nos. 148, 341; J. S. Brewer *et al.*, eds., *Letters and Papers of Henry VIII*, London, 1862, I, No. 1410. Edmonston on December 11, 1506, was representing David Sim against whom Robert had taken action before the Lords of the Council (*A.D.C.*, XVIII: 2, at date.) The lands of Edmonston lay east of Craigmillar and south of Niddry

(J. Russel, "Bonnington: Its Lands and Mansions," *The Book of the Old Edinburgh Club*, Edinburgh, 1933, XIX, 148). Elizabeth and Gilbert had founded the Chapel of St. Barbara in the Church of the Virgin Mary in Leith (1497), now the Parish Church of South Leith (*Reg. Grt. Seal*, II, No. 2496).

53 Belief that Robert married Elizabeth Crawford about this time is based upon the fact that in *The Letters of James IV* (Nos. 148, 341) there appear two requests of the king that the pope grant Elizabeth and Robert a dispensation to marry, since they were afraid that their acting as godparents to each other's children by their previous partners would make their marriage null and void. R. K. Hannay has dated these letters as 1507 and 1510. The first date is ruled out by the statement of the letters that they were already married, and it is quite certain that Elizabeth would have been mentioned in the grant of Over Barnton, if the marriage had taken place by 1508. Moreover, she would also have been mentioned in Robert's charter of the same year to her sister Janet and brother-in-law, Sir James Logan, son of the Laird of Restalrig, granting them some of the lands of Over Barnton (*Reg. Grt. Seal*, II, Nos. 3198, 3214). It may even be that Elizabeth employed her influence with her future husband to obtain the grant for Sir James and his wife. Thus it would seem that the proper date for both the letters is 1510, by which time Robert and Elizabeth could have been married for a year as the letters state.

54 *Reg. Sec. Seal*, I, No. 2318.

55 *Ibid.*, I, Nos. 2451, 2458.

56 Davison and Gray, *op. cit.*; M. P. Rooseboom, *The Scottish Staple in the Netherlands*, The Hague, 1910.

57 Unger, *Bronnen*, II, Nos. 289, 291 ff.; Smit, *Bronnen*, II, Nos. 1, 195, 203, 204, 207, 209, 214, 215, 217. S. T. Bindoff, *The Scheldt Question to 1839*, London, 1954, p. 62 f., 67; J. Yair, *An Account of Scotch Trade in the Netherlands*, London, 1776, p. 96; Davidson and Gray, *op. cit.*, p. 147; Rooseboom, *op. cit.*, p. 32; J. Gairdner, *Letters and Papers Illustrative of the Reigns of Richard III and Henry VII*, London, 1863, II, 262.

58 Unger, *Bronnen*, II, No. 294; Smit, *Bronnen*, II, Nos. 1, 238.

59 *Ibid.*, II, Nos. 238, 239, 241, p. 222, n. 1.

Notes to Chapter IV

1 T. Thomson, ed., *Acts of the Parliament of Scotland*, Edinburgh, 1817, II, 214, 224; T. Dickson *et al.*, eds., *The Accounts of the Lord High Treasurer of Scotland*, Edinburgh, 1877, I, cxii, 179, 199 f.; A. J. G. MacKay, ed., *The Poems of William Dunbar*, Edinburgh, 1893, III, 390 f.; *The Forty-Sixth Report of the Deputy Keeper of the Public Records*, London, 1867, Appendix, p. 52; A. de Teulet, ed., *Inventaire chronologique des Documents Relatives à l'Histoire d'Écosse*, Edinburgh, 1839, I, 54; *Mss. Dupuy*, Bibliothèque National de France, Vol. 468; W. S. Reid, "The Place of Denmark in Scottish Foreign Policy, 1470–1540," *The Juridical Review*, Edinburgh, 1944, LVIII, 183 ff.

2 *Treasurer's Accounts*, II, 145, 196; R. J. Hannay, ed., *Acts of the Lords of the Council in Public Affairs, 1501–1554*, Edinburgh, 1932, p. lix.

3 *Treasurer's Accounts*, II, 157.

4 Cf. G. Burnett, *et al.*, eds., *The Exchequer Rolls of Scotland*, Edinburgh, 1891, XII; *Treasurer's Accounts*, II.

5 Cf. *infra*, Chap. V.

6 *Treasurer's Accounts*, II, lxxvi ff., 380.

7 *Ibid.*, II, 281 f., 351, 356, 380, 413.

8 *Ibid.*, II, 281 f., 351.

9 *Ibid.*, II, 281 ff.; A. Boudier, *A travers les Siècles*, Dieppe, 1950, Ser. 3, p. 9.

10 *Treasurer's Accounts*, II, 356, 413 f.

11 *Ibid.*, II, 281 ff., 284.

12 P. F. Tytler, *The History of Scotland*, Edinburgh, 1864, II, 271 ff.

13 *Treasurer's Accounts*, II, xci ff., 431.

14 *Ibid.*, III, 138, 200; Tytler, *op. cit.*, II, 275.

15 *Treasurer's Accounts*, II, xlv, 437, 448.

16 *Ibid.*, II, lxxxix, 284 ff., 437. In June, 1505, it was "the king's ship" (*Ibid.*, II, 145). In 1506 the hire of a crew from Brittany was £107 (*Ibid.*, III, 341).

17 *Ibid.*, II, 449, 452, 461. The next year Merchamston was acting as Robert's assistant in hiring a crew for the *Lion* (*Ibid.*, III, 203).

18 *Ibid.*, II, 419; J. C. Irons, *Leith and its Antiquities*, Edinburgh, 1898, I, 112.

19 *Treasurer's Accounts*, II, 286 f.; III, 82, 129.

20 *Ibid.*, III, lxviii, 368.

21 *Ibid.*, II, 477; III, lix ff., 127.

22 *Ibid.*, II, 445, 461; III, lxv ff., 135, 182, 341.

23 J. Gairdner, *Letters and Papers Illustrative of the Reigns of Richard III and Henry VII*, London, 1863, II, 202.

24 Hannay, *Acts*, p. lxi.

25 *Acta Dominorum Concilii*, XVI, 266, 300.

26 *Ibid.*, 300 ff.; XVII, 42; XVIII: 1, 113, 133; XVIII: 2, no folios marked, proceedings of December 4 and 11.

27 *Registre de la Chancellerie de Bretagne*, 1506, fo. 59; A. de la Borderie, *Hervé Porzmoguer*, Quimper, 1855, p. 10.

28 *Treasurer's Accounts*, III, xvii, 55, 83 ff., 90, 91, 143, 150. The author has concluded that the ship referred to on May 26 and 27 was the *Jacat* mentioned in September and November (*Ibid.*, III, 162, 173). It may not have been, but it is significant that this is the only ship of which we have record, in which Robert and Makyson were both interested. Canon law forbade the taking of usury on a loan, but this type of transaction was by no means uncommon when men desired to evade such ecclesiastical regulations.

29 L. A. Barbé, *Sidelights on the History, Industries, and Social Life of Scotland*, London, 1919, pp. 163 ff.; *Treasurer's Accounts*, III, 87, 190, 196, 200, 340 ff.

30 *Ibid.*, III, 182; Gairdner, *Letters and Papers*, II, 218.

31 *Exch. Rolls*, XII, 400.

32 *Treasurer's Accounts*, III, 341, 342, 346.

33 Tytler, *op. cit.*, II, 279 f.

34 *Treasurer's Accounts*, III, 182, 312.

35 *Ibid.*, III, lxiii, 203, 326, 344, 347, 352.

36 *Lansdowne Mss.*, British Museum, "Caesar Papers," No. 171; J. Stedman, *Memorial of the Family of Barton*, Bath, 1857, p. 13. From the text of the letters of marque, at present in the *Lansdowne Mss.*, it looks as though James IV had made the grant a year earlier, since it is dated 1505, but there are a good many reasons for rejecting this date. In the first place, the year (1505) given in the ms. is a correction in Arabic numerals over Roman numerals which have been partially obliterated, but which look like "VI." The new date is probably a late sixteenth century alteration. Further support for 1506 is found in the fact that the regnal year is given as "in the nineteenth year of our reign," which points to November of that year since James ascended the throne in June, 1488. And last, but by no means least, the timing of the grant fits in perfectly with Andrew's position in the autumn of 1506. When going forth under the king's instructions to clear the seas of pirates, what could be more appropriate than that the letters of marque should be renewed?

37 J. Davidson and A. Gray, *The Scottish Staple at Veere*, London, 1909, p. 53; R. Holinshed, *Scottish Chronicle*, Arbroath, 1805, II, 126, James Balfour, *Historical Works*, Edinburgh, 1824, I, 227.

38 *Treasurer's Accounts*, III, 46, 298, 335, 378.

39 *Ibid.*, III, 298, 403; IV, 76, 78.

40 T. Ruddiman, ed., *Epistolae Jacobi IV, Jacobi V et Mariae Regum Scotorum*, Edinburgh, 1722, I, 91, 120 f.; Gairdner, *Letters and Papers*, II, 274–76; *Extracts from the Records of the Burgh of Edinburgh*, Edinburgh, 1869, p. 119.

41 *Treasurer's Accounts*, IV, 40, 45, 72, 82, 97, 104, 114.

42 *Ibid.*, IV, 40; *Mayne Letter Book* (ms.), H.M. General Reg. House, Edinburgh, No. 95.

43 Gairdner, *Letters and Papers*, II, 258 f.; R. L. Mackie *et al.*, eds., *The Letters of James IV*, Edinburgh, 1953, No. 157.

44 *Treasurer's Accounts*, IV, 46, 114; *Reg. Chanc. Brit.*, 1509, fo. 22; de la Borderie, *op. cit.*, p. 4.

45 *Letts. Jas. IV.*, No. 208; Gairdner, *Letters and Papers*, II, 274 ff.; H. J. Smit, ed., *Bronnen tot de Geschiedenis van den Handel met Engeland, Schotland en Ierland*, The Hague, 1942, II, No. 308; *Extrs. Edinb. Recs.*, p. 119 f. The year 1508 would seem to be the proper date for James' letters rather than 1507 as Smit, or 1510 as J. S. Brewer, *The Letters and Papers of Henry VIII*, London, 1862, I, Nos. 841, 1245. They were written from Jedburgh where James was in 1508 and they fit in with the circumstances most easily at this time.

46 *Letts. Jas. IV.*, No. 217.

47 Hannay, *Acts*, p. lxiv.

48 *L.&P. Henry VIII*, I, No. 20.

49 *Ibid.*, I, No. 117; Ruddiman, *op. cit.*, I, 106.

50 *Ibid.*, I, 103.

51 John Leslie, *Historie of Scotland*, ed., E. S. Cody and W. Murison, Edinburgh, 1895, II, 130.

52 *A.D.C.*, XXI, 13, 38 f., 45 f., 56 ff., 100, 102, 175.

53 *Ibid.*, XXI, 39, 61 f., 65, 66.

54 *L.&P. Henry VIII*, I, No. 1826.

Notes to Chapter V

1 R. L. Mackie *et al.*, eds., *The Letters of James IV*, Edinburgh, 1953, Nos. 259, 278, 286; *Forty-Sixth Annual Report of the Deputy Keeper of the Public Records*, London, 1886, App. II, 55.

2 *Ibid.*, *loc. cit.*; *Letts. Jas. IV*, No. 310; *Acta Dominorum Concilii*, XXII, 54.

3 *Ibid.*, XXII, 67, 78, 98, 112; R. K. Hannay, ed., *Acts of the Lords of the Council in Public Affairs*, Edinburgh, 1932, p. lxv.

4 *Letts. Jas. IV*, Nos. 320, 321, 324; D. Schafer, *Hanserecesse, von 1477–1530*, Leipzig, 1894, IV, 136; *Forty-Sixth Rep. Deputy Keeper*, App. II, 55; C. F. Wegener, *Aarsberetninger fra det Kongelige Geheimarchiv*, Copenhagen, 1852–55, I, 35.

5 *Letts. Jas. IV*, No. 387, 412; *Forty-Sixth Rep. Deputy Keeper*, App. II, 55; *Exch. Rolls.*, XIII, clxxxiii; *Hanserecesse*, IV, No. 183. It would seem that the ship *Jenny Pirwin* was the one built in the priest's yard at Dumbarton which Andrew may have commanded on a voyage to France for wine. It also appears that the Lords of the Council regarded the vessel as Andrew's own property, but if this were the case King James could hardly have given it to Hans of Denmark as Hans later claimed. It may be that Andrew felt he had a vested interest in the *Jenny* as he had commanded her since her launching and others had come to think of her as his possession. If this were so it would explain the cavalier way in which he carried her off from Denmark when he sailed to attack the Portuguese. On the other hand, that James gave her to Hans finds no support except in Hans' letters to Henry VIII after her capture. Claiming that she was a present from the Scottish king, he demanded, without effect, that Henry return the ship to her lawful owner—himself. (*A.D.C.*, XXII, 78; Edward Hall, *Chronicle*, London, 1809, p. 525; R. Holinshed, *The Scottish Chronicle*, Arbroath, 1805, II, 132).

6 *Letts. Jas. IV*, Nos. 315, 381; John Leslie, *Historie of Scotland*, ed. E. S. Cody and W. Murison, Edinburgh, 1895, II, 131 f.; J. S. Brewer, *et al.*, eds., *Letters and Papers of Henry VIII*, London, 1862, I, No. 1826.

7 *Ibid.*, I, No. 3619; Hall, *Chronicle*, p. 525.

8 *Ibid.*, *loc. cit.*,; A. G. Dickens, *The Register or Chronicle of Butley Priory, Suffolk, 1510–1535*, Winchester, 1951, p. 26; Leslie, *op. cit.*, II, 135.

9 *Percy's Reliques of English Poetry*, London, 1906 (Everyman), II, 42 f.

10 Hall, *loc. cit.*; Dickens, *loc. cit.*

11 *Letts. Jas. IV*, No. 381.

12 M. Wood, *Flodden Papers*, Edinburgh, 1933, pp. xv ff.; H. Hauser and A. Renaudet, *Les Débuts de l'Age Moderne*, Paris, 1946, pp. 86 ff.; P. W. Becker, *De Rebus inter Ioannem, Christianum II Daniae Reges ac Ludovicum XII et Jacobum IV Galliae Scotiaeque Reges*, Copenhagen, 1835, pp. 1 f., 7 ff., 75 ff.

13 *Ibid.*, pp. 23 ff., 58 f.; Wood, *op. cit.*, xxvii, xxxiii f.; G. Burnett *et al.*, eds., *The Exchequer Rolls of Scotland*, Edinburgh, 1893, XIV, cxxviii.

14 T. Dickson *et al.*, eds., *The Accounts of the Lord High Treasurer of Scotland*, Edinburgh, 1902, IV, *passim*, and 276, 284, 289, 301 f.; *Letts. Jas. IV*, No. 435.

15 *Treasurer's Accounts*, IV, 287, 289, 306, 317, 444.

16 *Ibid.*, IV, 236, 286.

17 Robert Lindsay of Pitscottie, *The Chroniclis of Scotland*, ed. A. J. G. Mackay, Edinburgh, 1899, I, 251 f.

18 Becker, *op. cit.*, pp. 30 ff.; *Treasurer's Accounts*, IV, 327 f.

19 Becker, *op. cit.*, pp. 33 ff., 66 ff.; *L.&P. Henry VIII*, I, Nos. 2076, 3138, 3225, 3628; *Letts. Jas. IV*, No. 427; *Treasurer's Accounts*, II, 334, 336 f.; Wood, *op. cit.*, p. xxiv, xxxi; 27, 38, 40.

20 *Treasurer's Accounts*, IV, 290, 331.

21 *L.&P. Henry VIII*, I, No. 3086; *Treasurer's Accounts*, IV, 289, 290, 294, 301 ff., 332, 341.

22 *Ibid.*, IV, 290, 299, 332; *L.&P. Henry VIII*, I, No. 2050.

23 Leslie, *op. cit.*, II, 135 ff. Dr. West was Dean of Windsor and Bishop of Ely.

24 *L.&P. Henry VIII*, I, No. 3347.

25 *Ibid.*, I, Nos. 3321, 3372; *Treasurer's Accounts*, IV, xxxi, 300, 305; Leslie, *op. cit.*, II, 138.

26 *Ibid.*, II, 137 f.; *Letts. Jas. IV*, No. 473; A. Spont, ed., *Letters and Papers Relating to the French War, 1512–1513*, London, 1897, p. 27.

27 *Treasurer's Accounts*, IV, 291, 372; *Mss. Français*, No. 2930, Bibliothèque Nationale, Paris; *L.&P. Henry VIII*, I, No. 3321.

28 *Ibid.*, II: 2, No. 1457; Spont, *loc. cit.*; *Letts. Jas. IV.*, No. 476.

29 *Ibid.*, Nos. 466, 467; *L.&P. Henry VIII*, I, Nos. 3321, 3326, 3346, 3347, 3372.

30 *Ibid.*, I, Nos. 3340, 3353; *Letts. Jas. IV*, No. 468.

31 *L.&P. Henry VIII*, I, No. 3412.

32 *Ibid.*, I, Nos. 3359, 3412; Wood, *op. cit.*, p. xlii f.

33 *Ibid.*, pp. 55, 57; Spont, *op. cit.*, pp. xxix–xxxi; Becker, *op. cit.*, pp. 78, 80, 84–86; *L.&P. Henry VIII*, I, Nos. 3577, 3617, 3633; *Letts. Jas. IV*, No. 459; *Treasurer's Accounts*, IV, 355, 400, 402, 406; *Forty-Sixth Rep. Deputy Keeper*, App. II, 56; Mackay, *Poems of Dunbar*, III, 396 f.; *A.D.C.*, XXIX, 178.

34 *Treasurer's Accounts*, IV, 293, 298 f., 398, 459.

35 *Ibid.*; M. Livingstone and D. H. Fleming, eds., *Register of the Secret Seal of Scotland*, Edinburgh, 1908, I, No. 2455.

36 Wood, *op. cit.*, p. liii.

37 R. Brown, ed., *Calendar of State Papers Relating to Venice*, London, 1864, II, 230; *L.&P. Henry VIII*, I, Nos. 3678, 3752.

38 *Ibid.*, I, No. 4330; Spont, *op. cit.*, p. 92 f.

39 *Hanserecesse*, VI, 442; *Treasurer's Accounts*, IV, 529, Appendix, *passim*.

40 *L.&P. Henry VIII*, I, No. 3838.

41 *Ibid.*, I, Nos. 3838, 3882; Spont, *op. cit.*, p. 75.

42 *L.&P. Henry VIII*, I, xlvii, No. 3882; Spont, *op. cit.*, p. 169.

43 *L.&P. Henry VIII*, I, No. 4169; Wood, *op. cit.*, p. 80.

44 *Treasurer's Accounts*, IV, 480; Wood, *op. cit.*, pp. lxvii ff.

45 Spont says that he left on May 22, but the contract for victualing his ship is dated the 24th, which would seem to indicate that he sailed a day or so later. Spont, *op. cit.*, pp. xliii, 125, 178; *Fond Français*, Cote 26, 113, pp. 1.189–1.306, Bibliothèque Nationale, Paris.

46 *L.&P. Henry VIII*, I, No. 3339; *Letts. Jas. IV*, No. 560; R. Holinshed, *Scottish Chronicle*, II, 135 ff.; *Treasurer's Accounts*, IV, 413, 488 ff.; *Exch. Rolls*, XIII, clxxxv; I. A. Taylor, *The Life of James IV*, London, 1913, p. 260 f.

47 Leslie, *op. cit.*, II, 139; Lindsay, *op. cit.*, I, 255 ff.; *Exch. Rolls*, XIII, lxxiv.

48 Taylor, *op. cit.*, Chaps. XVIII–XX; P. F. Tytler, *History of Scotland*, Edinburgh, 1864, II, 289 ff.; R. L. Mackie, *op. cit.*, Chap. X.

49 *A.D.C.*, XVIII, 65.

50 *Treasurer's Accounts*, IV, 531; Spont, *op. cit.*, pp. 178 ff.

51 *Treasurer's Accounts*, IV, 483 ff.; *L.&P. Henry VIII*, I, No. 4556; Spont, *op. cit.*, p. xliv; A. de Teulet, *Inventaire Chronologique des Documents Relatives à l'Histoire d'Écosse*, Edinburgh, 1893, p. 59.

Notes to Chapter VI

1 G. Burnett *et al.*, eds., *The Exchequer Rolls of Scotland*, Edinburgh, 1893, XIV, xxxviii; R. K. Hannay, ed., *Acts of the Lords of the Council in Public Affairs*, Edinburgh, 1932, p. 9.

2 R. S. Rait, *The Parliaments of Scotland*, Glasgow, 1924, pp. 39, 151; *Exch. Rolls*, XIV, xl f.; P. F. Tytler, *History of Scotland*, Edinburgh, 1864, II, 295 f.

3 M. Wood, ed., *Flodden Papers*, Edinburgh, 1933, pp. lxxxvi, 88 f.; P. W. Becker, *De Rebus inter Ioannem, Christianum II, Daniae Reges, ac Ludovicum XII et Jacobum IV Galliae Scotiaeque Reges*, Hafniae, 1835, pp. 89 ff.; Hannay, *Acts*, p. 3; H. Ellis, *Original Letters Illustrative of the History of England*, 2d ed., London, 1825, Ser. 1: 1, 99; [Thomas Ruddiman, ed.], *Epistolae Jacobi IV, Jacobi V et Mariae Regum Scotorum*, Edinburgh, 1722, I, 214; D. Calderwood, *History of the Kirk of Scotland*, ed. Thomas Thomson, Edinburgh, 1842, I, 58.

4 J. S. Brewer, *et. al.*, eds., *Letters and Papers of Henry VIII*, London, 1862, I, No. 4844; Wood, *op. cit.*, p. 101.

5 *Ibid.*, pp. lxxxi, 107 ff.

6 *Ibid.*, pp. lxxxv f.; Hannay, *Acts*, p. 20; T. Rymer, ed., *Foedera, Conventiones et Acta Publica*, The Hague, 1741, VI: 1, 64 ff.

7 Becker, *op. cit.*, p. 93.

8 H. Maxwell, *History of the House of Douglas*, London, 1902, II, 56 ff., 65 f.; Calderwoood, *op. cit.*, I, 58; *Exch. Rolls*, XIV, xlii.

9 Maxwell, *op. cit.*, II, 66.

10 *Exch. Rolls*, XIV, 223; Tytler, *op. cit.*, II, 299.

11 Wood, *op. cit.*, p. lxxxviii f.; *Exch. Rolls*, XIV, 223; *L.&P. Henry VIII*, II: 1, Nos. 261, 287.

12 *Ibid.*, II: 1, No. 344; *Acta Dominorum Concilii*, XXXII, 42; Tytler, *op. cit.*, II, 297. Robert loaned Lord Fleming, one of the Scottish embassy, 80 gold crowns while in Paris.

13 J. MacKinnon, *The Constitutional History of Scotland*, London, 1924, p. 219; *Exch. Rolls*, IV, xliii; Maxwell, *op. cit.*, II, 58, 67 ff.; J. N. Charteris, "The Tudor Dealings with Scotland," (unpublished thesis, McGill University), Chap. III; *L.&P. Henry VIII*, II: 1, Nos. 401, 541, 588, 850, 1011; *Royal Correspondence, Scotland* (ms.), Danish Royal Archives, A II, Reg. 14,287, Nr. 30 n.

14 *Rothes Cartulary*, (ms.) H.M. General Register House, Edinburgh, pp. 76, 79; *A.D.C.*, XXVII, 47, 103, 107, 130. Wheat was selling at 18s. the boll, bere (a coarse barley) at 14s. the boll, meal at 13s. 4d. the boll, and fowl at 8s. the dozen.

15 *A.D.C.*, XXVII, 111.

16 *Ibid.*, XXVII, 114, 115, 185.

17 *Ibid.*, XXVII, 57.

18 *Ibid.*, XXVII, 54, 56.

19 *Ibid.*, XXVII, 57, 60, 65; Hannay, *Acts*, p. 55.

20 *A.D.C.*, XXVII, 66 ff.

21 *Ibid.*, XXVII, 168, 171, 200, 209, 232.

22 H. J. Smit, ed., *Bronnen tot de Geschiedenis van den Handel met Engeland, Schotland en Ierland*, The Hague, 1942, II: 1, Nos. 305 f.; Hannay, *Acts*, pp. 19, 64; *A.D.C.*, XXVII, 144; *L.&P. Henry VIII*, II: 2, No. 2730.

23 *A.D.C.*, XXVII, 89, 213; XXX, 92 f.

24 *Ibid.*, XXVIII, 7.

25 *Ibid.*, XXVII, 69.

26 J. C. Irons, *Leith and its Antiquities*, Edinburgh, 1898, I, 149, 152; *Charters, etc., Relating to the City of Edinburgh, 1143–1540*, Scottish Record Society, Edinburgh, 1871, p. 159.

27 T. Dickson, *et al.*, eds., *The Accounts of the Lord High Treasurer of Scotland*, Edinburgh, 1903, V, 41, 42; Maxwell, *op. cit.*, II, 69.

28 Hannay, *Acts*, p. 63.

29 *L.&P. Henry VIII*, II, No. 1553, cf. also *Treasurer's Accounts*, V, 75.

30 *Ibid.*, V, 68 f., 72 f.

31 *A.D.C.*, XXVII, 192.

32 M. Livingstone and D. H. Fleming, eds., *Register of the Secret Seal of Scotland*, Edinburgh, 1921, I, No. 2694.

33 *Exch. Rolls*, XIV, 489, 494.

34 *Ibid.*, XIV, xxxi, 134, 155 ff.

Notes to Chapter VII

1 T. Dickson, *et al.*, eds., *The Accounts of the Lord High Treasurer of Scotland*, Edinburgh, 1877, I, xiv–xxii; *Excerpta e Libris Domicilli Jacobi Quinti, 1525–1533*, Bannatyne Club, 1836, p. v.

2 M. P. Gilmour, *The World of Humanism*, New York, 1952, p. 124; *Treasurer's Accounts*, IV, 447.

3 G. Burnett *et al.*, eds., *The Exchequer Rolls of Scotland*, Edinburgh, 1893, XIV, xxx ff. A list of the lands still held by the crown included among other properties the earldoms of Fife, Bute, Strathearn, and Moray, and the lordships of Ross and Ardmanach, Galloway, Balincreif, Glencairney, Urquhart, Glenmoriston, and Abernethy. Crown lands in Stirlingshire, and Linlithgow, along with the earldom of March and the Forest of Ettrick were the Queen's dowry (p. xxxiii).

4 *Acta Dominorum Concilii*, XXVIII, 95; cf. also *Exch. Rolls*, XIV, xxx, 116 f., 214 ff.; R. S. Rait, *The Parliaments of Scotland*, Glasgow, 1924, p. 363.

5 *A.D.C.*, XXVIII, *loc. cit.*

6 *Ibid.*, XXVIII, 53, 71 ff.

7 *Ibid.*, XXIX, 19.

8 *Ibid.*, XXVIII, 53, 89, 95; R. K. Hannay, ed., *Acts of the Lords of the Council in Public Affairs*, Edinburgh, 1932, p. 127.

9 *A.D.C.*, XXIX, 5; XXXIV, 61.

10 Hannay, *Acts*, p. 72; *Exch. Rolls*, XIV, 245, 258, 490.

11 *Treasurer's Accounts*, V, 114 f., 124.

12 *A.D.C.*, XXIX, 91 f., *Exch. Rolls*, XIV, xxxiii, 417 ff.

13 Hannay, *Acts*, p. 81.

14 *Ibid.*, pp. 76, 82; *A.D.C.*, XXVIII, 57, 59; XXIX, 197, 198; XXX, 178.

15 *Ibid.*, XXIX, 33.

16 *Ibid.*, XXIX, 37.

17 Hannay, *Acts*, p. 96; *Extracts from the Records of the Burgh of Edinburgh, 1403–1528*, Edinburgh, 1869, p. 168; R. K. Hannay, "Incidents and Documents, A.D. 1513–1523," *The Book of the Old Edinburgh Club*, Edinburgh, 1916, IX, 19 f.

18 *Rothes Cartulary* (ms.), H.M. General Register House, Edinburgh, p. 40, 625, 627.

19 *Ibid.*, XIV, 225, 243, 260, 263, 268; *A.D.C.*, XXX, 134. Many pages of the *Exchequer Rolls* are taken up with such items.

20 *Exch. Rolls*, XIV, xxx, 116 ff., 214 ff., 279 ff.

21 J. S. Brewer *et al.*, eds., *Letters and Papers of Henry VIII*, London, 1864, II: 2, No. 2742; M. Wood, ed., *Flodden Papers*, Edinburgh, 1933, pp. xcvi, 123 ff.

22 H. Maxwell, *History of the House of Douglas*, London, 1902, II, 58, 71; *Exch. Rolls*, XIV, lx.

23 *A.D.C.*, XXX, 159. Feu-farming was the system of granting land for a very large initial payment, and small subsequent yearly rents. The grant might be for a period of years, a period of lives, or in perpetuity.

24 *Ibid.*, XXX, 211, 215.

25 *Ibid.*, XXX, 222.

26 Hannay, *Acts*, pp. 124, 126, 127; *A.D.C.*, XXXI, 122, 123.

27 *Ibid.* XXXI, 105.

28 *Ibid.*, XXX, *passim*.

29 *Ibid.*, XXX, 216.

30 Hannay, *Acts*, p. 117.

31 *L.&P. Henry VIII*, III: 2, No. 1898.

32 *Exch. Rolls*, XIV, 358.

33 *Ibid.*, XIV, 344 ff.

34 M. Livingstone and D. H. Fleming, eds., *Register of the Secret Seal of Scotland*, Edinburgh, 1921, I, No. 3016; T. Thomson, ed., *Acts of the Parliament of Scotland*, Edinburgh, 1814, II, 320; *Treasurer's Accounts*, V, 141; *L.&P. Henry VIII*, III: 2, No. 1898.

35 *A.D.C.*, XXXI, 174. This Margaret Crichton was the illegitimate daughter of Lord Crichton and Lady Margaret, only daughter of the unfortunate James III, and so was a cousin, although illegitimate, of Albany. During James IV's reign she had received certain privileges from the king, and these show her to have been something of a business woman. She married first William Todrig, a wealthy Edinburgh merchant, then George Halkerstone, a burgess of the same city. Her second husband died at Flodden but she carried on his business and his activity as "custumar" of Edinburgh probably until Robert Barton assumed the office. In 1517 she entered into an irregular marital arrangement with the Duke of Rothes, but he divorced her in 1520, after which he had a succession of wives. Finally in 1542 they were reunited and Margaret died as Countess of Rothes in 1546. By her first marriage to the duke she had borne him a son, Norman who became Master of Rothes and was involved in the murder of Cardinal Beaton. During her second marriage she bore him other children. (M. W. Stuart, *The Scot Who Was a Frenchman*, London, 1940, p. 70 f.)

36 *Rothes Cart.*, p. 621.

37 Hannay, *Acts*, p. 128. The King of France's granting of special privileges to Scottish merchants in 1518 may have stimulated him to increase his business. (Stuart, *op. cit.*, p. 298.)

Notes to Chapter VIII

1 R. K. Hannay, ed., *Acts of the Lords of the Council in Public Affairs*, Edinburgh, 1329, p. 128.

2 *Acta Dominorum Concilii*, XXXII, 5 f.

3 *Ibid.*, XXXII, 107.

4 *Ibid.*, XXXII, 149.

5 *Ibid.*, XXXI, 104; Hannay, *Acts*, p. 133; J. S. Brewer *et al.*, eds., *Letters and Papers of Henry VIII*, London, 1864, II: 2, No. 4677.

6 *Ibid.*, II: 2, Nos. 4056, 4117, 4157, 4172, 4201, 4241, 4244; W. E. Collins, "The Scandinavian North," *Cambridge Modern History*, Cambridge, 1907, p. 603 f.; R. N. Bain, *Scandinavia*, Cambridge, 1905, p. 18 f.; C. F. Allen, *Histoire de Danemark*, Copenhagen, 1878, I, 268 ff.; Thomas Ruddiman, ed., *Epistolae Jacobi IV, Jacobi V et Mariae Regum Scotorum*, Edinburgh, 1722, I, 301; G. Burnett *et al.*, eds., *The Exchequer Rolls of Scotland*, Edinburgh, 1893, XIV, cxxxii f.

7 *Royal Correspondence, Scotland*, (ms.), Danish Royal Archives, A II, Reg. 14,288, Nr. 31c; *Forty-Sixth Annual Report of the Deputy Keeper of the Records*, London, 1886, App. II, 57.

8 *L.&P. Henry VIII*, III: 1, Nos. 112, 143; Ruddiman, *op. cit.*, 1, 313 f.; *Exch. Rolls*, XIV, cxxxiii.

9 *Ibid.*, XIV, cxxxv; Hannay, *Acts*, pp. 144 f.

10 *Exch. Rolls*, XIV, cxxxiv, 459, 461; *L.&P. Henry VIII*, III: 1, No. 268.

11 *Royal Correspondence, Scotland* (ms.), Danish Royal Archives, A II, Reg. 14, 287, No. 31b; 1507, No. 1. The latter document, although dated 1507, cannot possibly be of that date since Christian II was not King of Denmark, nor did Robert sell him the *Lion*, at this time. The only dating of the letter which meets fully the requirements of both the internal and external evidence is 1519.

12 *L.&P. Henry VIII*, III: 1, No. 341; *Exch. Rolls*, XIV, cxxxiv; Ruddiman, *op. cit.*, I, 320.

13 cf. note 11 *supra*.

14 H. Maxwell, *The History of the House of Douglas*, London, 1902, II, 72 f.

15 *L.&P. Henry VIII*, III: 1, Nos. 381, 396, 1024. Her lands were worth £6,000 (Scots) per annum, (*Ibid*, II, 2721).

16 J. B. Paul, *The Scots Peerage*, Edinburgh, 1910, VII, 45, *The Drummond Writs*, H.M. General Register House, Edinburgh, box II.

17 Hannay, *Acts*, p. 148; *Exch. Rolls*, XIV, 403.

18 *Ibid.*, XIV, ix f.; D. Calderwood, *The History of the Kirk of Scotland*, ed. T. Thomson, Edinburgh, 1847, I, 62; Maxwell, *op. cit.*, II, 59.

19 *L.&P. Henry VIII*, III: 1, Nos. 859, 964, 1127; Maxwell, *op. cit.*, I, 74; *Treaties with France* (ms.), H.M. General Reg. House.

20 *Lettres Missives* (ms.), Archives Départementales, Département du Nord, Lille, Ser. B., No. 34, 733; Hannay, *Acts*, p. 500; *L.&P. Henry VIII*, XV, No. 9; M. Livingstone and D. H. Fleming, eds., *Register of the Secret Seal of Scotland*, Edinburgh, 1921, II, No. 3235; *Exch. Rolls*, XIV, 464.

21 *Ibid.*, XIV, 492 f., 500 f., 505, 511.

22 *Ibid.*, XIV, lxiv, 459; *L.&P. Henry VIII*, III: 2, No. 1919.

23 *Exch. Rolls*, XIV, 451.

24 P. F. Tytler, *History of Scotland*, Edinburgh, 1864, II, 317; Maxwell, *op. cit.*, II, 74.

25 *Exch. Rolls*, XIV, lxiv, 459.

26 E. H. Dunkley, *The Reformation in Denmark*, London, 1949, pp. 21 ff.; Collins, *op. cit.*, pp. 606 ff.; Allen, *op. cit.*, I, 280 ff.; J. Jorgensen, *Geschichte der Danischen Literatur*, Munich, 1908, p. 20 f.; *Royal Correspondence, Scotland*, Dan. Archives, A II; *Forty-Sixth Rep. Deputy Keeper*, App. II, 57.

27 *L.&P. Henry VIII*, III: 2, App. No. 33.

28 *Exch. Rolls*, XIV, 346 ff., 451 ff.

29 *L.&P. Henry VIII*, III: 2, No. 1898.

Notes to Chapter IX

1 P. F. Tytler, *History of Scotland*, Edinburgh, 1864, II, 320; T. Dickson et al., eds., *The Accounts of the Lord High Treasurer of Scotland*, Edinburgh, 1903, V, 202; J. S. Brewer et al., eds., *Letters and Papers of Henry VIII*, London, 1867, III: 2, No. 2542; *Chambre des Comptes de Lille* (ms.), Archives du Département du Nord, Lille, Ser. B, 594/22.064.

2 *L.&P. Henry VIII*, III: 2, Nos. 2568, 2622, 2764.

3 *Chroniclis of Scotland*, ed. A. J. G. Mackay, Edinburgh, 1899, I, 304 f.

4 Tytler, *op. cit.*, II, 321.

5 *Acta Dominorum Concilii*, XXXIII, 93.

6 J. C. Irons, *Leith and its Antiquities*, Edinburgh, 1898, I, 154 f., 157; *A.D.C.*, XXXIII, 37, 47.

7 R. K. Hannay, ed., *Acts of the Lords of the Council in Public Affairs*, Edinburgh, 1932, pp. 159, 161.

8 *Ibid.*, pp. 159 f.

9 *Ibid.*, 161 f.

10 *Ibid.*, 162, 164, 167.

11 *A.D.C.*, XXXIII, 151.

12 H. J. Smit, ed., *Bronnen tot de Geschiedenis van den Handel met Engeland, Schotland en Ierland*, The Hague, 1942, II: 1, Nos. 222, 267, 278, 290, 291, 302 note 1; S. T. Bindoff, *The Scheldt Question to 1839*, London, 1954, p. 75; *L.&P. Henry VIII*, I, No. 4743; M. P. Rooseboom, *The Scottish Staple in the Netherlands*, The Hague, 1919, Appendix No. 38.

13 *L.&P. Henry VIII*, II, Nos. 1727, 1755, 1938, 2520; Smit, *op cit.*, II: 1, Nos. 309, 310, 319; pp. 234 note 1; 241 note 1.

14 *Ibid.*, II: 1, No. 318.

15 *Ibid.*, II: 1, Nos. 321, 322, 325, 327, 329–39, 386, 389; W. S. Unger, ed., *Bronnen tot de Geschiedenis van Middelburgh in den Landsheerlijken Tijd*, The Hague, 1923, I, Nos. 302, 303, 482; III, No. 469; J. Davidson and A. Gray, *The Scottish Staple at Veere*, London, 1909, p. 151; Hannay, *op. cit.*, p. 164.

16 Smit, *op. cit.*, II: 1, Nos. 327, 395; Rooseboom, *op. cit.*, p. 39.

17 Hannay, *op. cit.*, p. 177; Smit, *op. cit.*, II: 1, Nos. 396, 401, 402. The suggestion of Hannay ("Shipping and the Staple," *The Book of the Old Edinburgh Club*, Edinburgh, 1916, IX, 68–70) that the ship was arrested because Albany had taken over the money promised by Middelburg seems to have no foundation. From Cottis' letter we know

that the money had not been paid even after the arrest, and the process at Middelburg shows that the action was taken at the instigation of Kadde.

18 *The Letters of James V*, calendared R. K. Hannay, ed. D. Hay, Edinburgh, 1954, p. 177.

19 *L.&P. Henry VIII*, III: 1, No. 1301; III: 2, Nos. 2833, 2846, 2851, 2856, 2869, 2881, 2885, 2886, 2974; R. Brown, ed., *Calendar of State Papers Relating to Venice*, London, 1869, III, 637; G. Burnett *et al.*, eds., *The Exchequer Rolls of Scotland*, Edinburgh, 1895, XV, xxxix.

20 *L.&P. Henry VIII*, III: 2, No. 3110; Hannay, *Acts*, p. 175.

21 *L.&P. Henry VIII*, III: 2, No. 3237.

22 *Ibid.*

23 D. Calderwood, *The History of the Kirk of Scotland*, ed. T. Thomson, Edinburgh, 1847, I, 66; Hannay, *op. cit.*, pp. 176, 182, 188; Tytler, *op. cit.*, II, 324 f.

24 *Exch. Rolls*, XV, lxv–lxvi, 70, 71, 98 f., 188, 442, 448.

25 *A.D.C.*, XXXIV, 61, 140, 153, 157.

26 *Exch. Rolls*, XV, 84 ff.; *Treasurer's Accounts*, V, 192 f.

27 *Ibid.*, V, 238 f.; *Exch. Rolls*, XV, lxv f.

28 *A.D.C.*, XXXIV, 174.

29 *L.&P. Henry VIII*, IV, 68; H. Ellis, ed., *Original Letters Illustrative of English History*, London, 1825, Ser. 1: I, 244, 246; T. Thomson, ed., *A Diurnal of Remarkable Occurrents which have Passed within the Country of Scotland*, Edinburgh, 1833, p. 9.

30 J. B. Paul *et al.*, eds., *Register of the Great Seal of Scotland*, Edinburgh, 1883, III, No. 254.

31 *A.D.C.*, XXXIV, 167 ff., 189.

32 J. B. Paul, *The Scots Peerage*, Edinburgh, 1910, VIII, 388; *A.D.C.*, XXXIV, 183 ff. This indenture was published in *The Scottish Historical Review*, XXVIII (1949), 58 f.

33 "Calder Writs," *Lord Torphichen's Muniments* (ms.), Bundle XV, 1, 2; *Reg. Grt. Seal*, III, No. 279.

34 Hannay, *op. cit.*, p. 204 f. Gonzolles in a letter to Albany (Sept. 3, 1524) reported the country to be in chaos as the pro-Albany party headed by the chancellor who was the Archbishop of St. Andrews, the bishops of Aberdeen, Brechin, and Dunblane, and one or two abbots did not feel that they should renounce obedience to the duke until it was shown that he would not be back within his allotted three months. The bishops of Dunkeld and Galloway and the abbots of Holyrood and Paisley wished to declare him to be no longer regent. St. Andrews and Aberdeen were arrested as they attempted to slip out of Edinburgh. The earls of Argyle, Lennox, and Moray who were also on the duke's side were retiring to their estates, while Lord Fleming, his son, and the Master of Glamis had fled in fear of their lives. The fact that the Albany faction was under such pressure makes it all the more obvious that Queen Margaret and her supporters felt Robert was absolutely indispensable, or they would never have kept him. (*L. & P. Henry VIII*, IV: 1, No. 670.)

Notes to Chapter X

1 R. S. Rait, *The Parliaments of Scotland*, Glasgow, 1924, p. 40 f.; H. Maxwell, *The History of the House of Douglas*, London, 1902, II, 77; J. S. Brewer *et al.*, eds., *Letters and Papers of Henry VIII*, London, 1870, IV: 1, Nos. 613, 631, 670, 817.

2 R. K. Hannay, ed., *Acts of the Lords of the Council in Public Affairs, 1501–1554*, Edinburgh, 1932, p. 211.

3 *L. & P. Henry VIII*, IV: 1, No. 685.

4 *Ibid.*, IV: 1, No. 870.

5 *Ibid.*, IV: 1, Nos. 766, 768, 797.

6 *Ibid.*, IV: 1, Nos. 768, 797.

7 *Ibid.*, IV: 1, No. 817; J. Stevenson, *Illustrations of Scottish History from the 12th to the 16th Centuries*, Glasgow, 1834, p. 101.

8 *L. & P. Henry VIII*, IV: 1, No. 817.

9 *Ibid.*, IV: 1, Nos. 917, 919, 943; Stevenson, *op. cit.*, p. 119.

10 J. Stedman, *Memorial of the Family of Barton*, Bath, 1857, p. 26.

11 P. de Gayangos, ed., *Calendar of State Papers Relating to Spain*, London, 1873, III: 1, 4; *L.&P. Henry VIII*, IV: 1, Nos. 870, 1029.

12 Stevenson, *op. cit.*, p. 122; P. F. Tytler, *History of Scotland*, Edinburgh, 1864, II, 333.

13 *L.&P. Henry VIII*, IV: 1, No. 1027.

14 *Cottonian Mss.*, British Museum, Cal. B II, fo. 133; Tytler, *op. cit.*, II, 334; Maxwell, *op. cit.*, II, 80.

15 *L.&P. Henry VIII*, IV: 1, No. 1056.

16 *Ibid.*, IV: 1, Nos. 1105, 1111, 1446.

17 Rait, *op. cit.*, p. 42; Tytler, *op. cit.*, II, 336 ff.

18 *Acta Dominorum Concilii*, XXXV, 18 f.

19 *Ibid.*, XXXV, 22 f.

20 *Ibid.*, XXXV, 19, 22. That the guarantee of Angus, Arran, and Fleming to Robert, which was registered first on May 6, was cancelled "by order of the King," probably because Robert's agreement with the queen had not been produced, would seem to verify this hypothesis. Only after the latter document was registered was the guarantee permitted to stand.

21 Hannay, *Acts*, p. 216.

22 M. Livingstone and D. H. Fleming, eds., *Register of the Secret Seal of Scotland*, Edinburgh, 1921, I, No. 3284.

23 *A.D.C.*, XXXV, 97.

24 W. E. Collins, "The Scandinavian North," *Cambridge Modern History*, Cambridge, 1907, II, 607 f.; C. F. Allen, *Histoire de Danemark*, Copenhagen, 1878, I, 283 f., 288; H. Zimmern, *The Hansa Towns*, London, 1889, pp. 233 ff.; E. H. Dunkley, *The Reformation in Denmark*, London, 1948, pp. 37 ff.; *Forty-Fifth Annual Report of the Deputy Keeper of the Public Records*, London, 1886, App. II, 7 ff., 57; *L.&P. Henry VIII*, III: 2, Nos. 2886, 2971, 3142, 3153, 3165; IV: 1, Nos. 747, 777, App. No. 10; R. N. Bain, *Scandinavia*, Cambridge,

1905, p. 29; *Royal Correspondence*, Danish Royal Archives, A II; C. F. Wegener, ed., *Aarsberetninger fra det Kongelige Geheimarchiv*, Copenhagen, 1865, III, 110, 113, 118.

25 *Diplomatarium Norvegicum*, Christiana, 1847, XVI, No. 430.

26 R. K. Hannay, "Shipping and the Staple," *The Book of the Old Edinburgh Club*, Edinburgh, 1916, IX, 60 f.; Hannay, *Acts*, p. 202.

27 *Ibid.*, p. 212.

28 *Ibid.*, p. 215, 232 f.; *A.D.C.*, XXXV, 7–9.

29 *Ibid.*, XXXV, 21, 29 f.; Hannay, *Acts*, p. 220 f.

30 *Ibid.*, p. 219.

31 D. Schafer *et al.*, eds., *Die Hanserecesse*, Leipzig, 1913, Ser. 3, IX, No. 82.

32 *Diplom. Norweg.*, XII, No. 364.

33 Hannay, *Acts*, p. 224.

34 *Ibid.*, p. 226; "Shipping and the Staple," p. 66.

35 *A.D.C.*, XXXIV, 199; S. Cowan, *The Lord Chancellors of Scotland*, Edinburgh, 1891, I, 263.

36 *A.D.C.*, XXX, 234; T. Dickson *et al.*, eds., *The Accounts of the Lord High Treasurer of Scotland*, Edinburgh, 1902, IV, 142, 264, 447; V, 55; G. Burnett *et al.*, eds., *The Exchequer Rolls of Scotland*, Edinburgh, 1893, XIV, 44, 57, 137, 234; XV, lxi.

37 *Ibid.*, XV, 584.

38 *A.D.C.*, XXXV, 30.

39 *Ibid.*, XXXV, 31.

40 *Exch. Rolls*, XV, 559.

41 *A.D.C.*, XXXV, 140 f.; *Exch. Rolls*, XV, 125, 143.

42 *A.D.C.*, XXXV, 110 ff.

43 *Excerpta e Libris Domicilii Jacobi Quinti, 1525–1533*, Edinburgh, 1836, p. vi.

44 *L.&P. Henry VIII*, IV: 1, No. 1545; *Exch. Rolls*, XV, lxii f.

45 *Ibid.*, XV, 84, 194 f., 197 f., 211.

46 *Ibid.*, XV, 184, 194, 282 ff.; *L.&P. Henry VIII*, IV: 1, No. 1592.

47 Hannay, *Acts*, p. 66; *A.D.C.*, XXXV, 150.

Notes to Chapter XI

1 T. Thomson, ed., *Acts of the Parliament of Scotland*, Edinburgh, 1814, II, 294; W. Fraser, *The Douglas Book*, Edinburgh, 1885, II, 220 f.

2 *Ibid.*, II, 212, 222 f.; *Acta Dominorum Concilii*, XXXVI, 9.

3 R. K. Hannay, ed., *Acts of the Lords of the Council in Public Affairs*, Edinburgh, 1932, p. 227. Robert may have returned temporarily to office at this point, for he was called the comptroller on August 16. (*A.D.C.*, XXXV, 148). Colvile, however, was apparently eventually satisfied.

4 *A.D.C.*, XXXV, 177 f.; Fraser, *op. cit.*, II, 204.

5 Fraser, *op. cit.*, II, 224 ff.; Robert Lindsay of Pitscottie, *The Chroniclis of Scotland*, ed. A. J. G. Mackay, Edinburgh, 1899, I, 318 f.; *A.D.C.*, XXXVI, 67, 73.

6 *Excerpta e Libris Domicilii Jacobi Quinti, 1525–33*, Edinburgh, 1836, p. 6.

7 *A.D.C.*, XXXV, 187. As Murray failed to appear before the Lords in his own defense, the latter ordered him to restore the goods he had taken.

8 *Liber Introitus de Edinburgh*, (ms.), H.M. General Register House, Edinburgh, 1528.

9 *Ibid.*; *James Colvile's Customes Book, Edinburgh, 1528* (ms.), H.M. General Register House, Edinburgh; G. Burnett *et al.*, eds., *The Exchequer Rolls of Scotland*, Edinburgh, 1895, XV, 440.

10 *A.D.C.*, XXXVI, 66, 67, 72, 80, 81, 87; *A.P.S.*, II, 306.

11 *A.D.C.*, XXXVIII, 87, 134 f.

12 H. J. Smit, ed., *Bronnen tot de Geschiedenis van den Handel met Engeland, Schotland en Ierland*, The Hague, 1942, II: 1, Nos. 406, 409, 416; W. S. Unger, ed., *Bronnen tot de Geschiedenis van Middelburgh in den*

Landsheerlijken Tijd, The Hague, 1926, II, No. 309; J. H. de Stoppelaar, *Inventoris van het Oud Archief der Stat Middelburgh*, Middelburg, 1883, No. 1290.

13 Smit, *op. cit.*, II: 1, Nos. 426, 430 ff., 440, 441; Unger, *op. cit.*, III, No. 511; Hannay, *Acts*, p. 222.

14 M. P. Rooseboom, *The Scottish Staple in the Netherlands*, The Hague, 1919, p. 42; Hannay, *op. cit.*, p. 236; Smit., *op. cit.*, II: 1, Nos. 452 ff.

15 *Ibid.*, II: 1, Nos. 458 f., pp. 351 n.1, 352 n.1; *A.P.S.*, III, 305.

16 Hannay, *Acts*, pp. 243, 246 f.; *Exch. Rolls*, XV, lxx; *A.P.S.*, II, 315.

17 *Ibid.*, II, 314; *Exch. Rolls*, XV, lxxi; T. Dickson *et al.*, eds., *The Accounts of the Lord High Treasurer of Scotland*, Edinburgh, 1903, V, 307.

18 *A.P.S.*, II, 313 f.; Smit, *op. cit.* II: 1, 354n. 2; Hannay, *Acts*, p. 253.

19 *Lettres Missives*, Archives du Département du Nord, Lille, Ser. B, No. 34,733; J. S. Brewer *et al.*, eds., *Letters and Papers of Henry VIII*, London, 1870, IV: 1, Nos. 3778, 4101, IV: 2, No. 3612; M. J. Thorpe, *Calendar of State Papers Relating to Scotland*, London, 1858, I, 26, 27.

20 *A.D.C.*, XXXVI, 51, 129, 144.

21 *Ibid.*, XXXV, 148.

22 M. Livingstone and D. H. Fleming, eds., *Register of the Secret Seal of Scotland*, Edinburgh, 1908, I, Nos. 3347, 3348; J. Paul *et al.*, eds., *Register of the Great Seal of Scotland*, Edinburgh, 1882, III, No. 1002.

23 Hannay, *Acts*, p. 227.

24 *L.&P. Henry VIII*, IV: 1, 1592. The original, which contains more information, is in *State Papers*, 49, III, 23, Public Record Office, London.

25 Hannay, *Acts*, p. 258.

26 *A.D.C.*, XXXVIII, 74, 75.

27 Cf. *supra*, p. 192 f.; *L.&P. Henry VIII*, IV: 3, App. No. 97; *A.P.S.*, II, 313.

28 *A.D.C.*, XXXVII, 207 f.; Hannay, *Acts*, pp. 253, 271 f.

29 *Reg. Sec. Seal*, I, No. 3388; R. Pitcairn, *Ancient Criminal Trials*, Edinburgh, 1833, I: 1, *237.

30 *Reg. Sec. Seal*, I, No. 3568; J. Skene, *De Verborum Significatione*, Edinburgh, 1681, "assisa" and "schiereff."

31 *A.P.S.*, II, 320.

32 *A.D.C.*, XXXVII, 146; *Treasurer's Accounts*, V, 293.

33 *A.D.C.*, XXXVIII, 9, 26, 68, 70; *Inventory of Earl of Crawford and Balcarres Scottish Muniments at Haigh*, Vol. I, 79–80 (ms.), H.M. General Register House, Edinburgh.

34 *A.D.C.*, XXXVIII, 91, 111.

35 Hannay, *Acts*, p. 253; *Diplomatarium Norvegicum*, Christiana, 1847, VIII, Nos. 132, 561, 565; X, No. 546; XI, No. 460; XVI, No. 482; XV, No. 348; *L.&P. Henry VIII*, IV: 2, 2547, 2548.

36 *Ibid.*, XII, 395.

37 *L.&P. Henry VIII*, IV: 2, 3803; A. Teulet, ed., *Papiers d'état Relatifs à l'Histoire de l'Ecosse au Seizième Siècle*, Paris, 1851, I, 89.

Notes to Chapter XII

1 W. Fraser, *The Douglas Book*, Edinburgh, 1885, II, 238 ff.; R. K. Hannay, ed., *Acts of the Lords of the Council in Public Affairs*, Edinburgh, 1932, p. 277.

2 *Ibid.*, p. 281.

3 T. Thomson, ed., *Acts of the Parliament of Scotland*, Edinburgh, 1814, II, 322, 325, 327.

4 Fraser, *op. cit.*, II, 238; H. Maxwell, *The History of the House of Douglas*, London, 1902, II, 99; *A.P.S.*, II, 322 f.

5 *Diplomatarium Norvegicum*, Christiana, 1847, XVIII, No. 515; T. Thomson, ed., *Diurnal of Remarkable Occurrents*, Edinburgh, 1833, p. 12; J. S. Brewer *et al.*, eds., *Letters and Papers of Henry VIII*, London, 1872, IV: 2, No. 4923; Fraser, *op. cit.*, II, 237 f.

6 *Ibid.*, II, 251; D. Calderwood, *The History of the Kirk of Scotland*, ed. T. Thomson, Edinburgh, 1847, I, 99 f.; Hannay, *op. cit.*, p. 296; *Acta Dominorum Concilii*, XXXIX, 114, 132; XL, 23, 130, 166.

7 Fraser, *op. cit.*, II, 239 ff.; *L.&P. Henry VIII*, IV: 2, No. 4720.

8 T. Rymer, ed., *Foedera, Conventiones et Acta Publica*, The Hague, 1741, VI: 1, 110; *L.&P. Henry VIII*, IV: 2, No. 5289.

9 Fraser, *op. cit.*, II, 334; M. Livingstone and D. H. Fleming, eds., *Register of the Secret Seal of Scotland*, Edinburgh, 1906, I, No. 4104; Hannay, *op. cit.*, p. 306; Calderwood, *op. cit.*, I, 100; G. Burnett *et al.*, eds., *The Exchequer Rolls of Scotland*, Edinburgh, 1897, XVI, xxxviii.

10 *Reg. Sec. Seal*, I, Nos. 4109, 4117; Hannay, *op. cit.*, p. 308; *A.D.C.*, XXXIX, 171.

11 Hannay, *op. cit.*, p. 524; Calderwood, *op. cit.*, I, 100; Fraser, *op. cit.*, II, 241.

12 *Diplomatarium Norvegicum*, XVIII, No. 515.

13 *Supra*, p. 202; *A.D.C.*, XL, 53.

14 Hannay, *op. cit.*, p. 311.

15 *A.D.C.*, XL, 60.

16 J. Paul *et al.*, eds., *Register of the Great Seal of Scotland*, Edinburgh, 1882, III, Nos. 801, 806, 818.

17 T. Dickson, *et al.*, eds., *The Accounts of the Lord High Treasurer of Scotland*, Edinburgh, 1903, V, 390, 437 f.

18 *Exch. Rolls*, XV, 682.

19 *Ibid.*, XV, 513; *A.D.C.*, XL, 92 ff., 102, 105.

20 *Exch. Rolls*, XV, 390 f., 456 f., 529 ff., 531, 538 f.

21 Hannay, *op. cit.*, pp. 313 ff.

22 *Liber Introitus de Edinburgh*, 1528.

23 *Reg. Grt. Seal*, III, Nos. 801, 806.

24 *A.D.C.*, XXXIX, 21; *Crawford and Balcarres Muniments*, Box B, p. 79 f. There are other complaints of Crawford's sharp practices in the *Acts of the Lords*, cf., *A.D.C.*, XXXVIII, 157.

25 *Reg. Grt. Seal*, III, Nos. 765, 773.

26 *A.D.C.*, XXXIX, 84, 120. The case was first of all committed to "judge-ment arbitral," the arbitrators awarding Robert 200 marks, but when Dundas ignored the judgement he proceeded to demand definitive judgement, which he obtained on February 27.

27 *Ibid.*, XXXVIII, 136 f.; *Exch. Rolls*, XV, 581.

28 *A.D.C.*, XL, 111.

29 Hannay, *op. cit.*, pp. 232, 239, 242, 253, 310; *A.D.C.*, XXXVI, 13, 20, 113 f.

30 *Ibid.*, XLI, 77; Hannay, *op. cit.*, p. 327.

31 *Reg. Grt. Seal*, III, Nos. 848, 854, 855, 871, 882, 929.

32 Hannay, *op. cit.*, p. 327; *A.D.C.*, XLI, 35, 40, 90, 101.

33 *Reg. Grt. Seal*, III, No. 954.

34 Hannay, *op. cit.*, p. 331 f.

35 *Ibid.*, p. 338. The abbot was George Durie, Archdeacon of St. Andrews and nephew of James Beaton, Archbishop of St. Andrews (J. M. Webster, *Dunfermline Abbey*, Dunfermline, 1948, p. 59).

36 *A.D.C.*, XLI, 78, 102, 106, 107.

37 *Ibid.*, XLI, 104.

38 *Calendar of Writs Preserved at Yester House, 1166–1625*, Scottish Record Society, Edinburgh, 1917, No. 462.

39 *Treasurer's Accounts*, V, 333–56.

40 *Exch. Rolls*, XV, 553; XVI, 142 f. Colvile was granted one-third of the casualties of Ayrshire to repay him for the balance still owing. *Reg. Sec. Seal*, II, No. 307.

41 Hannay, *op. cit.*, p. 344; *op. cit.*, II, 307, 408. Colvile was not comptroller on September 2 nor apparently by October 30, while Robert had vacated that office by December 6.

Notes to Chapter XIII

1 A. F. Mitchell, ed., *The Richt Vay to the Kingdom of Hevine*, Edinburgh, 1888, pp. xi–xxii.

2 Cf. the author's articles: "Lutheranism in the Scottish Reformation," *Westminster Theological Journal*, VII (1945), 91 ff.; "The Middle Class Factor in the Scottish Reformation," *Church History*, XVI (1947), pp. 137 ff.; "Clerical Taxation, the Scottish Alternative to Dissolution of the Monasteries, 1530–1560," *The Catholic Historical Review*, XXXV, (1948), 129 ff.

3 G. Burnett *et al.*, eds., *The Exchequer Rolls of Scotland*, Edinburgh, 1897, XVI, 127, 141 ff.

4 R. K. Hannay, ed., *Acts of the Lords of the Council in Public Affairs*, Edinburgh, 1932, p. 344.

5 *Ibid.*, p. 361.

6 *Acta Dominorum Concilii et Sessionis*, (ms.), H.M. General Register House, Edinburgh, II, 172.

7 *Ibid.*, II, 176 f.

8 *Ibid.*, IX, 49, 77; Hannay, *op. cit.*, p. 456.

9 *A.D.C.&S.*, X, 190; XI, 228; Hannay, *op. cit.*, pp. 455, 474, 476.

10 *Ibid.*, pp. 419, 455, 470; *A.D.C.&S.*, X, 94; T. Thomson, ed., *Acts of the Parliament of Scotland*, Edinburgh, 1814, II, 325.

11 *Acta Dominorum Concilii*, XLI, 153, 157; *Protocol Book of Gavin Ros*, *1512–1532*, Edinburgh, 1908, No. 1170.

12 *A.D.C.*, XLII, 94, 119, 128 f.

13 *A.D.C.&S.*, IX, 2, 17, 25, 35, 104.

14 M. Livingstone and D. H. Fleming, eds., *Register of the Secret Seal of Scotland*, Edinburgh, 1906, II, No. 823; Hannay, *op. cit.*, p. 351; T. Dickson, *et al.*, eds., *The Accounts of the Lord High Treasurer of Scotland*, Edinburgh, 1903, V, 436, 437.

15 Hannay, *op. cit.*, pp. 407, 412; *Treasurer's Accounts*, VI, 151.

16 *Ibid.*, VI, 168, 231 ff.

17 *Reg. Sec. Seal*, II, No. 3235; J. Brewer *et al.*, eds., *Letters and Papers of Henry VIII*, London, 1896, XV, No. 9.

18 Hannay, *op. cit.*, p. 425.

21

19 *Ibid.*, p. 455 f.; *Treasurer's Accounts*, VI, lx, lxii, 454, 462.

20 *A.P.S.*, II, 357; J. Paul *et al.*, eds., *Register of the Great Seal of Scotland*, Edinburgh, 1883, III, No. 1779; *Moray Muniments*, Darnaway Castle, Morayshire, Box 31, Div. 1, Bundle 1.

21 *L.&P. Henry VIII*, IV: 2, No. 3803; *Royal Correspondence, Scotland*, Danish Royal Archives, Copenhagen, A II; C. F. Wegener, ed., *Aasberetninger fra det Kongelige Geheimarchiv*, Copenhagen, 1861–65, III, 150; *Forty-Sixth Annual Report of the Deputy Keeper of the Public Records*, London, 1887, II, 58; Hannay, *op. cit.*, pp. 299 ff.

22 *Diplomatarium Norvegicum*, Christiana, 1847, VIII, No. 640; D. Hay *et al.*, eds., *Letters of James V*, Edinburgh, 1954, pp. 198, 206.

23 C. F. Allen, *Histoire de Danemark*, Copenhagen, 1878, I, 306 f.

24 *L.&P. Henry VIII*, VIII, No. 1159; Wegener, *op. cit.*, III, 231.

25 *L.&P. Henry VIII*, XV, No. 396; Thomas Ruddiman, ed., *Epistolae Jacobi IV, Jacobi V et Mariae Regum Scotorum*, Edinburgh, 1722, II, 101.

26 *Treasurer's Accounts*, V, 461; VI, 153, 159, 163; *L.&P. Henry VIII*, VI, Nos. 143, 1069; P. de Gayangos, *Calendar of State Papers Relating to Spain*, London, 1882, IV: 2, 625, 698; *A.D.C.&S.*, III, 58.

27 *Tyningham Ms.*, Mar. 27, 1531; *Treasurer's Accounts*, V, 458, VI, 48.

28 *Liber Tronatoris Burgi Edinburgi*, 1537–38; 1538–39; *Customs Bk. Edinb.*, 1538–39; *Treasurer's Accounts*, VI, 381, 390, 394, 413, 421.

29 *A.D.C.&S.*, XI, 197, 248.

30 *A.D.C.*, XLIII, 88 f., 156. He was probably the "Evangelist," a Lombard, referred to in Gavin Douglas' letter to Wolsey of January, 1522. (Cf. H. Ellis, *Original Letters Illustrative of English History*, London, 1846, Ser. 3, Vol. I, No. cx.)

31 *A.D.C.&S.*, X, 105.

32 *A.D.C.&S.*, III, 12.

33 *Ibid.*, III, 67, 68, 135.

34 *Ibid.*, XII, 40.

35 *Reg. Grt. Seal*, III, No. 1777; *A.D.C.&S.*, XII, 199.

36 *Ibid.*, XI, 155; cf. E. J. Hamilton, *American Treasure and the Price Revolution in Spain, 1501–1650*, Cambridge, Mass., 1934.

37 *Treasurer's Accounts*, V, 400; VI, 2; *A.D.C.*, XLII, 17.

38 *Ibid.*, XLII, 121.

39 *Reg. Sec. Seal*, II, No. 1022.

40 *Reg. Grt. Seal*, III, No. 1064; *A.D.C.*, XLIII, 118. It may be, too, that he was the Robert Barton who was fined for not appearing at the court of the Abbot of Dunfermline on January 11, 1532, although there is no other record of his holding land in the prelate's regality. If he did, it would mean he had also acquired lands somewhere in the neighbourhood of Dunfermline. J. M. Webster and A. A. M. Duncan, *The Regality of Dunfermline Court Book, 1531–1538*, Dunfermline, 1953, p. 45.

41 *The Great Historic Families of Great Britain*, Dumfries, 1888, II, 88; *A.D.C. &S.*, VII, 111, 149; VIII, May 19, 1537, fo. no. missing; IX, 91, 112; *Drummond Writs*, Box 2, Bundle I.

42 D. Robertson and M. Wood, *Castle and Town*, Edinburgh, 1928, p. 281.

43 *A.D.C.*, XLII, 144; XLIII, 24, 72, 185; John Knox, *The History of the Reformation in Scotland*, ed. W. C. Dickinson, Edinburgh, 1949, I, 24; Pitcairn, *op. cit.*, I, *211. It is a little difficult to tell, from the wording of the statements about Dais, whether he burned his faggot or followed the example of some of his contemporaries and fled the country.

44 *A.D.C.&S.*, III, 31; D. Calderwood, *The History of the Kirk of Scotland*, ed., T. Thomson, Edinburgh, 1847, I, 107; Historical Manuscripts Commission, *Fifth Report*, London, 1876, p. 633.

45 *A.D.C.&S.*, XI, 197.

46 *Ibid.*, X, 140; XI, 52.

47 *Ibid.*, VII, 149 f. From Knox's account it would seem that the Bishop of Moray was noted for his attempts to exact tithes wherever possible. *Op. cit.*, I, 24.

48 *Reg. Grt. Seal*, III, No. 1020.

49 *A.D.C.*, XLIII, 80, 96 f., 99.

50 Lord Cooper, ed., *Regiam Majestatem*, Edinburgh, 1947, Bk. II, cap. 27.

51 *Treasurer's Accounts*, VI, 454, 462; *Royal Correspondence*, Danish Royal Archives, Copenhagen, A II, Reg. 14,289; *Forty-Sixth Rep. Deputy Keeper*, App. II, 59; *L.&P. Henry VIII*, XII: 2, No. 218; *Reg. Sec. Seal*, II, No. 3304; *Reg. Grt. Seal*, III, No. 2092.

52 *Ibid.*, III, 1934, 1954.

53 John Leslie, *Historie of Scotland*, eds., E. S. Cody and W. Murison, Edinburgh, 1895, II, 131; *L.&P. Henry VIII*, XV, No. 779.

54 *A.D.C.&S.*, XII, 194 f., 199.

Notes to Chapter XIV

1 T. Dickson *et al.*, eds., *The Accounts of the Lord High Treasurer of Scotland*, Edinburgh, 1907, VII, 483.

2 *Acta Dominorum Concilii et Sessionis*, XII, 194, 199.

3 Thomas Ruddiman, ed., *Epistolae Jacobi IV, Jacobi V et Mariae Regum Scotorum*, Edinburgh, 1722, II, 101.

4 M. Livingstone and D. H. Fleming, eds., *Register of the Secret Seal of Scotland*, Edinburgh, 1921, III, No. 3993; R. K. Hannay, ed., *Acts of the Lords of the Council in Public Affairs*, Edinburgh, 1932, p. 509; *Treasurer's Accounts*, VII, 483.

5 *Ibid.*, VIII, 106; *Expenditures for Royal Liveries, 1541* (ms.), H.M. General Register House, Edinburgh; *Protocol Book of Gilbert Grote, 1552–1573*, Edinburgh, 1914, No. 248; J. H. Burton, *Register of the Privy Council, 1545–1569*, Edinburgh, 1877, I, 161.

6 *Parliamentary Records of Scotland*, Edinburgh, 1804, I, 624.

7 J. Paul, *et al.*, eds., *Register of the Great Seal of Scotland*, Edinburgh, 1883, III, No. 2760; R. Keith, *An Historical Catalogue of the Scottish Bishops*, Edinburgh, 1824, 191; J. Dowden, *The Bishops of Scotland*, Glasgow, 1912, p. 225 f.

8 *Reg. Grt. Seal*, III, Nos. 355, 1311; *Protocol Book of James Nicholson, 1549–1579* (ms.), H.M. General Register House, Edinburgh, p. 48.

9 *Reg. Grt. Seal*, III, No. 1311.

10 "Calder Writs," *Lord Torphichen's Muniments*, Bundle XV: 6; Nicholson, *op. cit.*, p. 50; J. Paul, *The Scots Peerage*, Edinburgh, 1910, VIII, 387 f.

11 J. Spottiswoode, "An Account of all the Religious Houses in Scotland," in Keith, *op. cit.*, p. 439; *Scots Peerage*, VIII, 386 f.

12 Hannay, *op. cit.*, p. 500.

13 J. Brewer *et al.*, eds., *Letters and Papers of Henry VIII*, London, 1896, XV, Nos. 544, 779.

14 *Reg. Sec. Seal*, II, xiv; *Papiers d'Etat et de l'Audience* (ms.), Archives Générales de la Royaume de Belgique, Brussels, Nos. 4–6.

15 *Register of the Privy Council*, I, 161; T. Thomson, ed., *Acts of the Parliament of Scotland*, Edinburgh, 1814, II, 544; James MacKinnon, *The Social and Industrial History of Scotland from Earliest Times to the Union*, Glasgow, 1920, p. 88; J. Davidson and A. Gray, *The Scottish Staple at Veere*, London, 1909, p. 54.

Index